THE VOICE SAID, CRY

Also by Eric James:

*Judge Not: A Selection of Sermons
Preached in Gray's Inn Chapel,
1978–1988*
(available from Christian Action,
St. Anselm's Church Hall,
Kennington Cross, Kennington Road,
London SE11 5DU)

Word Over All: Forty Sermons, 1985–1991
(London: SPCK, 1992)

THE VOICE SAID, CRY

 Forty Sermons 1990–1993

ERIC JAMES

SPCK

First published in Great Britain 1994
Society for Promoting Christian Knowledge
Holy Trinity Church
Marylebone Road
London NW1 4DU

British Library Cataloguing-in-Publication Data
A catalogue record for this book is available from the British Library

ISBN 0–281–04730–8

Typeset by Parker Typesetting Service, Leicester
Printed in Great Britain by
The Cromwell Press, Melksham, Wiltshire

To Gwen Rymer

Contents

Preface

There is a famous David Langdon cartoon of a frail and aged vicar hanging over the edge of a pulpit and saying to the congregation 'Mind you: I'm no Billy Graham'. After having called this third book of sermons *The Voice Said, Cry* I am tempted to add: 'Mind you: I'm no Isaiah'.

I have loved the phrase 'The voice said, Cry' as long as I can remember, but I doubt whether I asked who Isaiah really was until I went to King's College, London, in the 1940s, where I learnt things like 'Isaiah 40—55 is the work of a prophet who lived in Babylonia during the middle years of the sixth century BC'. Clearly he was as much poet as prophet, but because some say he may have been a 'court prophet', as Preacher to Gray's Inn and a Chaplain to HM The Queen, I feel a special affinity and affection for him—and have, too, a painful awareness how fatally easy it is for the court prophet to become the court jester, who entertains, even decorates with his cap and bells, the Establishment and speaks too comfortably to it. (Conversely, Shakespeare wrote, in *King Lear*: 'Jesters do oft prove prophets.')

Another person who comes into my mind when I hear 'The voice said, Cry' is Joan of Arc—Bernard Shaw's *St Joan* rather than the Joan of history.

When Isaiah talks of the 'mouth of the Lord' it is as though he has been hearing a celestial voice—or voices—like St Joan. Joan's voices were sometimes illusory and failed her from time to time. Every preacher understands that. 'You must not talk about my voices' Joan says, awed and humbled by her gift. Captain Robert de Beaudricourt says to her concerning her voices: 'They come from your imagination.' 'Of course' says St Joan 'That's how the messages of God come to us.'

Shaw shows us he understood the preacher's vocation: the consecration, not least, of imagination. But that, of course, is not the preacher's vocation alone. Isaiah, St Joan, Shaw, T. S. Eliot, Van Gogh. . . . Who of us, man or woman, lay or ordained, has never heard the voice say, Cry?

But, above all, the model of the preacher is, of course, our Lord Himself. 'The Tortured Christ', sculpted in 1975 by the Brazilian artist Guido Rocha, is now in the All Africa Conference of Churches' Training Centre, Nairobi. No one can look at it and not hear the Voice crying— which He does wherever He is tortured in His body. And, as Pascal said, 'Jesus will be in agony even to the end of the world.'

*   *   *

I am aware, as I read through this volume of sermons, that in every case there was a friend or a group of friends waiting to greet me where I preached. I am grateful to all of them, not least to my friends at Gray's Inn, where I have now been privileged to be the Preacher for fifteen years.

Again I must thank the Council of Christian Action for their continued support—all royalties from the book will go to them—and to its Secretary, Mrs Jane Spurr, who has prepared the manuscript with her usual diligence and skill.

Eric James
Ascension Day
1993

Acknowledgements

Cover illustration: Vincent Van Gogh: *Pollard Willows and Setting Sun*, 1988. Reproduced by courtesy of the Bridgeman Art Library.

Sermon 1: Extract from 'Eurydice' by Edith Sitwell, published in *Collected Poems* (Sinclair Stevenson), reprinted by permission of David Higham Associates Ltd.

Sermon 2: Extract from 'Anger's Freeing Power' by Stevie Smith, published in *The Collected Poems of Stevie Smith* (Penguin 20th Century Classics), reprinted by permission of James Mac-Gibbon. Reprinted in the U.S. by permission of New Directions Pub. Corp.

'Fire and Ice' by Robert Frost, published in *The Poetry of Robert Frost* (Jonathan Cape), edited by E. C. Lathem, reprinted by permission of the publishers, with thanks to the Estate of Robert Frost.

'The Soldier's Dream' by Wilfred Owen, published in *The Collected Poems of Wilfred Owen* (Chatto & Windus), edited by C. Day Lewis, reprinted by permission of the publishers, with thanks to the Estate of Wilfred Owen.

Sermon 6: 'Journey of the Magi' by T. S. Eliot, published in *Collected Poems 1909–1962* (Faber and Faber Ltd.), reprinted by permission of the publishers.

Sermon 7: Gerard Manley Hopkins, translation of the 17th century Latin hymn *O Deus, ego amo te*, published in *The Poems of Gerard Manley Hopkins*, 4th edn, edited by W. H. Gardner and N. H. MacKenzie (1967), reprinted by permission of Oxford University Press on behalf of the Society of Jesus.

Sermon 9: Extract from *John Leonard Wilson: Confessor for the Faith* by Ron McKay (Hodder and Stoughton Limited), reprinted by permission of the publisher.

Sermon 11: Extract from *Journey from Obscurity* by Harold Owen (OUP, 1963), reprinted by permission of Oxford University Press.

Sermon 18: Extract from *The Zeal of Thine House* by Dorothy L. Sayers (Gollancz), reprinted by permission of David Higham Associates.

Sermon 19: Extract from *The Confidential Clerk* by T. S. Eliot, reprinted by permission of Faber and Faber Ltd.

Sermon 21: Extracts from 'Addiction as a Necessity and Opportunity' by Edwin H. Land, published in *Science*, Vol. 171, 15 Jan. 1971, pp. 513–15; copyright 1971 by the AAAS, reprinted by permission of the American Association for the Advancement of Science.

Sermon 24: Acknowledgements to the Estate of Eleanor Hull and the publishers Chatto & Windus for the versified Irish Hymn by Eleanor Hull.

Sermon 26: Extract from *Five Questions in Search of an Answer* by David Stafford-Clark (Curtis Brown, 1972). Not able to contact the copyright holder.

Sermon 30: Extract from 'East Coker' by T. S. Eliot, published in *Four Quartets* (Faber and Faber Ltd.), reprinted by permission of the publishers.

Sermon 32: Extracts from *The Spirit of Tolerance* edited by Katharine Moore (Gollancz), reprinted by permission of the publisher.

Sermon 34: 'The Transfiguration' by Edwin Muir, published in *Collected Poems* (Faber and Faber Ltd.), reprinted by permission of the publishers.

'Maundy Thursday' and 'At a Calvary near the Ancre' by Wilfred Owen, published in *The Collected Poems of Wilfred Owen* (Chatto & Windus), edited by C. Day Lewis, reprinted by permission of the publishers, with thanks to the Estate of Wilfred Owen.

Acknowledgements to the Estate of Wilfred Owen and the publishers Chatto & Windus for the poem 'The Parable of the Old Man and the Young' by Wilfred Owen.

Sermon 39: 'Hymn in Contemplation of Sudden Death' by Dorothy L. Sayers, published in *Dorothy L. Sayers: Her Life and Soul*, by Barbara Reynolds (Hodder & Stoughton, 1993), reprinted by permission of David Higham Associates.

The voice said, Cry.
And he said, What shall I cry?
All flesh is grass,
    and all the goodliness thereof is as the
        flower of the field . . .
The grass withereth,
      the flower fadeth:
      but the word of our God shall stand for ever.

Isaiah 40.6 & 8

1

IN MEMORIAM: THE REVD GILES STEPHEN ECCLESTONE

Great St. Mary's Church, Cambridge; 3 November 1990

When Imogen phoned me with the news of Giles' illness, and told me how serious it was—that, humanly speaking, he had only a few weeks to live—I was dumbfounded: as I expect most of you were when you heard the news.

I was privileged to be allowed to see Giles one day in Addenbrooke's: for a while with Imogen and the children, and then left alone with him, knowing I was saying farewell to him, and he knowing he was saying farewell to me.

I was aware that the last time I'd been in that particular ward was when Bishop John Robinson was dying, of that same fell disease; but now, there was Giles reading what John had to say on *Living with Cancer* and *Learning from Cancer*, and saying to me how grateful he was to John: how strengthened by what he had written.

No one in fact has helped me more, when in the depths of one sort and another, than Giles' revered father, Alan—to whom our hearts have gone out again and again in these last weeks. Alan has helped me, not least, by turning my attention to *King Lear*; so that it was not surprising that in that ward at Addenbrooke's, as I looked at Giles, the words uppermost in my heart and mind were the words of Kent at the end of *Lear*:

> I have a journey, sir, shortly to go;
> My master calls me, I must not say no.

Put it another way: It was clear that Giles was trying to say, with everything in him, his 'Yes to God': to all that lay ahead.

He was hearing the call:

1

> Darest thou now, O soul,
> Walk out with me toward the Unknown Region . . .

and, supported by the prayers and love of so many, family and friends, he was gathering all together for the journey.

His departure from us was not untroubled. How could it be? He did not 'go gentle into that good night'. He had his Gethsemane. But he died in faith.

And I find myself wanting to give thanks today for all who cared for him in his last weeks and days, in Addenbrooke's and at the Hospice; cared for him physically and spiritually.

Ten days later, some of us were privileged to be present at Giles' never-to-be-forgotten funeral and burial at Over. And I'd like simply to share with you some of my personal reactions and responses to that occasion.

I have to say that I was still very angry with God at Giles' death when I entered the church. It was, of course, full; but it was decorated for Harvest: for Harvest *Festival*.

In one way, that was marvellous. I thought immediately, as many must have done, of those lines of Edith Sitwell in her poem 'Eurydice':

> Love is not changed by Death,
> And nothing is lost and all in the end is harvest.

But, frankly, for me to accept at that stage that 'nothing is lost by death' was simply too much. And I thought suddenly of James Hilton's novel *Random Harvest*. That was more like it! 'Random Harvest' was much nearer the mark. I couldn't myself yet see much pattern or purpose in Giles' dying. There's a mysterious randomness at the very heart of much of our universe. There's certainly, to our eyes, a randomness and chance in cancer. And I found myself saying to the Heavenly Reaper, angrily: 'You seem to reap your harvest at mere haphazard.'

I'm not ashamed of that prayer. Prayer (Alan might have written—and probably did) is a kind of questioning—a kind of accusing—of God. There's plenty of that kind of prayer in, for instance, the Psalms:

> O God, wherefore art thou absent from us so long?
> Why is thy wrath so hot against the sheep of thy pasture?

As Giles' coffin was borne up the aisle, I was still wanting to say to God: 'God, what have you done with Giles?—harvesting him, surely, before the time of harvest, before the harvest is ripe.'

I confess, I didn't find it easy to join in the first hymn. I was rather short on 'gold of obedience and incense of lowliness' that day. But then we had read to us that incredible passage from the First Chapter of the Second Epistle of St Paul to the Corinthians.

Let me be honest, and tell you it was only at 2 o'clock the next morning—that's to say, in the middle of the night—that the significance of that passage really dawned on me. I woke up suddenly, wide awake, with the clear conviction that I must get up and read it again—which I did. Let me read it to you now; and note the recurrence, ten times in five verses, of the word 'comfort':

Blessed be the God and Father of our Lord Jesus Christ;
the Father of mercies and God of all *comfort*;
who *comforteth* us in all our affliction;
that we may be able to *comfort* them that are in any affliction;
through the *comfort* wherewith we ourselves are *comforted* of God.
For as the sufferings of Christ abound unto us,
even so our *comfort* also aboundeth through Christ.
But whether we be afflicted, it is for your *comfort* and salvation;
or whether we be *comforted*,
it is for your *comfort*,
which worketh in the patient enduring of the same suffering
which ye also suffer: and our hope for you is steadfast;
knowing that, as ye are partakers of the sufferings,
so also are ye of the *comfort*.

That reading seemed to me, I have to say, a message direct from God and from His son Giles. And I was comforted—at 2.00.a.m.—several hours after the service.

It was after the reading of that passage from Second Corinthians that the Bishop of Ely preached to us what was, I gather, only the second sermon he had yet preached at the death of one of his clergy. It was a most marvellous sermon that left no doubt he was a bishop, a shepherd, who knew his own sheep by name, that is to say, by nature.

'Giles spoke to me in hospital' he said 'of his family, of each of his children by name, with sensitivity, and love, and appreciation, and longing.'

The Bishop read again a passage which in his twenties Giles had copied into an exercise book: a passage from the great French spiritual director, of people like Charles de Foucauld, the Abbé Huvelin, which had been read to us just before the sermon. It says a great deal about Giles, and I must read it again to you now:

The Abbé Huvelin on Eternal Life

'We have to cast anchor, not below, but above: it is in God, in his goodness, that we have to found our hope. God, who might have created us directly, employs for this work our parents, to whom He joins us by the tenderest ties. He could also save us directly. But he saves us, in fact, by means of certain souls, who have received the spiritual life before ourselves, and who communicate it to us because they love us.'

That passage, which, as I say, Giles copied in his twenties, speaks of God 'joining us to our parents by the tenderest ties'.

That was certainly Giles' recognition of what he had received from his parents and his home. He knew how hugely he was indebted to them, not least for so much of what he believed and had made his own.

I knew Alan and Delia before I knew Giles, when Alan was the notable and notorious Vicar of Darnall, Sheffield, and Giles was a historian of promise at King Edward's School, Sheffield. It meant that when I first met Giles at Cambridge, when he was at Emmanuel, I was particularly delighted to meet the son of his father.

There's a sense that in these last weeks, to quote *Lear* again, 'The oldest hath borne most'. I felt that acutely as I watched Alan casting earth upon Giles' coffin.

Giles and I both went to South London from Cambridge. I saw something of Giles in his Clapham and my Camberwell years, when he was caught up with work at the House of Commons, and with the William Temple Association.

A namesake of mine, Cyril James, who worked with Giles in the House of Commons, wrote to me, after his death, a paragraph that to me rings totally true:

> My abiding mental picture of Giles [he wrote] is of his beaming at me across our desks. His good qualities? He was one of the most affable, amiable people I've met. This is not to say we always agreed. By no means; but disagreeing with Giles was a delight. He had integrity, compassion, intellectual honesty, dignity. For his religious convictions were not confined to liturgy and litany; they ensured that he would—in the Quaker saying—'walk cheerfully over the world, seeking that of God in every man' . . . I was allowed to know not just the intellectual Giles, but, perhaps less apparent but far more important, a loving, caring human being.

In time, Giles asked me to be his confessor. That fact, of course, fits a sort of silencer to me. But I can say, aloud, how thankful I was for Giles and Imogen and their home, and their children, at Grove Park, in South London. Both he and I were aware that he was on a journey that went on for the rest of his life; of bringing his intellect and his feelings together.

I said to Imogen the other day: 'I always so loved Giles showing me the garden.' 'Yes,' she said, with a smile: '*I* did most of the gardening!' I loved meals with them all.

When Giles came to make his confession—often in the Retro-choir of Southwark Cathedral—you'll not be surprised if I say it was a civil servant's compulsively detailed confession.

The obituaries of Giles in the national press have paid tribute to his work in the Commons: 'Mastery of Parliamentary procedure allied to administrative powers and a thoughtful personality made him a valued and popular servant in the House.' They have also spelt out his contribution to the Church through the Board for Social Responsibility. Here and now I simply want to record the major publications that Giles either wrote completely or in large part:

1977: *Planning for Community: the Planning Process and Human Needs*
1977: again: *The Irish Problem and Ourselves*
1977: again: *Prisons and Prisoners in England Today*
1979: *Homosexual Relationships: A Contribution to Discussion*
1981: *The Church of England and Politics*
1982: *The Church and the Bomb: Nuclear Weapons and Christian Conscience*

For Giles, these were not just written reports. He took part, for instance, in a visit to the Maze Prison around the time of the Hunger Strike, and met prisoners 'on the blanket', as it was called.

On Brenda Stanley's first day as Giles' Secretary at the Board there was a posy of fresh flowers on her desk, and he had cancelled all his engagements: to put her 'in the picture'.

I don't think there can be any doubt that Giles was a truly great Secretary of the Board. But I'd want to say also that there were times when Imogen and the family saw very little of him, when he spent evening after evening, and week-end after week-end, drafting lengthy reports. And any tribute to Giles must also be a tribute to Imogen.

I saw a good deal of Giles when he was wrestling with the decision to offer—or not to offer—himself for ordination. It wasn't, of course, an easy decision. He received lots of contrary and contradictory advice; but it was the kind of decision that had 'signs following'. Once the decision had been made, it was as though a great burden had been lifted from his shoulders, and he became much more relaxed and open. His eyes twinkled more often, and that crackle of a laugh of his crackled more often.

The rather important part that Westcott House now played in Giles' life was rather left out of his obituaries; so I've felt that I should give a good deal of space to a rather lovely letter I received from the Principal of Westcott House, Rupert Hoare. He wrote:

Giles was here as a student for two years, and he was a quite exemplary member of the House. Maggie Guite, our Doctrine teacher, said that she always gave his Doctrine Essays an A+ mark, and used to write on them how much *she* had learnt from reading them! So Giles' intellectual abilities were quietly but consistently demonstrated throughout his time as a student; but, of course, much more impressive was the quiet but wholly positive and responsible way in which he simply fitted into our life, making very valuable contributions, but with a quietness and humility that we came to appreciate very much.

(And from that time Imogen ran groups for our members and their spouses on sexuality and spirituality.)

Michael Mayne and I were able then to work out a scheme whereby Giles did two-thirds of his time with Great St Mary's, as his curate, and one-third at Westcott and the Federation. So he moved immediately from being a student member of the House to being a member of staff. Again, this was completely natural, and he fulfilled his staff role very well indeed. I always found it moving when he came to me to ask advice about things—for instance, the giving of a Compline address. He was very ready to take advice, and he made it easy for me to give it to him. He was a very good colleague on the staff, taking great care of his tutees, and adding a very important dimension through all his experience in the teaching of Ethics.

He and Imogen became real friends of Gesine and myself, and I remember vividly a lunch party the four of us had together on a punt in Grantchester Meadows, at the end of his three years with us and at Great St Mary's. I don't think I have ever felt the loss of anyone quite in the same way as I have Giles.

Michael Mayne added to that letter:

Giles brought to Great St Mary's and its wider floating population of graduates and undergraduates qualities which enriched all our lives. He preached thoughtfully and winningly, never safely, always carefully. He was at once recognized as a natural pastor, with a stillness and a readiness to give attention to whoever needed him. He was a perfectionist, which could be costly, but it resulted in worship prepared with care and thoughtful attention to detail. Undergirding his whole ministry was a spirituality and disciplined prayerfulness, and I must have been one of the many who learned from the still figure of Giles on his prayer-stool in St Andrew's Chapel.

A week before his priesting I was taken ill and effectively put out of action for the best part of a year. Giles took over the running of the parish with Hilary Oakley, the Girton Chaplain, and the then churchwardens, without apparent fuss. Never for a moment did I doubt his ability to do so, but I and many remain grateful for the confidence he imparted to us all.

Finally, there was Over. The letters the people of Over have written are eloquent beyond words.

It seems impossible to believe that we shall no longer see Giles cycling about the village . . . There is probably no one at all in Over who is untouched by his death. In the three years that he was Vicar here, he had become a central person in village life.

We all remember the early days of his ministry here, when he shared the old Vicarage with the surgery; many of us met him first in his own house, as we went to the doctor. That generosity of sharing we soon came to know was typical of Giles. . . .

Every day, around the village, I am confronted with more and more people who tell me, 'In my time of trouble Giles was there . . . He came cycling down, and he was there . . . I was feeling the church had forgotten me and he changed my life, he came to see me and I could talk to him as I've never talked to anyone before . . .

Some people have said that by Giles' death the Church of England lost a future bishop. I have to say I believe that was as far from Giles' mind as it was from George Herbert's; and I choose the comparison carefully, because in the parish, as a parish priest, Giles had reached his goal and the end of his journey: in a parish and in the particular parish of Over. 'Over' was an astonishingly appropriate place for Giles to end his journey.

But I want to read you one phrase or two more, written to Imogen, by someone who lives miles away from Over:

> Most importantly, the taking people seriously will have been one of the characteristics which so endeared Giles to the people of Over. I thought, two or three years ago, if I had something crucial that I needed to work through or sort out, it would be to Giles that I would turn . . . Giles has changed and grown so much in the sixteen years we have known each other. He always was a formidable person—in vision, grasp, articulation, certainly, but much of Giles was, on first acquaintance, only visible in a tantalising kind of way. A bit like coming across a walled garden with warmth, shelter, space, but only being able to see it through the wrought-iron gates. Over these years the gates have been opened, and more and more of what was your private domain has been shared and made available to the wider world . . . Sometimes people seem to change to become what they *weren't*. With Giles, I feel we have witnessed the unfolding of what he *is*; and seeing the possibility of that is the most powerful parable of the Kingdom.

I must draw this overlong address to a close. The time fails me to tell of the *Modern Churchman* and the Grubb Institute and editing *The Parish Church*, and so on.

How shall I end?

Last week-end I spent a couple of days in Bruges. It was there, amid the beauty of the medieval buildings and picturesque canals, and visiting its churches and galleries that I found the space and silence I needed to think out and write out most of what I have had to say to you today.

In what was the fourteenth century St Jan's Hospital, now the Memling Museum, there is a fifteenth century Pietà, by an unknown artist, which completely bowled me over. It's a Pietà focused upon the Trinity rather than on the Virgin. God the Father, crowned, sits in glory and splendour upon His throne. He has a face of infinite compassion, and in His arms He carries His Son, who lies within the Father's lap. The Father's face reveals how much He has suffered for and with His Son, but there is also a look of pride in the work of the Son.

As I looked at that Pietà, there seemed nothing more to be said in answer to the question to God: 'What have you done with your Son Jesus?' The wounds of Christ were still to be seen, but He was so clearly resting in the Father's ample love and care. So, to the question with which I began this sermon, 'God, what have you done with Giles?' there seemed also to be no other answer than: 'He is "in Christ" and Christ is in your care. He is with Christ in your arms; and you are all compassion.'

There was a detail to that painting, to that Pietà, which was unforgettable. John is holding a chalice, which Christ has clearly drunk to the dregs, but a horrible ludicrous little worm of a devil is still within the empty chalice. That devil is now of no consequence or power. The Father is all-powerful and reigning in the full power of His Love. The devil has had his day. His sting has been drawn.

Giles has suffered and has gone from us, ahead of us. The evil, the devil, of cancer reduced the length of his life with us and amongst us by some years. But Giles has had his Gethsemane. He has drunk his cup, and his death is not the end. Death is never the last word. Love is the last word: the sovereign Love of God, the triumphant power and wisdom of God's love.

Here, Giles knew in part. Now he knows, in Christ, that the last word is love: enthroned love.

2

ANGER

St John's College Chapel, Cambridge; 3 February 1991

This last week I had to go away with about twenty clergy, men and women, who come from the Deanery of Tower Hamlets in the East End of London. Their parishes all lie between the Isle of Dogs and the Tower of London.

They had given their annual residential conference the title 'An exploration of Anger within God's world and within ourselves', and had invited me to give them what help I could, by way of some addresses. I felt very privileged to do so, because I know well their places of ministry, and that they are a sorely tried and tested group of people.

In the very first session, I asked each member of the conference to say, in three minutes, what personal and social anger meant for them in their particular circumstances.

The first person told us that in the previous week every window of his home had been suddenly smashed by a gang of teenagers, and when he rushed out, they set on him, and he was left in the gutter with damage to his rib cage from which he will take several weeks to recover. It was good of him to come to our conference at all. He was still in considerable pain. He was a mild sort of man, but he was, very understandably, quite angry.

The second person talked of the double murder which had taken place a few doors away from the vicarage during the previous week. As it happened, he knew the family well, and was feeling a bit guilty at coming away from the parish to the conference at such a time of need. But, as he said, every week in that parish brings its fresh crop of violence.

Those first stories were not entirely untypical, I'm sad to say, of what most of the members of the conference had to report. They were clearly living in, and describing, a very violent society; and they themselves were, of course, not without violence in their reaction, however much they tried to control it and bottle it up.

And all this was taking place against the background of television, radio and newspapers, which reported the violence in the Gulf: missiles, air-raids, tanks, snipers, and so on. The second morning we were away together, almost every paper carried on its front page the photograph of a cormorant that was the helpless victim of an oil slick. You couldn't look at that photograph without anger.

There was therefore no doubt in my mind why this particular year that Deanery had chosen to take as its subject 'personal and social anger'. But their choice of subject did not make my task easy.

We are all familiar, perhaps too familiar, with the idea that the Christian gospel is of a loving God, and that our response to it should be, by God's grace, to love our neighbours as ourselves. But my task was to face the reality of anger: to answer the question: 'Can Christianity also be a *gospel* of anger? And could being angry with our neighbours also be a part of the Christian life?'

I have long believed that anger and love are not as far apart as some sometimes maintain. I have little doubt that in many a pastoral situation anger can be a potent influence for good. But finding the positive side of anger is not always an easy task, especially since, traditionally, it is so often associated with punishment and revenge; and human anger has most often undeniably destructive and damaging aspects.

In the Book of Job we are confronted by what has been called the 'enigma of the angry God'. But it's not only in the Bible that we confront that enigma. Jungian analysts are all too familiar with it. Specifically, in his work *Answer to Job*, Jung himself argued that we cannot discard the dark side of God. The relationship between love and what Jung called the 'rage and jealousy of God' is to be regarded, he says, not as an irreconcilable split in his nature but as a necessary antinomy. According to Jung, 'God is not only to be loved but to be feared.' He 'fills us with evil as well as good', Jung writes. To ignore the dark side is to ignore both the complexity of human nature and the mysterious nature of God.

Dr Anthony Storr, the English Jungian analyst, wrote in 1970 in his book *Human Aggression*: 'The sombre fact is that we are the cruellest and most ruthless species that has ever walked the earth'; and that, 'although we may recoil in horror when we read in newspaper or history book of the atrocities committed by man on man, we know in our hearts that each one of us harbours within himself those same savage impulses which lead to murder, to torture and to war.'

If the psycho-dynamic investigation of our warlike propensity has any advantage over other approaches it is that it gets closer to the core of the question. It underlines the truth that wars do not start simply in senates, parliaments and pentagons, but in the minds of people like ourselves. It demonstrates that the rational use of strategy to attain military goals is based on an irrational substratum in the human organism which makes military behaviour an available resource at the disposal of government, tyrants, warlords and people not unlike ourselves. On this foundation of unreason do our reasoned strategies proceed.

What is, I believe, one of the most important books of our time, by the Spalding Professor of Eastern Religions and Ethics at the University of Oxford, R. C. Zaehner, he simply called *Our Savage God*.

Dr Jim Garrison, the American theologian, who spent a good deal of time in Cambridge writing a book he called *The Darkness of God: Theology after Hiroshima*, wrote:

> Vengeance and repentance alone do not suffice to explain the wrath of God. There is something deeper going on within the Godhead itself. Something that defies conventional morality or even covenantal promises. It suggests a certain intention on the part of God to give vent to a dark side of the Divine. . . .

I do not want this evening only to encourage you to love God and to love your neighbour as yourself. I want to invite you to explore the complex nature of your own anger and to see that within the gift of God. There is an impressive book called *The Gospel of Anger* by Alastair Campbell, who lectures in the Department of Christian Ethics and Practical Theology in the University of Edinburgh, for those who want to pursue the subject further than a single sermon can possibly take them.

But I have found quite often that literature is as great a help as what I will call 'pure theology'. The dark side of God is not something human nature has suddenly and recently come across. Did not the great poet John Donne sing out in a sonnet, four hundred years ago, the invitation:

> Batter my heart, three person'd God; for, you
> As yet but knocke, breathe, shine, and seeke to mend;
> That I may rise, and stand, o'erthrow mee, and bend
> Your force, to breake, blowe, burn, and make me new . . .
> > . . . For I
> Except you'enthrall mee, never shall be free,
> Nor ever chast, except you ravish mee.

There is an invitation to the violence of God, by one who sees God's anger as part of His care and cure.

A worse alternative to the anger of God could be His utter indifference.

It's now nearly forty years since the novels of the Italian writer Guareschi—the world of Don Camillo—burst upon England. So often they're about creative anger, anger in the service of love. Don Camillo, in affectionate battle with the communist mayor, and with God, suggests that anger may have a positive as well as a negative role.

Certainly it's the poets as much as the psychologists who can help us on this particular subject, for often they not only accurately observe but long ponder before they put pen to paper.

I wonder do you know Wilfred Owen's poem of the First World War, 'The Soldier's Dream':

> I dreamed kind Jesus fouled the big-gun gears;
> And caused a permanent stoppage in all bolts;
> And buckled with a smile Mausers and Colts;
> And rusted every bayonet—with His tears.

> And there were no more bombs, of ours or Theirs,
> Not even an old flint-lock, nor even a pikel.
> But God was vexed, and gave all power to Michael;
> And when I woke he'd seen to our repairs.

And there's the American Robert Frost's poem 'Fire and Ice', a nine-line meditation on the alternative forms of destruction:

> Some say the world will end in fire,
> Some say in ice.
> From what I've tasted of desire
> I hold with those who favour fire.
> But if it had to perish twice,
> I think I know enough of hate
> To say that for destruction ice
> Is also great
> And would suffice.

Stevie Smith's poem 'Anger's Freeing Power' describes a dream she had of a pet raven 'imprisoned' in a room with only three walls. Despite her entreaties to the bird that it 'made a prison of a place that is not one at all', and despite encouragement to fly free through the open wall, it remains in its self-imposed captivity. Only when two fellow ravens make it angry, by mocking its stupidity, does the bird escape its prison. I find the last lines of Stevie Smith's poem particularly moving:

> And in my dream I watched him go
> And I was glad, I loved him so,
>
> Yet when I woke my eyes were wet
> To think Love had not freed my pet.
>
> Anger it was that won him hence
> As only Anger taught him sense.
>
> Often my tears fall in a shower
> Because of Anger's freeing power.

My meditation this evening on Anger—Curse or Blessing: Curse and Blessing—could go on for much longer before the subject began to be exhausted. I want in fact to end it in a rather odd way.

I've come up to Cambridge for several reasons. In the last few days, I've had a book published about a Cambridge don, which I've called a 'symposium', concerning the Reverend Canon F. A. Simpson: Historian, Preacher and Eccentric. I've entitled it *A Last Eccentric*. I knew him well when I was Chaplain of Trinity in the 60s. I expect that most people will like the book—if they like it—because of the anecdotes of Simpson's antics. And they were many. But, in fact, his prose, in my judgement, is unsurpassed in this century; and there's some evidence that much of his madness resulted from the experience of visiting in Cambridge the casualties of the First World War. Simpson did not go to the Somme: the Somme came to him in the terrible wounds of those who lay in the temporary hospital under the arches of Nevile's Court, Trinity. He said in a university sermon in 1914 that at such a moment some would feel that Christianity was bankrupt, and went on:

> Now, behind any such feeling as that there lies at once an admission and an assumption: the one true, the other unhappily false. The admission is that in the abstract, our present ultimate method of settling international disputes is contrary to the mind of Christ. That is probably true. The assumption is that in the face of that fact there is something exceptional in the concrete approbation of war by organised Christianity. That is certainly not true.
>
> Our present latest and greatest European war is in one thing, at any rate, not exceptional: but typical, to wit, that on the eve of it organised Christianity lifted hardly a little finger to avert it; and that on the outbreak of it, it was at once ready to assure every country concerned in it that its particular participation in it was right. War in general may be wrong, perhaps; but this particular war, so long as it lasts, is always right; and always equally right for both sides. That has been the general contribution of the vast majority of Christian teachers and preachers in all wars between Christian peoples: an admirably impartial alacrity to bless the banners of both sides.
>
> When you hear, for example—and it is an experience from which none who are called upon to hear sermons can expect this time to be exempt—when you hear ministers of Christ proving how Christian a thing it is that men should fight in this war, on our side; then I do not say that you should think them wrong. But I do say this: that hearers of the Word would do well to remember what preachers of it sometimes forget; that at that very moment, with no whit less fervour and sincerity, other Christian preachers of equal eminence, accounted by *their* audience equally well-informed, are engaged in proving to the champions of the opposite side the peculiarly Christlike character of their cause, with the assurance of God's especial favour towards them.
>
> That is a wholesome and sobering thought to have in mind; and one which may even carry in its train a tinge of penitence, if we go on to remember that as it is in this war so it has been in all great inter-Christian wars since Christ was lifted up upon the Cross: Christ, whom by our wars we crucify afresh in the body of his Church: Christ, whom by our perpetual justification of them, we put to open shame in the eyes of all the heathen. With what heart, with what hope, with what *right*, can we carry his gospel to the ancient civilisations of the East . . . if that, indeed, is what it spells? A Christianity so clean cut off from Christ would become a thing not merely incapable of defence, but unworthy of defending.

It is not only Simpson's prose I admire in that passage—it's his courage; but above all it's his ice-like anger—which, I believe, echoes the anger of God.

❧ 3

C. F. ANDREWS

Pembroke House, Walworth;
13 October 1991

He was touching hearts wherever he went, for there were few who could resist
him. He went to Cambridge, and was pleased to find himself walking in the
gardens of Trinity College with Charlie Andrews. Nehru had attended Trinity
College; so had Newton, Bacon and Tennyson, but Gandhi was not concerned
with them. He was delighted to be walking along the paths Nehru had
trodden.

Those words come from *The Life and Death of Mahatma Gandhi* by
Robert Payne. Let me repeat one sentence of that paragraph: 'He went
to Cambridge, and was pleased to find himself walking in the gardens of
Trinity College with Charlie Andrews.' But whoever was 'Charlie
Andrews'?

Charles Freer Andrews was born in 1871 in Newcastle. He went to
school, where his family moved to, in Birmingham, to King Edward VI
School. His father had left the Methodist ministry to become an
Irvingite—a member of the Catholic Apostolic Church.

In a set of brilliant contemporaries at King Edward's School, C. F.
Andrews was outstanding. He went up to Cambridge, to Pembroke
College, in 1890. His tutor there was undoubtedly a great man and a
great influence on him: C. H. Prior.

Andrews was a devout young man. He went to chapel every morning.
He rowed hard, talked hard and worked hard. He joined the company of
evangelical Christians in Cambridge called the C.I.C.C.U. But he was
soon revolted by what they then preached about Hell, and by the way
they took every word of the Bible as literally true.

Andrews could never pocket his intellect when it came to believing—
indeed, all his life he was wrestling with his intellectual doubts and
difficulties; and, at Cambridge, he swallowed eagerly all that Gore, later
Bishop Gore, had to say in his lectures on 'the fearless application of the
principles of scientific enquiry to every part of the Bible'.

While he was up at Cambridge he threw himself wholeheartedly into
the work of the Cambridge branch of the Christian Social Union, dominated at the time by people like Canon Scott Holland, who wrote the
hymn 'Judge eternal, throned in splendour'.

It was natural with his involvement in the Christian Social Union that

14

Andrews should spend many of his vacation weeks in South London at his College Mission, and he was an enthusiastic member of the Mission Committee in Cambridge.

In 1895 he won the Burney Prize with an essay on 'The Relation of Christianity to the conflict between Capital and Labour'.

Andrews' greatest friend at Cambridge was Basil Westcott, the son of the great Bishop of Durham; and Bishop Westcott was also clearly a very great influence on Andrews, when he went to stay with the bishop and his family, and went on holiday with them.

Andrews records the bishop saying to him one day: 'Remember, Andrews, *nothing, nothing* that is *truly human* can be left outside the Christian faith without destroying the very reason for its existence.'

Andrews and Westcott talked a good deal about industry and industrial conflicts and social problems. It was Westcott who in 1892 had intervened in the miners' strike, and was asked to act as arbitrator between the owners and the men, and it was Westcott who first turned Andrews' thoughts towards India. Westcott maintained that India could be the Greece of the modern world: the thinking nation and the religious nation combined in one.

In 1893, Andrews got a First in Classics, and in 1895, a First in Theology, and then he left Cambridge for six weeks to think out what his future should be—furnished with the advice of Bishop Westcott, of C. H. Prior, and of Forbes Robinson, uncle of Bishop John Robinson.

Andrews decided he would probably get ordained, but to do first a year's preparatory work as a layman, working things out for himself in Bishop Westcott's diocese of Durham, in a Sunderland shipyard parish, at Monkwearmouth, a few miles from where he'd been born.

Next year, in 1896, C. H. Prior wrote to Andrews asking him to become the Pembroke Missioner in South London. So it was that on 21 April 1896 Andrews arrived in Walworth, amid the slums of the Elephant and Castle and, six weeks later, he was ordained deacon by Edward Stuart Talbot, Bishop of Rochester, soon to be the first Bishop of Southwark.

What South London meant to C. F. Andrews he has recorded in his book *What I owe to Christ*, which went through five editions in its first six months. There is a whole chapter in that book on Pembroke College Mission.

It was in June 1897 that Andrews was ordained priest, in Southwark Cathedral—but, it is good to record, only after an agonizing struggle to square his conscience with the Thirty-Nine Articles.

Two years later, his health broke down. He had had rheumatic fever as a child, and clearly he had just worn himself out in Walworth. Pembroke College was kind to him, and elected him to a Fellowship of the College, and he became at the same time Vice-Principal of what is now Westcott

House: the theological college in Jesus Lane.

When Andrews returned to Cambridge, C. H. Prior was dying of cancer and, shortly after, Basil Westcott died of cholera, in Delhi.

Basil's death in India turned Andrews' attention in that direction. He felt he must literally take Basil Westcott's place. So, in spite of the fact that he was enormously used in Cambridge, in 1904 he went out to India.

There is a biography of Andrews by an Indian, Bernarsidas Chaturvedi, published in 1950, which covers particularly well his years in India and is tremendously worth reading.

Then there are Andrews' own books: *Mahatma Gandhi at Work*; *Mahatma Gandhi: his own story*; *Mahatma Gandhi's ideas*; and, as I've said, his autobiography, *What I owe to Christ*. Obviously, this evening I can only speak of Andrews' life in India fragmentarily.

From 1904 to 1907 he was at St Stephen's College, Delhi. From that period comes the saying of Andrews that I like most of all: 'Charity', he said 'is the careful inquiry into the need of one's fellow men that enables one to give the exact help needed.'

In the latter part of his time at St Stephen's College, Andrews became a campaigner against racial exclusiveness and social injustice. But the spirit of the *battlefield* was foreign to him. It was as much *Indian* writings as the New Testament which were now influencing him. He was particularly fond of quoting a passage which could almost have come from the New Testament, and which he set alongside the Beatitudes:

> Farid, if a man beat thee,
> Beat him not in return, but kiss his feet.
> Farid, if thou long for the Lord of all,
> Become as grass for men to tread on.
> Farid, when one man breakest thee
> And another trampleth on thee,
> Then shalt thou enter the Courts of the Lord.
> Let a man overcome anger by love,
> Let him overcome evil by good,
> Let a man overcome greed by liberality,
> Let him overcome the liar by the truth.

Already Andrews was seeing how Christianity and Hinduism *had* to be friends. He became great and lifelong friends with the poet Rabindranath Tagore, and was always quoting his writings. In 1910, in a pamphlet on *India in Transition*, he was quoting approvingly from Tagore:

> If Christianity is to succeed it must not come forward primarily as an antagonist and a rival to the great religious strivings of the past. It must come as a helper and a fulfiller, a peacemaker and a friend. There must no longer be the desire simply to capture converts from Hinduism, but to come to her aid in the needful time of trouble, and to help her in the fulfilment of duties she has long neglected.

In 1914, Andrews heard that in South Africa, in Natal, Indians had been fired on. He felt constrained to go there immediately and do what he could. When he arrived at Durban, Gandhi, a small slight figure wearing the coarse dhoti of an indentured labourer, was waiting for him on the dock side. It was their first meeting, and Andrews' first act on landing was to bend swiftly down and touch Gandhi's feet. This gesture of reverence, though made as quickly and as unobtrusively as possible, caused an uproar in the white press. Andrews wrote to Tagore: 'They boil over with indignation that I—an Englishman mind you—should have touched the feet of an Asiatic. When I remind them that Christ and St Paul and St John were Asiatics they grow restive and say that things were altogether different then.'

Andrews describes a memorable scene one evening in Durban:

> The strain of a long day of unwearied ministry among the poor was over. In the still afterglow of twilight, Mahatma Gandhi was seated under the open sky. He nursed a sick child on his lap, a little Muslim boy, and next to him was a Christian Zulu girl from the mission across the hill. He read us some Gujarati verses about the love of God, and explained them in English. Then these Gujarati hymns were sung by the children's voices. He asked me to sing 'Lead, kindly light' as the darkness grew deeper, and in the silence which followed its close, repeated quietly the last lines:
>
> > And with the morn those angel faces smile,
> > Which I have loved long since, and lost awhile.

It is clear that within two or three days Andrews was a very close friend of Gandhi. And ten years later the friendship of Andrews was still central to Gandhi's life. Gandhi writes to him in a memorable letter on 20 October 1924: 'I have missed you every moment today. Oh your *love!*'

In that letter I find the secret of all true missionary work—the love and understanding of the people to whom you are missionary.

When I was travelling the world some years ago I came across a C. F. Andrews School in Uganda, for African Asians, and another in Fiji for Indians of the Pacific Islands. In Calcutta, I visited Andrews' grave in Lower Cemetery Road. Around the kerbstone were the words 'Deenabandu Friend of the Poor'. In Delhi, I visited St Stephen's College where Andrews taught, and the church whose service register he signed when he came back to celebrate the Holy Communion for the first time after his long conscientious severance from the priesthood. While I was in India there was a centenary stamp to mark C. F. Andrews' birth. In that Hindu country the Indian Government and Indian people desired to pay their tribute to the man from whom they had learnt so much of Christian love—love in action.

In the sixties we named a Canon's Stall in Southwark Cathedral—his Cathedral—after Charles Freer Andrews. We did not want merely to draw attention to him as a man of the past. We found ourselves thinking of him as a very modern man, with his doubts about the Creeds and his sitting loose to the institutional side of religion, but with, nevertheless, a fierce love for the dignity of human beings whatever their race or their class and a profound religious faith and commitment. We wanted to say that this sort of human being, this sort of Christian, has been and is now needed in South London, and England and in the world. He is needed in Delhi, and Durban—and in the Walworth Road—and today humanity has need of such men as Andrews.

At all events, I hope you now understand who Charlie Andrews was and why I should have wanted to thank God for him this evening, and to bubble over about him to you.

4

TREVOR HUDDLESTON

Sermon before the University of Oxford; 20 October 1991

Lytton Strachey once wrote: 'It is perhaps as difficult to *write* a good life as to *live* one.'

At the moment I am trying to write a good life of someone who I have little doubt has lived one: Bishop Trevor Huddleston.

It was at the seventieth birthday party of Diana Collins, the widow of Canon John Collins, erstwhile Dean of Oriel and Canon of St Paul's and founder of Christian Action, that Trevor Huddleston, who had been reading my biography of Bishop John Robinson, made the kind observation that he would much like me to write his biography; but, he added, 'I'm not having one written while I'm alive.' I rather approved of that; but I did not see why we shouldn't meet regularly, so that I could at least begin the task and perhaps preserve memories which might otherwise be lost. So, for the last four years, Bishop Trevor and I have met roughly every six weeks for a meal and a talk together.

But what has happened as I have got on with the work is that I have realized, as I did when writing the biography of John Robinson, that you cannot write a life of such a person without confronting some taxing questions of theology, spirituality, and of faith in relation to life. And all I propose to do this morning is to share with you some of those 'confrontations'. But, first, let me give you a 'Brief Life' of Trevor Huddleston.

He was born in 1913, the son of Captain Sir Ernest Whiteside Huddleston, who eventually commanded the Indian Navy. 1913 was, of course, the year before the First World War, and Captain Huddleston was absent in India when Trevor was born. He did not see his father till he was seven. His mother, too, was often absent in India. Trevor could only remember two or three times when his parents were at home together in England before his father's permanent return when he was twelve.

He was brought up, in Hampstead, by a wealthy widowed aunt; and Trevor would maintain he had an idyllic childhood. His devout Anglo-Catholic Hampstead home and church were powerful influences upon him, and early in his childhood he began to think he was called to the priesthood. Later, there was the huge influence of Lancing College; and here, at Christ Church, and under the influence of the Church in Oxford, Trevor felt the call to be a monk as well as a priest.

His Anglo-Catholicism was widened and deepened through the Lancing College Mission's work in the slums of South London. Pusey House also put him in touch with *East* Enders through work in the summer vacations in the hopfields of Kent; and there was the Anglo-Catholic Summer School of Sociology, with speakers like T. S. Eliot and Nicholas Berdyaev.

Though Trevor only obtained a Second in History, to read History under the personal tuition of J. C. Masterman and Keith Feiling was a privilege that would stand him in good stead for many succeeding years.

After Oxford, Trevor spent some invaluable time out in Ceylon, as it then was, and up the Irrawaddy, and in India and, finally, in Palestine, in the steps of Charles de Foucauld. During his time at Wells Theological College, he was greatly influenced by a rather eccentric nearby village priest, J. F. Briscoe, who edited *The Priest's Book of Private Devotions*, who would write in his diary when one of his protégés married: 'One gone'. Trevor was ordained in 1936, at the height of the Depression, to a curacy in the railway town of Swindon.

It was in 1939 that Trevor, now twenty-six years of age, went to Mirfield, to test his vocation to the Community of the Resurrection. Fr Edward Keble Talbot, the Superior, a man of considerable wisdom and stature, warned Trevor that for him having no children would prove the most costly demand of the Religious Life.

Those wartime reclusive years at Mirfield, when every other able-bodied young man was being called up, were testing indeed. It is significant that none of his fellow novices saw in Trevor a future leader. He was in fact the last person they could imagine defying authority—though a visitor once asked concerning Trevor: 'Who is that novice with the face of an angel who would gladly go to the fires of Smithfield?'

What transformed Trevor was one of those unpredictable events which are the stuff of human biography. Raymond Raynes returned from South Africa to be Superior of the Community. He arrived unexpected and unannounced. Trevor was Servitor, that is to say, on kitchen and front-door duty. He opened the door to Raymond, who was clearly ill, and who was put to bed. Trevor took up Raymond's meals to his sick-room for a week or so, and was ordered to stay and talk. Soon it was announced that Raymond had decided that Trevor should be his successor in South Africa as priest-in-charge of Sophiatown and Orlando, Johannesburg.

He might never have got there, for the ship sailed for Cape Town, in convoy, in 1943, but the convoy was bombed, off Portugal, and one ship was sunk and the ship in which Trevor was sailing was narrowly missed.

Most of you will know a good deal about Trevor's twelve years in South Africa, for his book concerning those years, *Naught for Your*

Comfort, became a best seller, and is still in print, and has sold well over a quarter of a million copies.

It was in 1955 that Raymond Raynes took the difficult decision to recall Trevor to England. He would probably have been expelled from South Africa anyhow. Then followed two unhappy years, with Trevor trying to be Guardian of Novices at Mirfield and at the same time to cope with his bereavement of Africa and with the deluge of correspondence and invitations to speak that followed *Naught for Your Comfort*. Then came two more years as Prior of the London House of the Community, near to the scene of the Notting Hill Riots. That, too, was a drowning time.

Evelyn Baring, then Lord Howick, was one of those who believed that Trevor should go back to Africa. Lord Howick, in his days as High Commissioner to South Africa, had come to know Trevor very well. In 1960 he was chairman of the Universities' Mission to Central Africa, and thought Trevor just the man to be bishop of a diocese in Tanganyika, the fourth poorest country in the world, then on the verge of independence, under the leadership of Julius Nyerere. What Lord Howick thought coincided with what those in authority in the Community of the Resurrection thought, so in 1960 Trevor was consecrated Bishop of Masasi.

I have just returned from three weeks there, assessing Trevor's achievement as bishop of a rural African diocese utterly unlike urban Johannesburg. I am clear that insufficient attention has been given to Trevor's ministry in Masasi in those eight years 1960 to 1968. They have been overshadowed by his achievement in South Africa. It is to my mind very significant that Nyerere, a Roman Catholic, simply called Trevor 'our bishop'. They worked together as partners.

Here, and now, I should remind you that it was in the midst of his years in Masasi that Trevor returned to Oxford, in 1963, to conduct the Mission to this University, delivering addresses which were thought worthy to be published as a Fontana paperback, *The True and Living God*.

Then, after Masasi, there followed for Trevor a gruelling decade as Bishop of that most exacting of all suffragan sees, Stepney, with all the problems and possibilities of the East End of London. And I have never heard anyone question that Trevor was a great Bishop of Stepney.

Finally, that is to say, the final phase of Trevor's ministry before his retirement, so-called, was five years as Bishop of Mauritius and Archbishop of the Indian Ocean, with Madagascar and the Seychelles within his care and jurisdiction. But in his eight years of retirement he has been a very active President of the Anti-Apartheid Movement and Chairman of the International Defence and Aid Fund.

Well: that must suffice as a 'Brief Life' of Bishop Trevor. And now I must turn to some of what I have called the 'confrontations': the questions of theology, spirituality and faith in relation to life. Let us begin at the beginning.

In a post-Freudian age, a biographer is bound to pay particular attention to his subject's infancy and childhood. Trevor Huddleston maintains he had an 'idyllic' childhood: seeing little of his parents until he was twelve and being brought up by a wealthy widowed aunt. But he also describes in graphic detail his imaginary companion, whom he called by the rather odd name 'Gilkert'. He played with him, and talked with him, rather as Jung used to talk with his fantasy figure Philemon. Trevor retained a very vivid mental picture of Gilkert: a wraith-like, wispy figure, with fair, almost white, hair.

I cannot myself believe that an 'idyllic' childhood and such a figure sort well together. Such a figure surely betokens an inner aloneness, at least at that time. But one is not surprised to encounter in later years a somewhat reclusive person. And as one ponders Trevor the man of prayer—and from his youth up his disciplined daily prayer is one of his most notable characteristics—one is bound to ask how much that prayer is essentially an extension, development and transmuting of his relationship with his childhood companion.

A second area of questioning arises for me in the realm of Trevor's vocation and calling. Trevor from an early age felt called to the priesthood; and, indeed, when his sister, four years older than himself, was confirmed in St Paul's, Bedford, by Bishop Furse of St Albans, resplendent in cope, Trevor clearly remembers looking at him in wonder and saying to himself: 'I am going to be a bishop.' From his Oxford years he felt called to be a monk.

When you write the biography of someone like Trevor, you cannot avoid answering the direct question: 'Does God call particular people to a particular work?' And, what precisely does that mean? Is it a fairly isolated phenomenon? Does he call only men—and people who have been to places like Lancing and Christ Church? Or does he call men—and women—from the housing estates of Stepney and the villages of Masasi? The phenomenon of the able-bodied Trevor at Mirfield resisting call-up to the armed forces because God had called him to be a monk is worthy of our attention. It meant more to Trevor than a simple statement that to be a monk was the best way of using his gifts. He meant what he said. He believed God had called him.

It is, of course, easy to be wise after the event: after looking at the way Trevor was used in South Africa and Central Africa, and to say: 'Clearly God called and empowered him.' Certainly his gifts have been hugely used. Shakespeare assures us 'there's a special providence in the fall of a sparrow'. In Trevor's case you need to believe there was a special providence in his being on duty as Servitor at Mirfield when Raymond Raynes returned from South Africa; even a special providence in Raymond's sickness when the ship came home.

Another area of question arises concerning the remarkable transformation that took place in Trevor once he had got to Africa: the
change from Trevor the recluse to Trevor the scourge of apartheid; from
Trevor obedient to authority to Trevor the reformer and, indeed, the
revolutionary. In a sense, the scandal of the situation that greeted him is
sufficient to account for the change in him. Indelible in his memory were
the words of Basil Jellicoe he had heard as a boy of twelve from the
pulpit of All Saints' Margaret Street: 'Slums are the outward and visible
sign of an inward and spiritual disgrace.' But something psychophysical
seems to have happened in Trevor. It is more than just a guess to say that
the affection, physically expressed, that Trevor received daily from the
children of Sophiatown did much to effect that change. Archbishop
Desmond Tutu has written recently

> If Trevor wore a white cassock, it did not remain clean for long, as he trudged
> the dusty streets of Sophiatown, with little urchins and grubby fingers always
> waiting to touch him, and calling out 'Fader' with obvious affection in their
> little voices. He loved us—tremendous! He was fond of letting you sit on his
> lap, and in 1978, when I told people at the Lambeth Conference that I used to
> sit on Trevor's lap, they looked at me, looking so decrepit, and him still very
> sprightly, and I don't think they believed me.

One of the most crucial areas of confrontation in Trevor's life was
through his relations with the Archbishop of Cape Town, Geoffrey
Clayton, who had first been his Bishop in Johannesburg. Both were
enemies of apartheid; but Clayton was a gradualist, Huddleston an
absolutist.

Clayton was undoubtedly a good and holy man, but *he* believed it was
the duty of the Church in South Africa to resist the Government of South
Africa to the point of breaking the law only if the State prevented black
and white *worshipping* together.

Trevor believed that to protest only when black and white were forbidden to *worship* together and not to protest when they were forbidden to
live together was pietism.

It has to be said that when the South African Government brought in a
bill that would prevent mixed worship, Clayton gathered the bishops
together and said he would go to prison rather than agree to such a
measure. They spent Shrove Tuesday and Ash Wednesday 1957 drafting
a letter to the Government. Having signed and posted the letter, Clayton
believed he might indeed be arrested; but that fateful day when the
anxious Clayton put his signature to the letter, he had a heart attack and
died.

Not only the Archbishop of Cape Town, but the Archbishop of Canterbury, Geoffrey Fisher, told Huddleston that his methods were entirely

wrong. But of the three, only Trevor had *lived* in a native location. And Trevor could never forget the words of Frank Weston, Bishop of Zanzibar, to the Anglo-Catholic Congress of 1923: 'You cannot claim to worship Jesus in the tabernacle if you do not pity Jesus in the slum . . . It is folly, it is madness, to suppose that you can worship Jesus in the Sacrament and Jesus on the throne of glory, when you are sweating Him in the bodies and souls of his children.'

Trevor Huddleston is certainly a character of contradictions. It is curious, is it not, that Trevor Huddleston, son of Captain Sir Ernest Whiteside Huddleston, commander of the Royal Indian Navy, should be sent out as a *white* priest, with little training for the job, to be priest-in-charge of a parish of 80,000 *black* people; and, just when every white civil servant was preparing to leave Tanganyika, should become the *white* bishop of an overwhelmingly *black* diocese? There seems to me here a kind of consecrated imperialism: the kind of imperialism that found money for the education of this individual and that in Masasi, for hospitals there, for schools for the blind, and so on. At the end of an era of paternalism 'Father' Huddleston, rejecting as utterly offensive the description of black Africans as 'children' and working with and alongside black leaders, and treating them as equals, retained nevertheless not only paternal but paternalistic attitudes in conforming himself to a paternalist system. Trevor could compromise when the gospel demanded it.

His enthusiastic support for the policies and politics of President Nyerere and the Arusha declaration was based on Christian convictions and principles; yet when one sees the dismal state of Tanzania's economy, as I have seen it recently in Masasi, there are questions that cannot be avoided. By the Church in the person of Trevor endorsing State policies, were these policies promoted for longer than would otherwise have been the case? In Tanzania today, exports have collapsed; roads, schools and hospitals are in a parlous state; transport is chaotic; and the country has become dependent on aid. Agriculture, the mainstay of the Tanzanian economy, has suffered from political programmes and policies. Above all, the loss of incentives has caused the decline in production. Moral exhortation to produce for the collective good has been shown to be no substitute for material incentives, in Tanzania as in Eastern Europe. By the 1980s, many of Nyerere's original ideas were corrupted. The party had become a means of controlling the people. The urban educated élite were imposing their ideology on the rural peasantry. Corruption and inefficiency had become the norm.

All this has to be set against considerable social and political achievements. There is a genuine pride in nationhood in Tanzania which transcends tribal differences: an uncommon thing in Africa. Tanzanians point out that they have been at peace since independence. So although significant improvements in health in Masasi Diocese since Bishop

Trevor's time are as hard to find as improvements in the quality of education, there have been huge, if unquantifiable, benefits from the Nyerere years; and Bishop Trevor only did what any prophet and conscientious Christian leader would have done in giving President Nyerere his full support.

Trevor Huddleston is often portrayed as inflexible. Certainly at first, having been brought up as a rather sectarian Anglo-Catholic, he was for many years opposed to that first fruit of the Ecumenical Movement, the Church of South India. But in the later years of his ministry he has been much involved in the latest and most radically ecumenical movement: that which is concerned with the mutual understanding of the major world religions. Meeting, for instance, Muslims, and working with them, in South Africa, Masasi, Mauritius and Madagascar, the sectarian Anglo-Catholic ceased to have institutional Christianity as his chief concern and has become more Catholic in its profoundest sense: concerned with the universal.

Similarly, at the outset of his ordained ministry he was utterly opposed to the ordination of women, but in his later years he has seen clearly that there is more than one apartheid in this world, not least that which makes of women a 'lesser breed without the law'. Those who speak of the inflexibility of Trevor usually mean he is inflexibly anti-apartheid. He would gladly plead guilty to that.

No one who knows Trevor Huddleston intimately can deny one fact: that he is in a rather old-fashioned sense a man of God. Living in a few rooms at the top of the Vicarage of St James's Piccadilly, he looks for all the world like a solitary, and there is still much of the monk about him. He not only maintains his prayer and spiritual discipline; prayer remains the very centre of his life.

But 'for all the world' is not an unimportant phrase. Close to Piccadilly Circus, he is available to the media and to such leaders of the world as seek him out: people like Julius Nyerere, Nelson Mandela, Sonny Ramphal. And, if they press him, he will fly to the ends of the earth. He is undoubtedly a man of God—at God's disposal—and therefore a man of and for the world.

It is surely one of the most remarkable facts of our time that after all that the black people have suffered, it was a white Christian bishop whom the ANC asked to open their first conference in freedom in South Africa only a few weeks ago.

When I asked myself why they made Trevor their choice, it is, again, Archbishop Tutu who I think provides the best answer. He says: 'I was in hospital for twenty months with TB, and if Father Huddleston was in Johannesburg he made it a point to visit me at least once a week during those twenty months. I was just a nonentity, thirteen years old, and yet he paid so much attention to me.' And he adds, almost as an afterthought, 'And you could have knocked me down with a feather, young as I was at the time, when this man doffed his hat to my mother. I couldn't understand a white man doffing his hat to a black woman, an *uneducated* black woman.'

It may not be easy but it is undoubtedly a privilege to write the life of such a man.

5

BLESSED ARE THE PEACEMAKERS

*Gray's Inn Chapel;
Remembrance Day,
10 November 1991*

'Blessed are the peacemakers.'

Matthew 5.9

Each year, Armistice Day is subtly, or not so subtly, different. Subtly, the word Armistice itself becomes more ancient, antique, even out-of-date, out of the experience of the young. Not so subtly, each year has its new casualties of 'man's inhumanity to man' to be not only remembered, but faced and acknowledged.

This year, we might so easily have been having to face—to recall and remember—a blood-bath in the Gulf, with huge casualties, civilian and military, on every side. There is understandable relief that this is not so; but that very relief may cause us to underestimate and refuse to face just what did happen in the Gulf such a short time ago.

The University of Illinois, charged with making a special study, speaks of the lives of 170,000 children alone having been lost. Conservative estimates require at least another 100,000 Iraqi soldiers to be added to the list of the dead; probably 30,000 Kuwaiti soldiers killed, and those of other nationalities. But what was spent on weapons is the equivalent of a world disaster in terms of the diversion of funds from the hungry of the Third World, with literally incalculable consequences.

I speak with both knowledge and feeling on this aspect of the price of war, for, as some of you know, I've recently returned from the Tanzania/ Mozambique border, and have seen with my own eyes the state of hospitals with, for instance, the one operating table of one hospital broken down, beyond repair, and only two doctors for 300,000 people— one on duty at a time—and not able to afford more.

In our one world today, peace is indivisible; because so, too, in our one world, is war. It affects the whole world, though with appalling inequality.

So I am myself glad that there is still one Sunday of the year on which those who will can deepen their understanding of peace*making*. And a profound *remembrance* is, I believe, the gateway to peace*making*—just because the conflicts of the present are always rooted in the past, sometimes the recent, and sometimes the ancient past.

William Faulkner said succinctly: 'The past is not dead and gone: it isn't even past.' Put another way, we might say that getting past our past is a prerequisite for getting into our future.

That process of 'getting past our past and getting into the future', in the Christian vocabulary—but not in the Christian vocabulary alone—is called 'forgiveness'.

The Jewish philosopher Hannah Arendt has argued: 'Without being released from the consequences of what we have done, our capacity to act would be confined to a single deed from which we could never recover. We could remain the victims of its consequences for ever.'

Hannah Arendt—who, I say again, is a Jewish philosopher—goes on, somewhat surprisingly: 'The discoverer of the role of forgiveness in the realm of human affairs was Jesus of Nazareth. The fact that he made this discovery in a religious context and articulated it in a religious language is no reason to take it any less seriously in a strictly secular sense.'

I find myself smiling a little at that somewhat self-conscious and defensive secularity. Hannah Arendt continues:

> Only through this constant mutual release from what they do can humans remain free agents, only by constant willingness to change their minds and start again can they be trusted with so great a power as that to begin something new.
>
> Forgiving, in other words, is the only reaction which does not merely *re*-act but acts anew and unexpectedly, unconditioned by the act which provoked it, and therefore freeing from its consequences both the one who forgives and the one who is forgiven.

Thus, to the secular Hannah Arendt, forgiveness is one way of facing, and remembering, and responding to, and dealing with, the past.

The American poet Robert Frost in his poem 'The Star-Splitter' puts the matter with stark simplicity. He says: 'To be social is to be forgiving.'

Without forgiveness at the personal level, hurts go unchecked, and we recycle failures, resentments, bitterness and mistrusts in our lives. Without forgiveness there can be no real peace and no lasting reconciliation.

But it is not only at the individual and the personal level that forgiveness must be brought to bear, but at the political level, that is to say, at the social level of the structures of society; for politics is simply the way we individual human beings organize ourselves in groups, locally, nationally and internationally, to determine and distribute the use of resources, often in short supply—and the way we handle the institutions we create for doing this.

It is forgiveness which has to be worked out at this very moment, with such care and such pain, in Yugoslavia, in Ireland, in Zaire, in Israel and Palestine, and elsewhere.

Sometimes instead of talking of forgiveness in personal and social relationship I find it better to talk of 'seeking justice'. And I'm sure that Archbishop William Temple was right to say that

> one reason why the church has counted for comparatively little in public affairs in recent times is that its spokesmen have talked a great deal too much about love and not nearly enough about justice. Justice [he says] is the first expression of love. It is not something contrary to love, which love mitigates and softens. It is the first expression of it, that must be satisfied before the other and higher expressions can rightly find their place.

Yet justice can sometimes seem a rather impersonal concept. We talk, for instance, of retributive justice, and the scales of justice seem to be built visibly but impersonally into the phrase; but love, mercy and forgiveness suggest personal initiatives that may in fact secure justice, and without them justice may not be secured.

Certainly, in the final analysis, forgiveness does not contradict justice. The Biblical scholar Norman Snaith, in his book *The Distinctive Ideas of the Old Testament*, in which he studies, for instance, the Hebrew word for justice—*tsedeq*—says that it means 'more than sound ethical conduct, and shows a persistent tendency to topple over into benevolence, and easily to have a special reference to those who stand in dire need of a Helper'. 'As author of justice,' he says 'God loves justice, but, even more, he loves human beings and their restoration to just relationships. Insofar as forgiveness requires the identification and condemnation of behaviour that has alienated two or more parties to a conflict, it safeguards the majesty of the law.' The sanctions that are being imposed upon Yugoslavia at this moment can be seen as part of that identification and condemnation which is a prerequisite of forgiveness.

I was wondering how I might illustrate all that with something else contemporary when I was asked to read something which Desmond Tutu, Archbishop of Capetown, has recently written.

> On 20 March 1990 [he writes] I was one of thousands in the Windhoek Stadium waiting for the clock to strike the midnight hour, when Namibia would become an independent nation. Just before this auspicious hour, the South African State President, Mr de Klerk, made a very good speech which was received with very warm applause. But I thought then that he missed a golden opportunity to have made a speech that would have set the world agog. He failed to say two things which would have stamped his speech as outstanding and epoch-making. Had Mr de Klerk added something like, 'If we have caused you any pain in the past, I apologise, and to help you celebrate your richly deserved independence we are giving you Walvis Bay', the stadium would have erupted ecstatically. (The port of Walvis Bay is a bone of

contention between South Africa and Namibia, it is Namibia's only natural outlet to the outside world.) Mr de Klerk would have dealt with the horrible entail of the past, a legacy of potential hostility, anger, bitterness, and vengefulness that augured ill for future relations between the neighbouring countries. He would have done so by repenting on behalf of his people and would have demonstrated his sincerity by the token reparation of abandoning South African claims to Walvis Bay.

On 6 August 1985 I was present in Hiroshima, with many thousands, as the Japanese commemorated the dropping of the atom bombs on Nagasaki and Hiroshima. As guests, with other Nobel laureates, of the City of Hiroshima, we had been to the commemorative museum and seen the exhibits and the films recording the levels to which we are capable of sinking in our inhumanity to one another. We met with several disfigured survivors of that horrible obscenity, perpetrated forty years earlier, and we were devastated. I asked what purpose was being served by recalling such a traumatic experience, and I was deeply touched when the Japanese said, without bitterness or rancour, that they commemorated it because this awful thing had happened to them and they did not want it ever to happen again to others. I found their willingness to forgive, and their concern for humankind, quite staggering.

I myself have no doubt that repentance and forgiveness are indispensable for setting right relationships between those who have been wronged and the wrongdoers, within nations and between nations. Unless you deal with the past in a creative and positive manner, you run the risk of having no future worth speaking about. The past can have a baleful or beneficent impact on the future. This is a fact that is absolutely crucial for South Africa at the present time. It stands on the threshold of exciting possibilities of creating a new, democratic, non-racial, and non-sexist society largely because of the new initiatives of Mr de Klerk. And yet that possible future will be seriously undermined if those who benefited from the obnoxious apartheid system, perceived as the oppressors, will not ask for forgiveness for the awful things done under apartheid and if the victims, the oppressed, do not offer forgiveness.

Repentance and forgiveness do make new beginnings possible. They have an inner dynamic which can set off critical acts which then develop a momentum towards new possibilities. I have no doubt that the the nature of the meetings that Mr de Klerk and his colleagues had with Nelson Mandela and other long-term political prisoners must have played an important role in the decisions that Mr de Klerk subsequently made. Had they encountered embittered people, hell-bent on revenge, looking to get their own back on those who had treated them so unjustly, it is doubtful whether Mr de Klerk would have risked releasing them and embarking on the course which makes the emergence of a democratic dispensation a strong probability.

Many believe that you cannot just let bygones be bygones, when people have been subjected to the anguish of the injustices and atrocities of, say, apartheid; when three and a half million people have been forcibly uprooted from their traditional homes and dumped, many of them in poverty-stricken Bantustan homeland resettlement camps, or relocated in crowded ghetto townships many miles from their places of work when formerly they had lived in mixed residential areas near the cities where they worked; or when they have suffered the trauma of learning of the mysterious deaths in detention of their loved ones. The pain of these searing experiences goes deep, and the wounds are raw and open. Part of the soothing balm that can be poured over them to assuage the agony is without doubt the expression of repentance at having been part of a community or a system that caused the hurts of oppression and inhumanity.

It was on a recent Remembrance Day, you may remember, that there was a terrible bomb outrage in Northern Ireland; but you will also remember, this Remembrance Day, that act of forgiveness of Gordon Wilson after his daughter died as a result of that outrage. The Queen in her Christmas broadcast that year made specific mention of that act.

Blessed are the peace*makers*: They will always be thinking of new creative acts they might be making when and where relationships, social and personal, have broken down or are likely to break down. Of course, such acts will rarely be without cost. But Christians remember, whenever they take some initiative for reconciliation, small or large, Him who as *the* Peacemaker, at such cost, took such an initiative, and made on Calvary such an act of reparation and reconciliation for the healing of the nations and peoples of our so divided world.

6

THE JOURNEY
OF THE MAGI

Gray's Inn Chapel;
19 January 1992

It seems singularly appropriate that we should begin our new term and new year here in Chapel by welcoming our new Treasurer with his reading to us the story of the Wise Men bringing their 'costliest treasures' to the Infant Christ.

Often, on this particular Sunday, I find myself having in mind that revered member of this Inn, Bishop Lancelot Andrewes, commemorated in the stained glass of the Chapel window. He was James I's favourite court preacher, and I associate him inseparably with T. S. Eliot, who thought Andrewes' sermon on the Epiphany one of the finest examples of English prose, and, under its inspiration, wrote that poem which is arguably one of the finest of this century: *Journey of the Magi*.

Let me read just a few paragraphs of that Andrewes' sermon:

It was no summer progress. A cold coming they had of it, at this time of the year, just the worst time of the year to take a journey, and specially a long journey in. The ways deep, the weather sharp, the days short, the sun farthest off, *in solstitio brumali*, the very dead of winter. . . .

And these difficulties they overcame, of a wearisome, irksome, troublesome, dangerous, unseasonable journey; and for all this, they came. And came it cheerfully and quickly, as appeareth by the speed they made. It was but *vidimus, venimus,* with them—they saw and they came; no sooner saw, but they set out presently. So as upon the first appearing of the star, as it might be last night, they knew it was Balaam's star; it called them away; they made ready straight to begin their journey this morning. A sign they were highly conceited of His birth, believed some great matter of it, that they took all these pains, made all this haste, that they might be there to worship Him with all the possible speed they could. Sorry for nothing so much that they could not be there soon enough, with the very first, to do it even this day, the day of His birth. . . .

And we, what should we have done? Sure these men of the East shall rise in judgment against the men of the West, that is us, and their faith against ours in this point. With them it was but *vidimus, venimus*; with us it would have been but *veniemus* at most. Our fashion is to see and see again before we stir a foot, specially if it be to the worship of Christ. Come such a journey at such a time? No; but fairly have put it off to the spring of the year, till the days longer, and the ways fairer, and the weather warmer, till better travelling to Christ. Our Epiphany would sure have fallen in Easter week at the soonest.

As I have said, it was that sermon, preached before the King's Majesty, at Whitehall, on Christmas Day 1622, which, three hundred years later, inspired T. S. Eliot: inspired him to write a poem. But it not only inspired him to write *Journey of the Magi*. That poem occupies a pivotal place in Eliot's poetic development but also in what I will call Eliot's personal journey.

It is, of course, a commonplace today to describe human life as a journey and the Christian life as a pilgrimage. In the context of Eliot's life and work these images have a particular meaning.

Eliot was born in 1888 in Missouri. His upbringing was morally strict rather than profoundly spiritual. It was tinctured with the vagaries of Unitarianism. His early poems reflect an absorption with his private experience, though in his student days at Harvard he was already seeking a more ancient and more vigorous discipline, one unclouded by the mists of American liberal sentiment. That search led him first to the philosophy of F. H. Bradley, the Oxford Idealist, whose philosophy greatly influenced Bertrand Russell and Wittgenstein.

But it was in the interpretation of his past that Eliot was ultimately to discover well-springs of living water. In 1914 he journeyed to England, and in the pursuit of his own origins, he began to discover a framework for the assimilation and interpretation of his own personal experience.

Years later, in 1940, in his poem *East Coker*, he refers to the family into which he was born, which is to be found in *Burke's Distinguished Families of America*. Andrew Eliot of East Coker in Somerset left England in the late seventeenth century. The ashes of T. S. Eliot were, at his end, interred at East Coker.

But it was in 1927 that Eliot wrote *Journey of the Magi*. Earlier that year he had been prepared for confirmation by W. F. Stead, an American priest who was Chaplain of Worcester College, Oxford. On 29 June Eliot was baptized at Finstock Church in the Cotswolds, and the next day he was confirmed in the private chapel of the then Bishop of Oxford, T. B. Strong.

Eliot's biographer, Peter Ackroyd, calls *Journey of the Magi* 'the poem of a convert'. That is not an inaccurate description; but I would prefer to call it simply a 'thank-offering'.

When you read the first lines of the poem it becomes immediately clear that they are to some extent autobiographical.

A cold coming we had of it . . .

Eliot uses the dramatic imagery and careful alliteration of Andrewes to describe, and include, the experience of which he himself had written in his earlier poems *The Waste Land* and *The Hollow Men*.

The year before his confirmation, that is to say, the year before he wrote *Journey of the Magi* (1926) he had written an essay entitled *For Lancelot Andrewes* in which he extolled the virtues of a man who was for him the epitome of English Christianity. 'The voice of Andrewes', he wrote, 'is the voice of a man who has a formed visible Church behind him, who speaks with the old authority and the new culture . . . Andrewes is the first great preacher of the English Catholic Church.'

Journey of the Magi, I would say, is Eliot's testimony to his home-coming. His was not a conversion from unbelief to belief but from a pattern of spiritual self-reliance and individualism to the life of dependence on the grace of God ministered not only but not least through the sacraments. The dogmatism of the Roman Catholic Church left him no space to breathe. In Anglicanism Eliot found order and an inexhaustible talent for the blessings of compromise.

It is no accident that Eliot's rather idealistic attachment to the English Church went hand in hand with his preoccupation with his own family history and roots.

But *Journey of the Magi* is much more than a paean of praise for the Church of England. It is a poem about the gospel. If Eliot's journey begins in winter, if its geography is at first the geography of despair and of darkness, with the night fires going out; and continues into times of temperateness, below the snow-line, leading finally to the landscape of the nativity, into that landscape he projects darker images of betrayal and crucifixion. There are 'three trees on the low sky'. At the tavern door are to be seen 'six hands . . . dicing for pieces of silver'. Calvary and the foot of the Cross are thus to be seen from Bethlehem.

Finding the place, for the Magi, was, Eliot says 'satisfactory'; but even that rather ironical word, uttered with something of a smile, may indicate the way in which those three trees on the horizon speak to Eliot of Him who made there, what the Prayer Book Communion service describes as 'his one oblation of himself once offered, a full, perfect and sufficient sacrifice, oblation and *satisfaction*, for the sins of the whole world.' 'It was (you may say) satisfactory'.

Eliot speaks elsewhere of

> A condition of complete simplicity
> (Costing not less than everything)

which describes what happened at that 'satisfactory' time and place as well as what is asked of us in response.

> All our costliest treasures bring
> Unto Christ our heavenly King.

May I now read you the whole poem *Journey of the Magi*; but I hope you will be clear that my purpose this morning is not to give you an

English lesson, or a lecture on Eliot, or indeed a poetry reading. On this first Sunday of our new year, I am suggesting we each of us think of our life's journey in the light of the journey of the Magi and of Christ's own journey to His cross, and think also of the gifts, the costly treasures we have to bring to Christ our heavenly King.

A cold coming we had of it,
Just the worst time of the year
For a journey, and such a long journey:
The ways deep and the weather sharp,
The very dead of winter.'
And the camels galled, sore-footed, refractory,
Lying down in the melting snow.
There were times we regretted
The summer palaces on slopes, the terraces,
And the silken girls bringing sherbet.
Then the camel men cursing and grumbling
And running away, and wanting their liquor and women,
And the night-fires going out, and the lack of shelters,
And the cities hostile and the towns unfriendly
And the villages dirty and charging high prices:
A hard time we had of it.
At the end we preferred to travel all night,
Sleeping in snatches,
With the voices singing in our ears, saying
That this was all folly.

Then at dawn we came down to a temperate valley,
Wet, below the snow line, smelling of vegetation,
With a running stream and a water-mill beating the darkness,
And three trees on the low sky,
And an old white horse galloped away in the meadow.
Then we came to a tavern with vine-leaves over the lintel,
Six hands at an open door dicing for pieces of silver,
And feet kicking the empty wine-skins.
But there was no information, and so we continued
And arrived at evening, not a moment too soon
Finding the place; it was (you may say) satisfactory.

All this was a long time ago, I remember,
And I would do it again, but set down
This set down
This: were we led all that way for
Birth or Death? There was a Birth, certainly,
We had evidence and no doubt. I had seen birth and death,
But had thought they were different; this Birth was
Hard and bitter agony for us, like Death, our death.
We returned to our places, these Kingdoms,
But no longer at ease here, in the old dispensation,
With an alien people clutching their gods.
I should be glad of another death.

7

THE DECADE OF EVANGELISM

Gray's Inn Chapel;
26 January 1992

I've recently been turning over in my mind how those of us who attend Chapel in Gray's Inn can respond to the call of the Archbishop of Canterbury and, indeed, first, of the Pope, to make this a *Decade of Evangelism*.

While, last week, I was musing on this theme, a memory returned to me. It was more than thirty-six years ago—1955—and I'd just gone up to Cambridge as Chaplain of Trinity. Until I was interviewed for the job I'd never set foot in Cambridge, and I was certainly a little flustered—more accurately, put in a 'flat spin'—when my fellow Chaplain, Simon Phipps, said that to my first lunch party I should invite, beside himself:

> Dr Burnaby, the Regius Professor of Divinity,
> Mervyn Stockwood, the then Vicar of the University Church,
> and Dr Billy Graham, who would be in Cambridge that week conducting a
> Mission to the University.

I agreed—I had little alternative; but I realized just how difficult my task would be when Dr Burnaby told me, immediately before the lunch, that he had been to hear all Billy Graham's addresses in Cambridge so far, and that he felt in conscience bound to point out to Dr Graham at lunch just where Billy's addresses were lacking and, indeed, where, in his opinion, they were wrong.

In fact, thanks not least to the courtesy of Billy Graham, who showed us all that there is no reason why an evangelist should not also be a gentleman, the lunch party went very well. Billy Graham took the wind out of Professor Burnaby's sails by saying to him, before he could utter a word of criticism, that he had a week off that December and would be glad if Professor Burnaby could provide him with a note of all the errors he had observed in what he, Billy, had said, and also a book-list for further reading.

At the end of that Billy Graham week, in November 1955, I had to preach my first sermon in Chapel: my first sermon in Cambridge. Again, I have to admit my knees were knocking, but when I turned up the sermon this week to refresh my memory on what I had said, to my surprise, I found I had said much of what I would want to say in relation to this *Decade of Evangelism*—as I say, thirty-six years later.

I'm not usually for reading old sermons from pulpits. But I'd quite like to share that sermon with you this morning—but not simply for *old*-time's sake.

I took as my text Acts 17.18: 'What will this babbler say? . . . And he preached unto them Jesus, and the resurrection.' And this is what I said:

A week ago Cambridge was wondering what Billy Graham would say. Now we know. He has preached unto us 'Jesus and the resurrection'.

He himself would be the first to say that he has left many things unsaid, and that many things he has said could have been better said—for those of us who have met him know well his humility. But certainly he has preached unto us 'Jesus and the resurrection'.

A week ago Cambridge was wondering what Billy Graham would do. (Would he 'do' for Cambridge?) One thing he has done: he has made us all *talk* about Jesus and the resurrection. He has made a number of us *do* something about Jesus and the resurrection.

Of course, he has had his critics. It wouldn't be Cambridge if he hadn't. And three main criticisms I have heard.

One there is which says he has preached a 'religion of fear'. He has pointed to global destruction, and said: 'If you want to escape this you'd better believe in Jesus and the resurrection.'

Well, those of you who have studied the Gospels will recognize this as one element in our Lord's preaching. He did not *rely* on fear. He did not *encourage* fear. He said that perfect love would cast out fear. (Or at least his disciples caught this message from him.) But he did say: 'Except ye repent, ye shall all likewise perish.' It may only have been one element in the gospel message, but it is an element we disregard at our peril. Fear, after all, is what keeps us from doing many foolish things: fear of the inevitable built-in retribution that evil deeds contain. Fear makes us look both ways when we cross a dangerous road.

Another form of this criticism is that Dr Graham has pointed to Hell and said, 'If you want to escape *this* you had better believe in Jesus and the resurrection.' Now he may have exaggerated this element, but again this *is* one element in the truth. 'Our God is a consuming fire.' And if we will not know His love as a *kindling* fire we must know it as a *destructive* fire. The same fire of love which burns so bright in the life of Him who was the light of the world is inevitably a refining fire to all that is evil. (And do I need to say that the fire of Christ's love is not a *place*?)

Dorothy Sayers, in her play *The Zeal of Thine House* says 'He' (that is, Christ) 'will purge the gold itself from dross, till all is gold.'

We dare not throw cold water on the consuming fire of God's love.

Yet a religion of love, of *burning* love, is much to be preferred (Christ preferred it!) to a religion of fear. Do you know Gerard Manley Hopkins' translation of the seventeenth-century Latin hymn *O Deus, ego amo te*?

> O God, I love thee, I love thee—
> Not out of hope of heaven for me
> Nor fearing not to love and be

> In the everlasting burning.
> Thou, thou, my Jesus, after me
>   Didst reach thine arms out dying.
> For my sake sufferedst nails and lance,
> Mocked and marrèd countenance,
>   Sorrows passing number,
>   Sweat and care and cumber,
> Yea and death, and this for me,
>   And thou couldst see me sinning:
> Then I, why should not I love thee,
> Jesu so much in love with me?
> Not for heaven's sake; not to be
> Out of hell by loving thee;
> Not for any gains I see;
> But just the way that thou didst me
> I do love and I will love thee:
> What must I love thee, Lord, for then?—
> For being my king and God. Amen.

If talk of destruction has not commended itself to you, make doubly sure that God's *love* has kindled a response in you.

A second criticism I have heard is that Dr Graham has stirred the emotions and given no place to the intellect.

Whatever the truth of that assertion (and remember, the author of *The Cloud of Unknowing* says 'By Love he may be gotten and holden, but by thought never') certain it is that our Lord has said: 'You must love God with all your heart, with all your *mind*, with all your soul and with all your strength.'

God wants you to bring your mind to Him. And my question really would be to those who have said that Dr Graham has appealed to the emotions: 'Well, have *you* in fact brought *your mind* to Jesus and the resurrection?'

I must admit that I have been saddened in these first weeks of mine in Cambridge to hear from otherwise very intelligent men remarks which have often so plainly revealed their ignorance of the Christian religion. So many never seem to have really grappled with the documents and traditions and claims of the Christian message—which, after all, whether you agree with it or disagree with it, has undoubtedly affected our history and culture as much as any other single factor, and merits therefore intelligent attention. Day after day I come up against the prejudices against religion which are so out-of-date as to be almost laughable: prejudices, most of which originated in a philo-sophical, scientific and theological generation which has long since passed away.

It is perhaps even sadder to meet so many Christians who would be reduced to purple embarrassment if challenged on a railway journey by a militant atheist to give a reason for the hope that is in them.

Bring your mind to Jesus and the resurrection. Bring your contemporary philosophy, your contemporary science. Dig deep down, and ask what is the authority on which, for instance, your morals exist, if not on Jesus and the resurrection.

God is Truth; and we must follow Him wherever He leads. Paradoxically, He may lead us into agnosticism. But for God's sake, for Truth's sake, let us not stand still. We can never finally say we have applied our minds to the truth if we have not wrestled with the claims of Jesus and the resurrection.

There has been a third criticism within my hearing (though I have discovered that the court of a Cambridge college is not always, in this era of the long-playing record, the best place for a sensitive ear!): 'Billy Graham talks a lot about giving your life to Jesus, but then you are left in mid-air.'

Billy Graham said to a few of us this week who were lunching with him that he conceives *his* vocation to be simply that of an *evangelist*. He would say that it's up to the churches to care for and instruct those people whom God has influenced *through him*.

It is therefore my duty to say what from the Bible would appear to be the guidance for anyone who is anxious to know what their next steps should be. The last ten verses of the second chapter of the Acts of the Apostles are a good guide for us here. They describe the pattern of the life of the early Church.

First, those who had responded to the preaching of Jesus and the resurrection were baptized. That is, they were fully initiated into the Christian Church, the Christian community. (Is there anyone who has heard and received Billy Graham's preaching of Christ this week but who as yet is not fully initiated into the family of Christ? You will have little excuse for delaying *enquiry* about baptism and confirmation.)

Secondly, they 'continued steadfast in the apostolic teaching'. They asked for instruction. Well, why do you think a college appoints chaplains? And why do we all have a parish priest somewhere in England? At least one of the tasks of a parish priest or a college chaplain is simply to answer questions as helpfully as he can.

Thirdly, they all met together as Christians in fellowship. Cambridge offers at least as much opportunity for meeting your fellow Christians as any other place, and probably more. Only a Christian who doesn't really mean business will be able to escape the Christian fellowship!

Fourthly, they met together for the breaking of bread each first day of the week—probably a working day for many of them. And I suppose that may have meant getting up somewhat earlier than sometimes we do in Cambridge!

Fifthly, they were steadfast in prayer. Have you thought that in Cambridge, amongst all the other things you will learn you might resolve to learn to pray, or at least to begin to do so?

There is enough to go on with. It is in the Church that you can grow in the knowledge and love of Jesus and the resurrection.

Your faith will of course have to be hammered out in terms of *Christian action*—which, for the moment, for the most part, will mean working with integrity *here*, and playing your full part in the life of the community here. But Cambridge, I think I should underline, is not the whole world.

There will of course be some for whom this sermon may seem rather irrelevant. They have not *heard* Billy Graham. Perhaps they deliberately intended *not* to hear him.

Upon them lies a heavy responsibility, I think. Most of them will have judged, for reasons of varying integrity, that it was not of paramount importance that they should be assisted by Dr Graham to confront and be confronted by Jesus and the resurrection. Some of these will have been Christians already, others, non-Christians.

The *Christians* have a heavy responsibility, for they are asserting, albeit silently, that they have not *needed* this week to impress upon them the claims of Jesus and the resurrection.

The non-Christians, like the Epicurean and Stoic philosophers in Athens who encountered Paul, and wondered what this babbler would say, are claiming, again silently, I think, either that they have fully confronted Jesus and the resurrection and repudiated him, or said 'We still don't know', or they have said 'It's not really worth bothering about'.

Perhaps they, like the men of Athens, having not applied themselves to Jesus and the resurrection, worship still at the altar of an unknown God, who, they claim, gives them a purpose in life, an authority for their ethics, a power to fulfil them, better than Jesus and the resurrection.

But I think most of us (who admittedly do not by any means go all the way with Billy Graham) will remember this week chiefly because in one way or another we have been reminded again that none of us can ignore Jesus and the resurrection, and His claims upon our lives.

Many of us have been reminded (I know from those who have come and told me—and I know for myself) that 'Thou hast made us for thyself, and our hearts are restless till they find their rest in Thee.' There are in Cambridge this week, thank God, many who are the happier because they have committed themselves to Jesus. May they now find within the fellowship of his Church the power of his resurrection.

*   *   *

Well, as I say, that is a 36-year-old sermon. But the passing of the years adds, I find, a further dimension and perspective to that Billy Graham week of 1955.

I can still recall several undergraduates who came to see me as a result of Billy Graham's ministry, and one in particular, Paul Burrell.

Paul had been to Eastbourne College and had been brought up as a Christian Scientist. It was gone eleven at night when he knocked on my door and a couple of hours later when he left. He wanted to be prepared for confirmation and, not long after, he said he wanted to be ordained. We became great friends. I conducted his marriage and became the godfather of his first child, Mark. After his ordination, the interests fostered in childhood through Christian Science developed into a desire to be a hospital chaplain. He became chaplain of the Maudsley Hospital in South London. Eventually he moved to similar work in Portsmouth. Christmas week 1974 my phone rang. It was his wife Angela to tell me that Paul had had a sudden heart attack and died—at forty-one. I have to admit I was devastated by the news, and taking Paul's funeral in Portsmouth Cathedral was an ordeal beyond words. But it was one of those occasions which, if you dare to preach on the phrase 'Jesus and the resurrection', challenges you to practise what you preach.

The passing of thirty-six years has therefore, as I say, added a further dimension and perspective to that Billy Graham week of 1955. At the time, evangelism seemed to relate to the immediate years ahead. Now I can look back on the lives of many who heard Billy Graham that week, and see those lives—whether here or in the hereafter—all within the total continuum of the love of God. For me, 'Jesus and the resurrection' is a phrase which seems to sum up and articulate that total continuum of God's providence and love.

'What will this babbler say? . . . he preached unto them Jesus, and the resurrection.'

8

GRAHAM GREENE

Gray's Inn Chapel;
2 February 1992

Last April, Graham Greene died. He was nearly 87. Some of you may remember that, in July 1990, I preached on his novel—and play—*The Power and the Glory*, (*Word Over All*, SPCK, pp. 152–5) but I did not then say much about the author. This morning I want to redress that, for many would maintain Graham Greene is the most significant Christian author England has produced this century.

He was born on 2 October 1904, the fourth child of Charles and Marion Greene, and there were two more children to come. His biographer, Norman Sherry,* says that he was born into three worlds: the town of Berkhamsted; the family home attached to the School, and Berkhamsted School itself—of which Graham's father was at the time second master and a house master, and his mother was virtually matron of the house.

The family was fairly prosperous middle-class, with close connections with Greene King's, the brewery, at Bury St Edmunds and, in earlier times, estates in the West Indies.

The infant Graham was very impressionable. The first words he uttered were inspired by the death of his sister's dog; and when he was six there was another memorable confrontation with death: a man who wanted to kill himself rushed out of a cottage near the canal bridge at Berkhamsted; he had a knife in his hand, and people ran after him. That scene indelibly impressed itself on Graham's memory and he used it several times in his writings.

His biographer says that Graham had a mind so sensitive and an imagination so vivid, that the coming of evening raised up terrible possibilities, and all his nerves were ajump with the fear of bedtime, bringing him near to hysteria.

Minor ailments pleased him, for they confined him to bed and brought him a sense of peace, endless time, and a night-light burning in his bedroom, a feeling of security.

Fear of drowning, from which he also suffered, probably originated in an early attack of hay-fever brought on by playing in a haystack. His family was mystified by the illness as he lay awake coughing and gasping for

---

The Life of Graham Greene, vol. 1, 1904–1939

breath all night. 'Perhaps during that night I evolved my fear of drowning', Graham wrote, 'I was able to imagine my lungs filling with water.' He had dreams when he would feel himself drawn as if by a magnet to the water's edge, and later, in adolescence, they became so strong that they affected his waking life: he would find his feet would be actually attracted by the margin of a pond or river. This fear must have been strengthened by what he heard of reports of inquests in the *Berkhamsted Gazette* on people—often children of bargees—who had drowned in the Grand Junction Canal running through the town. It was believed locally that no one who fell into the locks on the canal could be rescued: 'I cannot to this day', wrote Greene, 'peer down ... the sheer wet walls, without a sense of trepidation.'

Graham's Aunt Eva—twenty-two when he was born—wrote, when she was almost a hundred years old:

> I never found it easy to understand young Graham. Once I remember when he was naughty, he refused to own up to the fact until he had persuaded us to say please. He must have been then 5 or 6 years old. He seemed as a boy completely inexperienced and yet he was not. He was very shy and yet he was not shy. He seemed to respond to us. I never knew, when he called at the Hall, whether he was happy or unhappy. He was certainly *different from any other child I have ever known.* He came over to the Hall very often during the time his father was Headmaster at Berkhamsted. I don't know, I think he just left me *puzzled.* I just never knew whether he was, as a child, pleased or unhappy, approved or didn't approve. I never knew.

It was in the year 1910 that Charles Greene became the headmaster of Berkhamsted School, and the family moved into *School* House. It was probably from that date that Graham began to get to know more intimately the town in which he lived for his first seventeen years. It occurs under other names in several of his novels.

On his seventh birthday Graham took part in a competition run by the *School House Gazette*. It meant answering a questionnaire:

> Q: What is your greatest aim in life? A: *To go up in an aeroplane.*
> Q: What is your greatest idea of happiness? A: *Going up to London.*
> Q: Who is the greatest living statesman? A: *Don't know any.*
> Q: Who is your favourite character in fiction? A: *Dixon Brett.*
> Q: What are the qualities you most admire in men? A: *Good looks.*
> Q: In women? A: *Cleanliness.*
> Q: What is your favourite pastime? A: *Playing Red Indians.*
> Q: What is your pet hobby? A: *Collecting coins.*
> Q: What is your favourite quotation? A: *'I with two more to help me will hold the foe in play'.*
> Q: Who is the author you like best and which book? A: *Scott. The Talisman.*
> Q: Who is the cricketer you most admire? A: *Herbert Greene.*
> Q: Which is your favourite holiday resort? A: *Overstrand.*

The two most interesting revelations are surely his admiration of good-looking men and cleanliness in women.

Norman Sherry is undoubtedly right in saying that Graham Greene's time as a boarder at Berkhamsted School was traumatic for him but seminal for his future as a writer. He returns to it again and again in his books.

On the face of it, Sherry says, there seems little to justify the emotive language he used to describe the situation in which he found himself. He was a 'foreigner' in a 'savage country of strange customs and inexplicable cruelties', he was 'a suspect', 'a hunted creature', 'Quisling's son' and there was 'loneliness, the struggle of conflicting loyalties . . . a great betrayal'. In fact, he was the *Headmaster's* son, had moved only a short distance from home to be a boarder where his cousins were also boarders and his brother Raymond was head boy.

His state of health *before* becoming a boarder was not good. In 'The Burden of Childhood' (1950) Greene wrote, 'There are certain writers . . . who never shake off the burden of their childhood' and they are those to whom life turned 'its cruel side' during the defenceless period of early childhood and all their later experience seems to have been related to 'those months or years of unhappiness'. He cites the cases of three writers to support his thesis: Charles Dickens, Rudyard Kipling and H. H. Munro ('Saki'). He might well have added his own name to the list. For him also childhood was a burden and his experiences had parallels with theirs. Greene writes about Berkhamsted: 'Memory often exaggerates, but some twelve years ago (1959), because I had started a novel about a school, I revisited the scene and found no change. I abandoned the novel—I couldn't bear mentally living again for several years in those surroundings.' Significantly, he went instead to a leper colony in the Congo.

A letter has survived, unknown to Greene, written in 1948 by his mother to his wife and kept secretly by her for forty years. In it, Graham's mother recalls the day he disappeared—and his peace-destroying note. Even though she was writing long after the event, her deep concern over her disturbed and sensitive son is apparent:

> He went as a boarder to St John's in September 1918. Raymond was still Head of the house but had no idea Graham was being persecuted by a particular boy. In what way I do not know, nor did Guest, who was a friend of Graham's. I cannot date when the crisis occurred but between 1919 & 1920. I think Graham was not well the morning he should have gone back to St John's— slight temperature and eyes peculiar. Doctor could not understand the eyes. I kept him in bed and went to do house-keeping & returned to find he was not there & a note to say he would not go back to St John's—had tried to poison himself with eye-drops (accounts for eyes) in vain, & had gone, & we should not see him again.
>
> You cannot imagine how we felt. We did not want to go to the police at

once, Uncle Eppy sent his bailiff whom he could trust to hunt along the canal. Dr McB. took me all over golf-links in his car—we searched woods, calling all the time. Then after lunch Molly said she had a feeling she should find him & taking Miss Arnell & some food they set out. And they found him sitting in the little wood where M. thought he might be. They brought him home & I put him to bed & told him he should never go back.

This letter confirms Greene's many attempts at suicide and his methods, but whereas he plays down the escape incident as a game of hide-and-seek (thus denying the feeling of terror which drives a young-ster to run away), merely holding out on the Common until his parents gave way, his mother's letter shows that it was much more serious and distressing and the note he left was much more disturbing than he suggests.

Greene's attitude to his upbringing, though he does not mention his father, comes out in his essay 'The Old School'. His criticism is of the public school system. At Berkhamsted his father was of course in charge of that system: 'At Berkhamsted, too often the system interferes, with its cult of suspicion and its abnormal fear of sexuality' wrote Graham. 'One is alternately amazed at the unworldly innocence of the pedagogic mind and at its tortuous obscenity.'

His breakdown was, therefore, the result of many pressures which brought him near to manic depression, of which he was showing the classic symptoms—loss of interest in or ability to experience pleasure, increasing feelings of worthlessness, and thoughts of suicide. There was also the delusion of being persecuted because of his apparent inad-equacy. He began to see persecution everywhere; whenever he 'entered the schoolroom' he wrote, 'an undertone of mockery seemed to creep into that endless chorus of voices . . . for twelve long weeks of term'.

He was also turned inward, unable to tell his family what was hap-pening or how he felt.

Thirty years after the events which drove him to breakdown, Graham Greene, writing on Charles Dickens, said 'The creative writer perceives his world once and for all in childhood and adolescence, and his whole career is an effort to illustrate his private world in terms of the great public world we share.' He had found his subject, which would appear in different guises in many of his more than thirty novels.

In his autobiographical volume *A Sort of Life* Greene describes the panic in his family after he ran away: 'Raymond was hastily summoned home for consultation: my father found the situation beyond him . . . My brother . . . suggested psychoanalysis as a possible solution, and my father—an astonishing thing in 1920—agreed.'

His crisis, culminating in psychoanalysis at sixteen or seventeen, is undoubtedly the *end of Graham's beginning*. But I should remind you that as yet he had not gone up to Oxford, fallen in love, nor become a

Roman Catholic, yet one can confidently say he had reached the end of his beginning.

I do not want to say any more today about the life of Graham Greene. I want simply to illustrate, by one of his short stories, the way that beginning I have described influenced his whole work as an author, as indeed the most significant Christian author England has produced this century.

The most famous of all Greene's novels, *Brighton Rock*, is, of course, about the theme of lost innocence, of the influence of our early impressions upon our later behaviour, of a child doomed through an early experience of corruption and evil. But I do not want to concentrate today on *Brighton Rock*. I would like to illustrate this theme of Greene's from another story of 'lost childhood'—which is the title Greene gave to the Prologue of his book of *Collected Essays* which he ends with a verse from a poem by the Irish poet 'AE':

> In ancient shadows and twilights
> Where childhood had strayed
> The world's great sorrows were born
> And its heroes were made
> In the *lost boyhood* of Judas
> Christ was betrayed.

It was on a cargo steamer on his way home from Liberia, that Graham Greene wrote a short story, published, in 1935, as 'The Basement Room', which had this theme of *lost childhood*. When it was made into a film, it was called *The Fallen Idol*.

While his parents are abroad, Philip, a small boy, is left in a large Belgravia embassy, in the care of Baines, the butler, and the menacing Mrs Baines. Baines has a girl-friend, and, soon, Philip is caught up in what Graham Greene calls 'other people's darkness'.

The film director, Carol Reed, in Greene's opinion, had an extraordinary feeling for the right face for the right part, and almost miraculously found a nine-year-old boy, Bobby Henrey—the son of the authoress Mrs Robert Henrey—to play the part of Philip to perfection—with Ralph Richardson as Baines.

The first shot of the film has the boy looking down through the stair-railing to the vividly chequered hallway floor below. It is very much the world of childhood as Graham Greene saw it. The stair-railing separates visually the world of innocence and the world of experience and establishes our sense of the child's imprisonment among adults. We frequently see the world from Philip's point of view and look with him through the railings. From behind these bars we often hear the Baineses argue. From this position we see the fight that precipitates Mrs Baines' fatal fall. (From the lower hall we catch the child's troubled face after

Mrs Baines has forced him to disclose the secret that he shares with her husband.) After the fall he enters the adult world and stands at the bottom of the stairs to tell his lies to the police—lies by which he hopes to protect his idol, Baines. '*After the fall*' is, of course, a significant phrase. No less significant is McGregor, Philip's pet *snake*, which is killed by Mrs Baines with a vengeance and violence she feels towards her husband and his girl-friend.

For a time, the bewildered Philip escapes from the embassy. Greene writes:

> He was wearing pyjamas and bedroom slippers when he came up into the square, but there was no one to see him. He climbed over the iron railings into the little garden: the plane trees spread their large pale palms between him and the sky. It might have been an illimitable forest into which he had escaped. He crouched behind a trunk and the wolves retreated; it seemed to him, between the little iron seat and the tree-trunk that no one would ever find him again. A kind of embittered happiness and self-pity made him cry; he was lost; there wouldn't be any more secrets to keep; he surrendered responsibility once and for all. Let grown-up people keep to their world and he would keep to his, safe in the small garden between the plane trees. 'In the lost childhood of Judas, Christ was betrayed.'

Greene is so clearly writing from his own painful experience. He is not only proclaiming how terrible a thing it is to cause little ones to stumble but is as eloquently pleading that they should be protected from cruelty. And this is surely a most deeply Christian theme.

It has to be said that sometimes Greene can be accused of cynicism and despair in his stories. There is no hope in this world in many of his situations and for many of his characters.

But Greene, the Catholic, might well respond that he is only being realistic about this world and say with St Paul 'If we have hope only in *this* world we are of all men most miserable.'

It would take more time than we have this morning *fully* to explore the claim I made at the outset that Graham Greene is the most significant Christian author England has produced this century.

In his last years Greene described himself as a Catholic agnostic. When in 1980 he wrote a second autobiographical book *Ways of Escape* he wrote: 'Those who believe that they believe in God, but without passion in their hearts, without anguish of mind, without uncertainty, without doubt, without an element of despair even in their consolation, believe only in the God Idea, not in God Himself.' And, interviewed in September 1989, fifteen months before he died, and asked the question 'What in the final analysis does your religion mean to you?' he raised his glass to his interviewer and, eyeing him mischievously, said, slowly and with some feeling, 'It's a mystery which can't be destroyed . . . even by the Church.'

That somewhat enigmatic response is one to which I imagine a good many of us would wish to raise our glass—maybe musing at the same time that Graham Greene's own life provides us with a good deal of hope: that a life which began with such wounds should in time bear such fruit.

🎗 9
SINGAPORE

The Chapel Royal,
St James's Palace;
16 February 1992

Yesterday was the fiftieth anniversary of the fall of Singapore. Winston Churchill described it as 'the greatest disaster to British arms that our history records'.

The defence of Singapore had undoubtedly been neglected. Japanese power and intentions had been greatly underestimated. Churchill himself admitted the Far East had been only in 'the twilight of his mind'. The British and American freezing of Japanese assets, and their attempts to deny *oil* to Japan, were almost bound to provoke a major Japanese response. And on 7 December 1941 that response came, with the Japanese attack on Pearl Harbour and the invasion of British Malaya. Only three days later the battleships *Repulse* and *Prince of Wales* were sunk by Japanese aircraft with huge loss of life. On 15 February 1942, the great island fortress of Singapore, with its garrison of some 70,000 men, surrendered to the Japanese, after a siege of only two weeks, and despite Churchill's impassioned exhortation that 'Commanders and Senior Officers should die with their troops'. 'The honour of the British Empire and British Army' he said 'is at stake.' The reaction here in Britain was one of anger and dismay. For the first time since he had assumed office in May 1940, Winston Churchill found his direction of the war the target of serious criticism from the press, the public and the House of Commons.

In this chapel, it is particularly appropriate that we should remember His Majesty King George VI. The ill-tidings of that black February week-end came as a severe shock to him.

'I am very depressed over the loss of Singapore . . .' he wrote to Queen Mary. 'We are going through a bad phase at the moment, and it will take all our energies to stop adverse criticism from the Press and others.'

To his uncle, the Earl of Athlone, then Governor-General of Canada, he wrote: 'I do wish people would get on with the job and not criticize all the time, but in a free country this has to be put up with.'

When Winston Churchill came to his weekly Tuesday luncheon with

49

the King, on 17 February, the King records in his diary that Churchill characteristically compared people's criticism of him to 'hunting the tiger with angry wasps about him'.

The King was careful to keep his despondency within the family, and there was no hint of depression in the letter which he sent to President Roosevelt a few days later by the hand of his brother-in-law, David Bowes-Lyon, then proceeding to Washington.

It was of course several years later that the truth of what happened *within* Singapore began to emerge, and *some* of the stories shine like jewels on the dark face of the history of those times.

I cannot myself forget how, when I was a young curate in Westminster, in 1953, a not very imposing man came to Evening Service one Sunday that October. He was in an ordinary suit: he introduced himself by name—Leonard Wilson—at the end of the service, and to my surprise invited me to lunch with him the next day at the National Liberal Club. What I learnt at that lunch was even more surprising: he was to be enthroned later that week as Bishop of Birmingham. I saw more of Leonard Wilson in the next years and we became friends. I learnt that in January 1941, when he was Dean of Hong Kong, he had been asked to be Bishop of Singapore. On 22 July 1941 he was consecrated bishop. By the beginning of August that year he had settled in the Bishop's House, Singapore. The next months he spent touring the diocese, and getting to know it, and only got back to Singapore itself in December 1941, the day after Pearl Harbour and the first landings in Malaya. In January 1942, his family left for the safety of Australia. Until March 1943 Leonard Wilson managed to stay out of internment; then he was taken to Changi Gaol and interned in squalid conditions with 3,000 others. Leonard Wilson himself never dwelt on the physical horror of the torture he suffered. But I think it helps us to know about it, not least in order to understand the dimensions of the forgiveness he practised.

One of the priests of his diocese, the Revd John Hayter, a fellow internee in Changi Gaol, left this written record:

> In the evening of his arrival, Leonard was questioned. The interrogation was punctuated with beatings, for between three and four hours. On the following morning he was again taken to the torture room, where he was made to kneel down. A three angled bar was placed behind his knees. He was then made to kneel on his haunches. His hands were tied behind his back and pulled up to a position between his shoulder blades. His head was forced down and he remained in this position for seven and a half hours. Any attempt to ease the strain from the cramp in his thighs was frustrated by the guards, who brought the flat of their hobnailed boots down hard on to his thighs. At intervals, the bar between his knees would be twisted, or the guards would jump onto one or both projecting ends. Beatings and kicks were frequent. Throughout the whole of this time he was being questioned. This was one of the times when he lost his nerve and pleaded for death.

The next morning, he was again brought up from the cells, and this time tied face upwards to a table with his head hanging over the end of it. For several hours he remained in that position while relays of soldiers beat him systematically from the ankles to the thighs with three-fold knotted ropes. He fainted, was revived, and then the beating was continued. He estimated that he must have received over three hundred lashes. The beating, he said, was far easier to bear than the excruciating pain of the previous day. It was not long before he lost all sense of feeling. The blows had lost their power to hurt, so dead were the nerves of his body. Finally he was taken down to the cells and thrown on the floor. There was no skin left on the front of his legs from his thighs downwards. He had no medical attention while he was in that state, and he said that if it had not been for the help of a fellow internee in his cell—who subsequently died from the treatment he himself received—he would not have survived.

It was on 13 October 1946—three years after the events just related—that Leonard Wilson, still Bishop of Singapore but on leave here in England, made an unforgettable broadcast on the BBC from which I want to quote at some length:

I remember Archbishop William Temple [said the Bishop] writing that if you pray for any particular virtue, whether it is patience or courage or love, one of the answers God gives to you is an opportunity for exercising that virtue. After my first beating I was almost afraid to pray for courage lest I should have another opportunity for exercising it, but my unspoken prayer was there, and without God's help, I doubt whether I could have come through. Long hours of pain were a severe test. In the middle of that torture they asked me if I still believed in God. When by God's help, I said 'I do', they asked me why God did not *save* me, and by the help of his Holy Spirit, I said 'God does save me. He does not save me by freeing me from pain or punishment, but he saves me by giving me the spirit to bear it.' And when they asked me why I did not curse them, I told them that it was because I was a follower of Jesus Christ, who taught us that we are all brethren. I did not like to use the words, 'Father, forgive them.' It seemed too blasphemous to use the words of Jesus, but I felt them, and I said 'Father, I know these men are doing their duty. Help them to see that I am innocent.' And when I muttered, 'Forgive them,' I wondered how far I was being dramatic and if I really meant it, because I looked at their faces as they stood around me and took it in turn to flog me, and their faces were hard and cruel, and some of them were evidently enjoying their cruelty. But by the grace of God I saw those men not as they were, but as they had been. Once they were little children, playing with their brothers and sisters, and happy in their parents' love, in those far-off days before they had been conditioned by their false nationalist ideals, and it is hard to hate little children; but even that was not enough. There came into my mind, as I lay on the table, the words of the communion hymn:

> Look, Father, look on His anointed face,
>   And only look on us as found in Him;
> Look not on our misusings of Thy grace,
>   Our prayer so languid, and our faith so dim;
> For lo! between our sins and their reward
> We set the Passion of Thy Son our Lord.

And so I saw them, not as they were, not as they had been, but as they were capable of becoming, redeemed by the power of Christ, and I knew it was only common sense to say, 'Forgive'.

It is true, of course, that there were many dreary and desolate moments, especially in the early mornings. I was in a crowded and filthy cell, with hardly any power to move because of my wounds, but here again I was helped tremendously by God. There was a tiny window at the back of the cell and through the bars I could hear the song of a bird—the Golden Oriole. I could see the glorious red of the Flame of the Forest tree, and something of God's indestructible beauty was conveyed to my tortured mind. Behind the Flame tree I could glimpse the top of Wesley's church in Singapore, and was so grateful that the Church had preserved so many of Wesley's hymns. One that I said every morning was 'Christ Whose Glory Fills the Skies'. The second verse began

> Dark and cheerless is the morn
> Unaccompanied by Thee;
> Joyless is the day's return
> Till Thy mercy's beams I see.

And I went on to pray,

> Visit then this soul of mine
> Pierce the gloom of sin and grief.

And, gradually, the burden of this world was lifted and I was carried into the presence of God and received from Him the strength and peace which were enough to live, day by day.

That spirit of courage and forgiveness and of the presence of God communicated itself from Leonard Wilson to others. A number of those in the cells with him asked him about the meaning of prayer. It was impossible to talk during the day, but at night, by keeping a careful watch, they were able to talk in whispers.

In 1947, after the War, Leonard Wilson, as bishop, took various services of baptism and confirmation in Singapore Cathedral for those who had been prepared, and he got permission for those who were serving sentences to be marched up from the prison. Amongst those whom he baptized and confirmed was one of the men of the Japanese military police who had been responsible, four years earlier, for torturing him. Leonard said he had seldom seen so great a change in a man. He looked gentle and peaceful, even though he was going back to serve a ten-year sentence and, later, he received communion at the bishop's hands in the prison.

So it was that what had begun so terribly, turned full circle, and at least some good came out of evil.

And so this particular Sunday, fifty years after the fall of Singapore, I for one, as I remember those who lost their lives there, Japanese as well as British, will also find myself thankful—as many of you I've no doubt will—for all the good that came out of all that evil, and not least for John Leonard Wilson—Bishop of Singapore and, later, Bishop of Birmingham, who departed this life 18 August 1970.

May we all live as courageously as he did, and show the kind of forgiveness he showed.

10

TO JERUSALEM

St Anselm's Kennington; 5 April 1992

'We are now going up to Jerusalem', Jesus said.

I wonder, when you heard that sentence in the Gospel, that saying of Jesus, what your reaction was?

One perfectly right reaction might have been: 'That was a saying of Jesus; and the sayings of Jesus are now nearly two thousand years old. They are part of history: central and fundamental to Christian history and, indeed, to the history of the world.'

There's another response—which I rather hope is how some of you may have responded—that every invitation of Jesus to His disciples, two thousand years ago, is in some way an invitation to us, His disciples, now; so that Jesus addresses each one of us today, as another Passiontide and Holy Week draws near, and He says directly to us: 'We are now going up to Jerusalem.'

Of course, we can ignore that invitation or turn it down. But I suspect that before any of us does that—or before we accept it—we shall need to think a bit what that invitation might involve and imply.

I wonder what the word 'Jerusalem' means to you? 'We are now going up to Jerusalem.'

It comes, of course, in many of the hymns we sing: 'Jerusalem, my happy home', 'Jerusalem, the golden'—and, here in Britain, we are especially fond of Blake's 'Jerusalem'; they sang it, in a jazzed-up version, this week, to end the Labour party's pre-election Sheffield rally.

On Friday I had to go up to Nottingham to visit a friend of mine who has been in prison for ten years now. I first of all popped into one of my favourite pubs, just by Nottingham Castle. It's called 'The Trip to Jerusalem'. It's said to be where pilgrims to Jerusalem would assemble, centuries ago, before they set out on their long pilgrimage, which was undoubtedly for them 'the journey of a lifetime'. There was no doubt of the importance of Jerusalem to them.

Yes: but what does Jerusalem mean to *us*, this year?

'We are now going up to Jerusalem'.

It could mean—I think for Christians it should mean—that just as at Christmas in heart and mind we go to Bethlehem, so at Passiontide— which begins this very day, Passion Sunday—we go up to Jerusalem; we go again to Gethsemane, and Calvary, and try to understand afresh the meaning and significance of Jesus' triumphant suffering and sacrifice. And there we bring the raw material of our own personal life to the cross.

In Nottingham, on Friday night, I stayed with a young priest whose friend—also a young priest—had been found dead last Christmas eve in tragic circumstances. I know this Passiontide and Easter will be very special for him. He rather desperately needs to take all that has happened to him in these last months to Jerusalem.

But all of us have something fresh to take to Jerusalem this year.

May I just say that with Andrew Grant leaving St Anselm's, and going off to Ghana to work, after having been such a good parish priest here for thirteen years, and the bereavement and loss there is bound to be to many of us—and with all that lies beyond Andrew's leaving: for Andrew himself in Africa, and for all of us—we all of us, here at St Anselm's, have a huge amount to take with us this year to Jerusalem.

But Jerusalem is never simply an individual and private affair. In many ways, I believe our journey to Jerusalem this year begins with our vote.

Roy, our new Bishop of Southwark, writes in his latest diocesan newsletter: 'Part of my Lenten discipline and of my spiritual realism will be to discover how many of our thirty-one prospective Members of Parliament are prepared to place housing and homelessness at the top of their agenda.'

He goes on: 'In the midst of our pre-election hullabaloo I have no doubt that we shall hear again that remarkable comment that religion and politics don't mix. What such a comment does to our religiously committed MP's I shudder to think—but what it says about our view of God is even more disturbing.' That's the Bishop. And I would add: 'What it says about the meaning of "Jerusalem" I shudder to think.'

Interestingly, Mrs Thatcher, in one of her interventions in the run-up to the election said: 'When will they learn you cannot build Jerusalem in Brussels?' Some of you may be a little surprised that I agreed with her question. But I would ask: 'When will they learn you cannot build Jerusalem in Brussels alone or in England alone?'

Last September I went to Africa, to Tanzania. If you've been to Africa recently you are bound to be dismayed that in Britain the election campaign has been unfolding amidst what can only be called national self-absorption. And Africa is the loser. It has been particularly since the Gulf War. In Africa, famine and disease and civil war and the collapse of civil administration stalk much of the continent—Somalia, Ethiopia, Liberia, Zaire. The misery of Africa covers huge tracts of its territory. You cannot build Jerusalem in Brussels alone or in London alone. We Christians have always to take our brothers and sisters with us when we go up to Jerusalem. That is why Andrew is going to Ghana not just by himself or for himself but on our behalf.

The silence of the politicians on Africa and the Third World these last weeks has been deafening, but Christians can never be silent about the rest of the family. 'We are now going up to Jerusalem'—together with the whole Christian family; and we take with us the whole human family. That is the meaning of intercession. We wear the rest of the family on our heart.

Jerusalem, as Christians conceive it, is nevertheless never simply a city, or a society, of this world. It's a vision that may be built with the bricks of this world but part of it will always lie beyond this world:

> Blessed City, Heavenly Salem,
> Vision dear of peace and love,
> Who of living stones upbuilded
> Art the joy of heaven above.

Jerusalem is in part vision and hope. So what should be decisive for us on Thursday—when we mark our ballot papers in the privacy of the booth, and cast our vote for a new government, as part of our Holy Week duties this year—is not what level of tax we should pay, important as that is, but what sort of society, what 'Jerusalem' we want to see, and who is most likely to realize something of that society in the here and now.

And I'm suggesting that this Passion Sunday we each one of us make a resolution: simply to accept the invitation of Jesus to his disciples—that's to say: to you and me—to travel afresh to Jerusalem, in this fortnight, which lies between now and Easter.

It will probably involve a special effort to hear what Andrew, our parish priest, has to say to us this last Holy Week he is with us. And the leaflet will suggest to us other opportunities we will have.

It will mean each one of us thinking really hard how, this way and that, we can this year make the 'trip to Jerusalem' with Jesus and his disciples. 'We are now going up to Jerusalem.' And there He will suffer many things of the powers that be, in Church as well as State. But Jerusalem in this world is not the end.

✵ 11

THE EASTER ENIGMA

Gray's Inn Chapel; 3 May 1992

The Easter Enigma is the title of a brilliant book, written by Michael
Perry, who was an undergraduate at Trinity College Cambridge when I
was Chaplain there, more than thirty years ago. He was a Senior Scholar
of the College and wrote most of the book while he was still an undergraduate. It was published by Faber and Faber in 1959. Michael is now
Archdeacon (not Bishop!) of Durham. One of his main interests from his
earliest years was psychical research. He is chairman of the Churches'
Fellowship for Psychical and Spiritual Studies.

His book was written from the assumption that it was inexcusable for
the philosophically minded enquirer into Christian truth to leave psychical research out of his reckoning when confronting the evidence for
the resurrection of Jesus.

> The Resurrection is central to the Christian faith [Michael Perry wrote]. It
> makes sense of all the rest and authenticates everything that preceded or
> followed it. But many people do not find it easy to believe that the facts, on
> which the doctrine of the Resurrection rests, really happened. If we can
> remove any unnecessary barriers to such a belief, we shall have done Christian
> apologetics a great service.

I hasten to add that Michael Perry is one of those who believes that
psychical research should be regarded as a science. Faced by the welter
of popular superstition and anecdotal exaggeration, he is at one with
those who believe psychical researchers should impose upon themselves
strict rules of evidence. Michael is no pushover. He is not credulous. He
is a very exacting researcher. He himself gained a First in both the
Natural Science Tripos and in the Theology Tripos at Cambridge.

It is never appropriate within the compass of a relatively brief sermon
to attempt to go through all the evidence for and against Christ's resurrection. I want simply to share with you some of the help that I believe
Michael Perry's book still offers.

After several chapters on subjects such as 'The written evidence for
the Resurrection *outside* the New Testament' and 'The written evidence
in the New Testament', and a chapter on 'The Empty Tomb', he has a

57

chapter on what is, I believe, an important subject, which is often excluded from the debate about the resurrection. He calls it 'Christ's Resurrection and Ours'.

Michael Perry reminds us that in the world of our Lord's day not everyone believed in resurrection or in a future life. The Greek idea was of the immortality of the soul. The specifically Jewish hope was very different. The body itself would rise from the dead at the Day of the Lord. In some parts of first-century Palestine, for instance, great expense was often incurred in ensuring that the dead were buried in appropriate clothes, ready for their resurrection.

This raises, of course, the crucial question of the degree of continuity between our present body and any future body which might be ours. Continuity of some sort there must be or the person who dies will not be the same as the one who rises. St Paul brings to life what might otherwise be a fairly abstract intellectual question by using the metaphor of the seed. What we sow, he says, is not the plant that rises: it is just a seed. A field of ripened corn is unimaginably different from the grains of wheat which were sown. And yet, there is undeniable, indeed, indispensable continuity, in this miracle of death and resurrection in nature: this natural experience of transfiguration and transformation. And, St Paul says, in *our* resurrection we shall be following Christ, the first-fruits of the harvest. Our resurrection will be in some way akin to and analogous to His.

Now Paul had caught a glimpse of the blinding glory of the resurrection body of our Lord on the Damascus Road, and realized that he was being shown something of an order of being entirely different from that of this physical world. Paul, who had never seen Christ in the flesh, was nevertheless clear he had seen the Lord. And, as a direct result, Paul the persecutor became not only Paul the convert but Paul the Apostle, Paul the missionary, and Paul the theologian of the Body. No one used the term 'the body of Christ' more than Paul, but it is of a transformed body that he speaks and writes.

Michael Perry, in his book, relates St Paul on the resurrection body to the subject of psychic appearances. He quotes several incidents from the publications of the Society for Psychical Research which could with justification be said to have something in common with the resurrection experiences. But I should like to quote to you now, not from Michael Perry's *Easter Enigma*, but from what I will call my own *favourite* psychic appearance, recorded in John Stallworthy's biography of Wilfred Owen, the poet of the Great War. Stallworthy records a remarkable incident at the very end of Wilfred Owen's life. Wilfred was killed in action in France on 4 November 1918. His parents did not receive the telegram announcing his death until the very day when the bells of Shrewsbury were ringing to celebrate the Armistice, on 11 November. That day found Wilfred's brother, Harold, on the Africa Station in the cruiser *Astraea*. He wrote:

> We were lying off Victoria. I had gone down to my cabin thinking to write some letters. I drew aside the door curtain and stepped inside, and to my amazement I saw Wilfred, sitting in my chair. I felt shock run through me with appalling force, and with it I could feel the blood draining away from my face. I did not rush towards him but walked jerkily into the cabin—all my limbs stiff and slow to respond. I did not sit down, but, looking at him, I spoke quietly: 'Wilfred, how did *you* get here?' He did not rise, and I saw that he was involuntarily immobile, but his eyes, which had never left mine, were alive with the familiar look of trying to make me understand; when I spoke, his whole face broke into his sweetest and most endearing dark smile. I felt no fear—I had not when I first drew my door curtain and saw him there; only exquisite mental pleasure at thus beholding him. All I was conscious of was a sensation of enormous shock and profound astonishment that he should be here in my cabin. I spoke again. 'Wilfred dear, how can *you* be here, it's just not possible . . .' But still he did not speak but only smiled his most gentle smile. This not speaking did not now, as it had done at first, seem strange or even unnatural; it was not only in some inexplicable way perfectly natural but radiated a quality which made his presence with me undeniably right and in no way out of the ordinary. I loved having him there: I could not, and did not want to try to understand how he had got there. I was content to accept him, that he was here, with me, was sufficient. I could not question anything, the meeting in itself was complete and strangely perfect. He was in uniform and I remember thinking how out of place the khaki looked amongst the cabin furnishings. With this thought I must have turned my eyes away from him; when I looked back, my cabin chair was empty . . .
>
> I felt the blood run slowly back to my face, and looseness into my limbs, and, with these, an overpowering sense of emptiness and absolute loss . . . I wondered if I had been dreaming, but, looking down, I saw that I was still standing. Suddenly, I felt terribly tired, and, moving to my bunk, I lay down; instantly I went into a deep, oblivious sleep. When I woke up, I knew with absolute certainty that Wilfred was dead.

That appearance of Wilfred Owen, after his death, to his brother Harold, surely has much in common with the appearances of our Lord described in the New Testament.

The disciples, behind locked doors, imprisoned in their fear, suddenly saw the Lord. He made His presence felt, without the doors ever being opened. His body was obviously very different from the body that had been buried in the tomb.

And the Emmaus story. Two friends walked all the way to Emmaus with a stranger. There was such *dis*continuity between the Jesus they had known and the stranger, that they did not recognize Him, though they walked together for several miles. But He made Himself known in the breaking of bread. The disciples had no more doubt that it was Jesus than Harold Owen had that it was Wilfred.

Now it is not Michael Perry's purpose to convince his readers that *all* the evidence supports the belief that our Lord's resurrection was like the apparitions of people after their death—which form a not insignificant part of the proceedings of the Society for Psychical Research. Michael Perry is too careful a scholar for that. But he does say that the evidence may make *one* aspect of the resurrection more credible to the sceptic, even though simply to categorize the resurrection as a psychic manifestation does not cover a thousandth part of what the Christian believes about the resurrection.

I would want to testify that in my pastoral experience over the last thirty and more years since the publication of *The Easter Enigma*, I have found, in dealing with the bereaved, what Michael Perry has written of very great help. I have found it of equal help in caring for the dying, when I have been posed the direct question: 'Do you think this life is the end?'

It was a previous Preacher to Gray's Inn in the 1920s—the much revered Walter Matthews, some time Dean of St Paul's—who in 1940 gave the Myers Memorial Lecture on Psychical Research and Theology. Michael Perry quotes Dean Matthews as saying in that Lecture: 'No one who understands what he is about would suppose . . . that God could be the conclusion of an investigation by scientific methods.' Perry adds: 'No one need ever fear that the totality of the beauty of Christianity will ever be expressed in a textbook on parapsychology.' And he continues:

> The fact that the Resurrection is so much more wonderful than 'just another case' of telepathic communication is no surprise to the Christian. He believes that the Resurrection was a unique act of the living God. Jesus of Nazareth is not only a man. He is Divinity incarnate, and so his Resurrection is so much greater than anything the world has experienced before or since. We may try to categorize the mode of communication of the Glorified Lord; we can never categorize the Resurrection or empty it of its significance.

But I believe that Michael Perry's approach may help us the more to surmount the barriers of the grave, and interpret what we believe Jesus himself has done. And who of us could say we have no need of such help?

✻ 12

THE WRECK OF THE DEUTSCHLAND

Gray's Inn Chapel; 10 May 1992

The genesis of a sermon is often complex. I think my sermon this morning probably began when I heard that you, Master Treasurer,* bear the title, a 'Commissioner of Wrecks'.

But there were several other contributory factors. There have been two biographies recently of Gerard Manley Hopkins—who, of course, wrote one of the best poems in all English literature on 'The Wreck of the *Deutschland*', and there has been another book published recently by Sean Street which spells out the details of that sad event.

A third reason for my sermon is probably that I went down to Harwich recently and looked out to sea to where the wreck of the *Deutschland* took place, off the Suffolk coast.

But I think there is probably another reason buried not all that deep in my psyche. When I was a child, my father used to sing Victorian ballads accompanied by mother, and such a lot of them seemed to be about lifeboats, and pilots, and storms at sea, and the safety of harbours, and 'Crossing the Bar'.

It was 1875, when a German ship—called, in fact, the *Deutschland*, though it was built in Britain, on the Clyde—ran aground, on a notorious sandbank: the Kentish Knock, in the mouth of the Thames. She languished there, at the mercy of the waves, for more than thirty hours, her propeller broken, and her distress signals ignored, before a tug, the *Liverpool*, arrived, from Harwich, to take off survivors.

More than fifty of the passengers and crew were drowned. It was one of the worst shipping disasters ever to occur off the coasts of Britain.

When a disaster like that takes place, there's never just a single story. There's the story, for instance, of the ship itself. Was she in good order? Well, yes; she was. She'd been launched only nine years before, in 1866: 320 ft long; 2,500 tons. She carried sail, but only to augment her engines. By 1875, the *Deutschland* was a veteran of many Atlantic crossings.

*Richard Stone QC

61

She'd been fully inspected only that autumn, and her compasses checked.

It was, in fact, the December weather that year that was the *Deutschland*'s downfall: driving snow, and a force-ten gale, and a maelstrom of conflicting currents, which made navigation hazardous beyond words. She was at the mercy of the waves, and, at the end, helplessly driven towards the sandbanks, less than thirty miles off the Suffolk shore.

As with all such disasters, there was, of course, an inquest, at the Three Cups Hotel, Harwich—which I was glad to find is still there—and an Inquiry, at the Board of Trade, in Poplar, East London. The reports of both still read graphically.

It's difficult now for us to realize just what a graveyard for shipping the East Coast was in 1875, particularly where the fingers of sand stretch out from the Thames Estuary into the North Sea. In those days, there was marine carnage.

'Why was there no lifeboat at Harwich?' asked the Inquiry. And, of course, as a direct result, there was one—from 1878—and there is still one, because of the wreck of the *Deutschland*, and thanks to the Royal National Lifeboat Institution.

The Inquiry had to investigate some very sombre subjects. 'Why did help never effectively reach the *Deutschland* in those thirty crucial hours?'

And an even more sombre subject: 'Did those who reached the *Deutschland* from the Suffolk shore, pillage and pilfer the contents of the ship and the possessions of the passengers?'

The salvage sales of goods from the ship, organized by the Receiver of the Wreck and held at Brightlingsea and Woodbridge, came in for criticism. Apparently, goods were first sold at knock-down prices but then re-sold at a huge profit.

Other questions were pressed to good and lasting effect: concerning communications, for instance, between lightships and land.

Of course, the primary tragedy was the loss of life: to passengers and crew; each life was a separate tragedy, including some very young children. Many of the passengers were emigrants—some virtually refugees, emigrating to America, because of the strutting and swaggering policies of Bismarck's Prussia.

There were five Franciscan nuns, whose religious order was virtually forbidden in Germany at the time. They were below decks when the *Deutschland* ran aground. All five were drowned.

The Harwich correspondent of *The Times*, on 11 December 1875, reported that one of the sisters called out loudly and often: 'O Christ, Christ, come quickly'. Other accounts said what she was actually crying was: 'O my God, make it quick, make it quick', and it wasn't clear whether she was meaning the arrival of help or the end of life. The grave of the five nuns is still to be seen in St Patrick's Roman Catholic Cemetery, Leytonstone, East London.

Now I've hardly yet mentioned one rather important outcome of the tragedy: Gerard Manley Hopkins' poem 'The Wreck of the *Deutschland*'. The whole tragedy would probably now have faded from the memory of all but a handful of people but for that poem.

The subject deeply moved Hopkins for several reasons. The fact is, he had been born, in 1844, across the road from the very church, St Francis, Stratford, East London, where, thirty-one years later, the funeral of those five nuns was to take place.

Secondly, Gerard Manley Hopkins' father was what's known as an Average Adjuster. He wrote a book called *A Manual of Marine Insurance* and a standard work called *A Handbook of Average*. The firm of average adjusters to whom he belonged—Manley Hopkins & Sons & Cookes Limited—still exists today in Folgate Street, in the City. Probably an average adjuster would have had to deal with the wreck of the *Deutschland*—maybe Manley Hopkins & Sons & Cookes Limited. Anyhow, Gerard Manley Hopkins would have known a good deal about wrecks because of his father's business.

Thirdly, by 1875, Gerard Manley Hopkins, a graduate of Balliol College, Oxford, had become a Roman Catholic and, indeed, was studying to become a Jesuit priest. He saw the account of the wreck of the *Deutschland* in *The Times*; and his superior at the Jesuit college in North Wales, where he was studying—St Bueno's—said he 'wished someone would write a poem on the subject'. And Gerard did.

In the world at large, Hopkins was virtually unknown as a poet for another thirty or forty years. It wasn't until 1918 that the first edition of his poems was published. They took a long while to sell. And not till 1940 was his significance as a poet really recognized. And I suppose, odd as it may seem, Hopkins has become known not least because of 'The Wreck of the *Deutschland*'. It isn't an easy poem that he penned, but T. S. Eliot wrote that 'the thrill of excitement from our first reading of a work of creative literature which we do not understand is itself the beginning of our understanding'.

Because 'The Wreck of the *Deutschland*' is long and, as I say, difficult, I shall read you only the first of its thirty-five verses.

> Thou mastering me
> God! giver of breath and bread;
> World's strand, sway of the sea;
> Lord of living and dead;
> Thou hast bound bones and veins in me, fastened me flesh,
> And after it almost unmade, what with dread,
> Thy doing: and dost thou touch me afresh?
> Over again I feel thy finger and find thee.

But now I want to read you a few paragraphs of prose which Gerard Manley Hopkins wrote—which, remember, he was writing as a Jesuit monk:

> The life I lead is liable to many mortifications, but the want of fame-as-a-poet is the least of them. I could wish, I allow, that my pieces could at some time become known but in some spontaneous way, so to speak, and without my forcing.
>
> Fame, the being known, though in itself one of the most dangerous things to man, is nevertheless the true and appointed air, element and setting of genius and its works.
>
> It is not that I think a man is really the less happy because he has missed the renown which was his due, but still, when this happens, it is an evil in itself and a thing which ought not to be, and that I deplore, for the good work's sake rather than the author's.
>
> We must then try to be known, aim at it, take means to it. And this without puffing in the process or pride in the success . . .
>
> What I do regret is the loss of recognition belonging to the work itself. For as to every moral act, being right or wrong, there belongs, of the nature of things, reward or punishment, so to every form perceived by the mind belongs, of the nature of things, admiration or the reverse . . . Nevertheless, fame, whether won or lost, is a thing which lies in the award of a random, reckless, incompetent and unjust judge, the public, the multitude. The only just judge, the only just literary critic, is Christ, who prizes, is proud of, and admires, more than any man, more than the receiver himself can, the gifts of his own making.
>
> Now if you value what I write, if I do myself, much more does our Lord. And if he chooses to avail himself of what I leave at his disposal he can do so with a felicity and with a success which I could never command.

I think those particular paragraphs have a great deal to say to us all today. But so, too, do the events I have been describing this morning. Almost each one of them raises questions about the meaning and mystery of life.

Accidents strike us all at some time, and often they bring good as well as evil. I like to think of those five nuns refusing to sit down under an alien government; but their resistance wasn't the *last* word. I like to think of the lifeboat as part of the good that came out of evil, but the evil in the world—not least the evil people who may have pillaged and pilfered and looted—has to be faced. I think it is as important for us to see the work of average adjusters and those involved in marine insurance—and commissioners of wrecks—as much within the providence of God as poets and priests. And it's important for all of us to face the question of the renown, the value and worth of the work we do, in the sight of God, and to wrestle with the mystery and meaning of the complex tapestry of life—of our own life and of life as a whole—so that Hopkins' phrase 'Thou mastering me, God' comes to mean something to us personally; and that other so powerful phrase of his: 'I feel thy finger and find thee.'

13
THE COMMUNITY OF THE RESURRECTION

Gray's Inn Chapel; 17 May 1992

In the last weeks, I have hardly been able to put down a book which has just been published and could not be more appropriate for the weeks after Easter: it's the Centenary History of the Community of the Resurrection, by a friend of mine, Canon Alan Wilkinson, erstwhile Principal of Chichester Theological College.

The Community of the Resurrection has probably been the most influential of all the Anglican Religious Communities. For a whole series of reasons, its history is bound to be of interest not only to ecclesiastics.

Its founder, Charles Gore, later Bishop of Worcester, then Birmingham, then Oxford, was an aristocrat by birth. His mother was Countess of Kerry. Most of the earliest members of the Community were in fact what one might call 'well connected': Etonians, Harrovians, who invariably went on to Oxbridge. And there I think is the first question this important book indirectly poses and presses: 'What was it that in the 1890s prompted a group of men to pass by on the other side of the major professions, of which they were quite likely to rise to the top, and to forsake marriage, and money, and many of the luxuries of life, and live together in Religious Community?' In fact, Gore did not live in Community for long. He was better at founding a Community than living as a member of it. He once said: 'All I have to do to make any institution prosper is to leave it.'

It needs to be made clear that although the Community of the Resurrection began in Oxford, it moved in less than ten years to Mirfield, near Huddersfield: to the heart of the industrial North, to the West Riding. And it did that as a matter of conscience. It knew that Oxford, indeed, rural Radley, was not the place for a Community of the Resurrection to rise in an industrial society. And in fact most of the Community, albeit gentlemen of means, were socialists: aristocratic socialists, members of the Christian Social Union—again, as a matter of conscience.

Beatrice Webb, the Fabian, quoted at that time Arnold Toynbee, then economics tutor at Balliol College, Oxford.

65

'We—the middle classes, I mean, not merely the very rich—we have neglected you' Toynbee said. 'Instead of justice we have offered you charity, and instead of sympathy we have offered you hard and unreal advice; but I think we are changing . . . we have sinned against you grievously . . . but if you will forgive us—nay, whether you will forgive us or not—we will serve you, we will devote our lives to your service . . . We are willing to give up the life we came for, the life with books and with those we love.'

It was from people with that sort of outlook that the Community of the Resurrection emerged. Its earliest members were, as I've said, gentlemen; and most of them, individualists; and it was no easy job for them to live together in community. That needed not only nature but grace. It was continually a difficult question how the Community life could both respect their individuality yet also produce a community. There had to be self-repression as well as self-assertion.

At Mirfield it was not long before the Community began putting up the kind of buildings which a growing community clearly needed. But such buildings had their dangers. It was all too possible for the Community to be in Mirfield but not of it. Yet, to be fair, the Community soon began to reach out far beyond Mirfield and Yorkshire. Though here in England, before the Great War, the Community was identified in the public mind with Christian Socialism, the Community never penetrated the Labour Party, or succeeded, then or later, in persuading the Church of England as a whole to take Socialism seriously; and by the 1930s the social conscience of the Community was largely focused upon the problems of South Africa, rather than upon those at home.

Gore, the Founder, had been succeeded as Superior, in 1902, by Walter Howard Frere, also a patrician and a scholar, later Bishop of Truro. But it was probably Edward Keble Talbot, who became Superior in 1922, who influenced the Community most. His father had been Bishop of Rochester, Southwark and Winchester. Keble Talbot and his brother Neville had been Chaplains in France in the First World War, and their brother Gilbert killed there, and in his memory Toc H was started. Soon the Community of the Resurrection began to be known in upper-class church circles as 'Ted Talbot's Community'. Ted was Winchester and Christ Church, Oxford, and was a superb raconteur. Bishop Trevor Huddleston, whose first year as a novice was spent with Talbot as Superior, said: 'In those days we all used to meet in the community room after supper, even the novices, and when Keble—Keble Talbot—wasn't in the house it was as dull as ditchwater. When Keble was there, it was as though a light had come on.'

I was myself fortunate enough when I was a student to go to one of the last retreats at Mirfield which Fr Talbot conducted, and I can still recall the beauty of his voice and his command of English. I can even now hear him saying:

There is a wonderful sentence written over the porch of the church at Staunton Harold in Leicestershire, built at the time of the Commonwealth in 1653, 'When throughout the nation all things sacred were either demolished or profaned, this church was founded by Sir Robert Shirley, Baronet, whose singular praise it is to have done the best things in the worst times and hoped them in the most calamitous'. Knowing that Christ is enthroned, *we* are to go on doing the best things even though the times be worst, and to hope, though in the worst calamity.'

I remember, in that same retreat, Fr Talbot quoting a saying of Mother Julian of Norwich: 'It is full great pleasure to our gracious Lord when the poor soul comes to him simply, plainly and homely.'

My last memory of Fr Talbot was in fact at Cumberland Lodge in Windsor Great Park. I was night porter there as a student in my summer vacations and Fr Talbot came in cassock to dinner with Lord Halifax. Alan Wilkinson records that Talbot gave invaluable support to the establishment of Cumberland Lodge and to its subsequent work.

I have said that the Community's work expanded. It did so in South Africa, in what was then Rhodesia, in Barbados, and in the British Isles. By 1958 the Community of the Resurrection had ten houses and eighty-five brothers.

When the history of South Africa comes to be written, I have little doubt the part that the Community of the Resurrection played will be seen to have been quite crucial. In 1903 there were forty-five state schools for whites in Johannesburg but none for blacks. By 1947, the Community of the Resurrection was looking after forty-four schools and 10,000 children in that area, almost all of them black. The Community ran the only secondary school for blacks in the Transvaal, St Peter's, Rosettenville, but pupils came from all over South Africa, and from Southern Rhodesia, and Portuguese East Africa—'The Black Eton', as it was called, produced people like Oliver Tambo, later, President of the ANC.

What Trevor Huddleston achieved in South Africa, he would say he only achieved—could only have achieved—as a member of a Religious Community like the Community of the Resurrection. And Mirfield's work at Penhalonga, Southern Rhodesia, was probably as important as its work in South Africa.

It was not only what the Mirfield Fathers did for Africans; it was also what Africa did for the Fathers which was important. I quote just one paragraph from the testimony of Fr Reginald Smith CR:

I knew that I had got to be nice to the African people and love them, but I was all stiff inside and I'd sort of smile and shake hands and I wouldn't really want to have anything to do with them. The change came one day when I was standing on the open space in front of the church at Penhalonga, and there were two small black toddlers and an ox broke away and charged across the

open space. The children screamed and rushed to me and held me round the
legs. I suddenly realized that they were not black but just children, so I picked
them up and kissed and comforted them and that changed my attitude. From
then on I was human with African people.

Much of what I have said so far is about what individual members of
the Community did as individuals and what the Community got up to in
various parts of the world. But I know that, without exception, if I were
to end there, every member of the Community from 1892 to 1992, would
rise up and say 'You have got us wrong. You have omitted the most
important ingredient. You have said little or nothing about our worship
and our prayer.'

One of his brethren told me that Trevor Huddleston, before he had to
face the Chief of Police in Johannesburg, would get up early and spend
an extra hour of silence in prayer in the chapel.

Trevor himself would say he owed much to the Mirfield Novice Guardian, Hubert Northcott, who wrote a book *A Venture of Prayer*. Yet even
Northcott wrote: 'Sooner or later our methods of prayer fail, we are left
once more face to face with God, helpless, "and with no language but a
cry".'

It would be wrong to let you think that the Centenary History of the
Community of the Resurrection is, page after page, a success story. It is
not. I've already hinted that people living adjacent to Mirfield might say
it had very little influence on them. I've hinted that there were some
fairly fundamental clashes and collisions within the Community, not least
between the needs of the individual and the need of his merging himself
in the Community.

I've said that the first members of the Community were gentlemen and
it may have remained too much a gentleman's club. And I wonder
whether the Community ever really related closely enough to the role of
the layman and to the world of work. But it has to be remembered that in
the 1920s more than half the bishops of the Church of England were
connected with the aristocracy. The Community of the Resurrection
bridged many gulfs. It made it possible for many working-class people to
get ordained, but it never really managed to become a genuinely multi-
racial community. And it was undoubtedly better at looking after people
and *giving to* them than *receiving from* them. And that means that the
Community created people dependent upon them. Princess Margaret
became the first *woman* to dine in the refectory when she attended the
Community's 75th Birthday in 1967. From 1976 other women guests
were also able to eat there.

Two Africans asked a penetrating question in the Community's own
magazine: 'Why do Missionaries seek to convert Africans but not white
imperialists?'

It cannot be said that this great Anglican Community, any more than the C of E in general, was all that good for most of its history at relating to other Christian denominations or to people of other religions.

And, at the end of the century, the work of the Community has had to be reduced to its House at Mirfield, and a House in London, and a much reduced House in South Africa. Its mission work in great cities has virtually come to an end.

In these last years the Community of the Resurrection has been part of a crisis in the monastic life that has been world-wide. Between 1960 and 1975 the number of Benedictines dropped by fifteen per cent. In 1969 alone some 6,500 nuns left their communities.

I think it is important to underline that what the Community of the Resurrection did and achieved in its hundred years of history is in no way denied or negated by the position in which it now finds itself. In all that century men faced God and His call and challenge, and their response still challenges each one of us. But this age has new challenges, some of which are old challenges that must be responded to in a new way.

One of the major gifts—and challenges—of this last century has of course been the advent of psychology; and there is no doubt that if men are to live together in community, a more profound psychology is now indispensable; and, indeed, a more profound understanding of sexuality, not least if the response of men and women to the gospel is seen as involving the renunciation of marriage. In fact, a more direct and rigorous confrontation of the subject of what holiness has to say about sexuality is required from the whole Church. Response to the gospel now requires something more profound and rigorous than the socialism of the turn of the century. The gospel still requires of all Christians that we live alongside the poor, and that cannot mean an easy carefree abandonment of all the insights of Christian Socialism. A Community of the Resurrection must mean a more profound and costly identification with other races and, indeed, a more profound understanding of other religions, if a Community of the Resurrection is to be a truly missionary community. Right from its earliest days the Community of the Resurrection contained within its company major theologians—not least as a sign and symbol of the fact that if you don't get the very nature of God right, and the Church and the world, you are in trouble. That often meant divisions within the Community, unavoidably. I love the story of a guest one day seeing one of the Fathers—who was always notoriously silent except when engaged in theological controversy—sitting at tea entirely isolated from the others. 'Who is that?' asked the guest. 'Oh, that is Fr Thornton. He is writing a great book on the Common Life in the Body of Christ.'

None of this, as I say, negates what happened through the Community of the Resurrection in the last hundred years, or releases other Christians like ourselves, lay or ordained, from recognizing the reality of the call of

God, and with realism responding to that call in our own way, in our own circumstances, with our own personalities and gifts. And all of us need support—the support of some kind of community—not simply to go it alone. We all need to be part of that Community of the Resurrection which is the Church itself if we are to be who we are meant to be and to live life at its best: the best we each one of us can be.

14

ASCENSION

*Sermon broadcast by the BBC
from All Souls' Langham Place;
Ascension Day, 28 May 1992*

It's over forty years now since I became a priest; and I have to tell you that I find preaching on Ascension Day as difficult now as I did when I was first ordained: if anything, it's *more* difficult.

I can put the difficulty in two words: words fail.

The words that are used to describe the ascension in the New Testament are undeniably part of an antique way of regarding the universe. In our space age we no longer believe that if people go up they will get to heaven. But the people of Jesus' time probably did believe that.

But let's be clear: the truth of the ascension is not essentially about a sort of divine astronaut who never came back. It's not about someone moving in space or into space, though a first look at the Bible, because of the cosmology of the time, might suggest that it is.

I say again: words fail; for if you don't put the truth of the ascension into the language of the Bible's cosmology the question still remains: what words should we use? What words shall we use this Ascension Day?

It sometimes helps if we remind ourselves that most of our language, our language today, is still picture language. We still talk, for instance, of 'going up' next year at school, and coming 'top' in examinations, and of people 'rising above' their circumstances. So it's worth asking: what were the Bible writers wanting to picture when they wrote of the ascension of Jesus?

In a sense, they were wanting to picture just what they described: an astronaut-type being: someone going up into the clouds; because that picture had no difficulty for them in their age; nor did it for quite a few centuries later; so that artists—great artists, like Raphael and Fra Angelico—when they painted the ascension, would paint a human being taking off from the earth. Often they would paint at the top of the picture a pair of feet disappearing into the clouds!

We have no need to be ashamed of such a picture, no need totally to discard it. It was useful to human beings of widely different cultures and civilizations and for century upon century. And, as I say, most of our language today is still picture language.

71

What I think we need to do is to go to the heart of the language and remind ourselves that the symbol of the ascension has two main meanings. A higher level in space signifies a higher value, but it also often corresponds with an upward impulse within us; so that mountains, or music moving from low to high, from bass to treble, and so on, seem to articulate some of our most profound human experience, and lift up our hearts—though there's some picture language again; we can't escape it. And the ascension of Jesus is really a way of speaking in spatial terms of the ascendancy of Jesus: that He is supreme; that He's 'the tops'. The *quality* that He is has been put into terms of space.

In some of what we say at Ascensiontide we use explicit picture language of height. Sometimes we use other pictures of supremacy. We say that Jesus is 'King': the King of Love. We take the top person in society as we know it and use that as a picture of God who rules with the power of love. We use that way to speak of his ascendancy.

So, on Ascension Day, quite a lot of the picture language we use is the language we still use of earthly coronations. 'Crown him with many crowns' is one of the most popular Ascension hymns. No one means it literally. We're lost for words, but we keep on trying to find them: find pictures that will fit what we are struggling to say.

I began by saying that on Ascension Day 'words fail'. They do so particularly if our language is literally spatial, crudely of this world, or when we think that only one kind of picture language will do.

I love Newman's hymn which begins:

> Praise to the holiest in the height,
> And in the depth be praise.

Sometimes, paradoxical as it may seem, depth is an even more profound picture of God's ascendancy than height. We say of someone when we really want to pay them a compliment: 'She's got great depth to her.' We speak of depth of feeling. We say of some music that it's particularly deep. But all our picture language of the ascension will be misleading if we think it literally describes some actual movement in space or some actual moment in time, or some earthly event or quantity instead of some quality.

The ascension, at its heart, is about the ascendancy of Jesus. It's about the ascendancy which Jesus revealed by the quality of His life and love, lived out on this earth.

We've just sung on this Ascension Day:

> The head that once was crowned with thorns
> Is crowned with glory now.

Well; that may sound all very theoretical—and be quite tough going. I began by saying that preaching on Ascension Day is never easy. But it's nevertheless a favourite day of mine because the theory, to my mind, has such practical implications.

You see: Jesus has blazed a trail for us. (There's picture language for you!) He has gone ahead of us. He has shown us how to achieve true ascendancy in this world: the ascendancy of love, forgiveness, goodness and truth; but He has shown us that it's not done cheaply: at no cost. His ascension cost Jesus the suffering of the cross.

We pray in the most familiar of all prayers—the Lord's Prayer—'Thy Kingdom Come!' That's a prayer that the rule of Christ, the sovereignty of Christ, the ascendancy of Christ, shall be clearly seen on earth.

But that rule will be manifest in very down-to-earth ways: in peace and justice between individuals and nations; in compassion for those in need: the hungry and the homeless; prisoners, imprisoned because of a miscarriage of justice, released; and so on.

That kingdom, that rule of Christ, that ascendancy, will not be achieved without cost today. It will mean individuals like us committing ourselves to costly peacemaking, in families, and on housing estates, and between warring nations. It will mean committing ourselves to securing *justice* for particular people, and taking practical measures to care for those who are hungry or homeless. That kingdom will only come about through the sovereign power of Christ at work in each one of us. His ascendancy has to be revealed on earth: and, paradoxically, in ways that are down-to-earth.

15

THE DIVINE DYNAMIC

The Mayor's Sunday,
St Mary-le-Tower, Ipswich;
31 May 1992

'Stay in the city till you are clothed with power from on high.'

Luke 24.39 49

The three English words *ENDUE*, *DYNAMO* and *DYNAMIC* all share a common Greek root, which lies in fact behind two of the words of my text this morning, the second half of which you could translate: '. . . till you are endued with divine dynamic'—stay in the city till you are endued with divine dynamic.

The claim to possess divine dynamic is made, I find, with alarming frequency by those who, alas, all too often these days are to be found roaming the streets of London, but who really need rather more care than they are getting for their mental disorder and distress.

Others who hang about the streets, manifestly under the influence of alcohol, when they spot my dog-collar, often suggest to me that it's *divine dynamic* which is influencing them, rather than the more obvious spirit.

And quite often these days, when, as an itinerant preacher, I visit this parish or that—as I do most Sundays of the year—someone will quite often confide in me that they believe themselves to be endued with divine dynamic—or words to that effect.

I always try to respond positively. After all, the gift of divine dynamic is precisely what we're promised shall follow our baptism.

Mercifully, I find there is one all but infallible way of sobering up those who make claims to possess that divine dynamic. I simply quote to them the main headlines of the BBC news of the day and ask them to let me know what the Spirit suggests to them should be their response to those headlines.

For instance, today: the tragic fighting in Serbia. What should the United Nations, what should we, do about that?—if we are filled with the divine dynamic. Likewise the situation between Arab and Israeli? Likewise Northern Ireland? And what should be done about the refugees

74

from Haiti? And closer to home, What should we do about bankrupt Canary Wharf?

Yes; and Monday, the Earth Summit opens in Rio de Janeiro. Jonathon Porritt, who knows that subject, is not hopeful about the outcome.

But 'Stay in the city till you are clothed with power from on high . . . endued with divine dynamic.' Then, presumably, we shall be given a few answers?

May I say that, wherever I go, I also try to find out in that particular locality, that town or city, what the main local problems are: in the realms of health, social care, housing, education and law and order; and I say to myself: 'That's certainly where people will need to be endued with divine dynamic if they are to come to grips with those problems.'

You will not need me to tell you that whenever people put on mayoral or aldermanic robes or take on offices of that sort and kind, there they are being clothed with a series of local responsibilities. Very often those responsibilities are considerable, sometimes complex beyond words, and not easy to fulfil; and coming to church—whatever else it may mean—represents at the least a kind of public admission and awareness of the dimensions of those responsibilities and reveals, let us say, humility in approaching them.

Some of those responsibilities fall on the shoulders of other officers and officials. And, of course, a good many of the burdens of local responsibility are not simply local: local government shares with those at a higher level, usually with the national level of government—which does not usually lessen or simplify them. And, local or national, the problems are mostly of such difficulty and complexity that they cannot be solved by some romantic idea of 'divine dynamic'. The solutions—if solutions there be—have to be detailed and down-to-earth.

I suppose what is taking place in London this very morning is as good an example of a national question of huge complexity as one is likely to find.

You will most of you know that at St Clement Danes' Church, at midday, after morning service, the Queen Mother is unveiling—amidst considerable controversy and, indeed, protest—a statue in memory of Sir Arthur—so-called 'Bomber'—Harris.

Those of us who are old enough to remember the days of the Second World War will remember that there was all but national unanimity that the war against Germany should be prosecuted with all possible power.

Again: there was all but national unanimity for the RAF raids on the mainland of Europe. It took a great deal of courage on the part of the then Bishop of Chichester, George Bell, to raise his lone voice in the House of Lords and question the value and indeed the ethics of the thousand bomber raids on places like Cologne, Dresden and Vienna.

Most of us, with the wisdom of hindsight, have come to see there was much more in the Bishop's protest than we were willing to acknowledge at the time. But the responsibility belonged, of course, finally to Sir Winston Churchill and the War Cabinet—who possessed so much more knowledge than we did. It was their final responsibility, not that of Bomber Harris.

But the question needs to be posed: had we been endued with divine dynamic, should we, in the fight against Nazism, have heeded the Bishop of Chichester rather than Churchill and Bomber Harris?

That painfully difficult question—particularly for those who confess and call themselves Christians—can be posed even more painfully.

Part of the problem was that at the beginning of the Second World War the kind of precision bombing for which we now have the capacity just did not belong to us. If crews managed to get within a few miles of their targets they were doing reasonably well.

But there was one lone inventor, in fact a refugee, Captain Lipschutz, who in 1939 had come up with a particular invention which has now played its part in giving us the possibility of a hitherto quite impossible precision in bombing. In 1939 that inventor's suggestion was dismissed out of hand. Had it been accepted by the Air Ministry, thousands of lives would have been saved, paradoxically, by *precision* bombing.

But it was not only, I imagine, the Air Ministry, in 1939, who dismissed Captain Lipschutz's invention. I cannot think that there were many Christian congregations in 1939 who would have supported huge sums of money being spent on research into *precision* bombing. Yet probably, as I say, thousands of civilian and service lives would have been saved had that invention been available and, indeed, the war itself may well have been more speedily terminated.

The single point I am trying to make this morning is that human decision-making is often complex and compromising. The questions of ethics which adult human beings are called upon to decide are often not only complex but involve compromise and ambiguity. When human beings grow up, that is the sort of world we have to learn to live in and live with—and yet keep our principles.

But all too often a Christian is pictured as someone privileged and favoured by being endued with divine dynamic which gives to him or her simple solutions. Faith, it is all too often suggested, provides Christians with a kind of escape from the torturing dilemmas that other people have to endure.

Not so.

Madam Mayor, you will know, as will your Council, that life in government is full of complex responsibilities. I know that the Vicar and Parochial Church Council here at St Mary-le-Tower rejoice that you have come amongst them this morning. We pray for God's guidance for you: that you will be endued with divine dynamic. Your coming reminds each one of us that you do not exercise your responsibility *instead* of any of us but as our representatives; and you remind us that we too need to be clothed with 'power from on high', with divine dynamic.

Let me just add that it may sometimes be the lone voice (like that inventor), the lone prophet (like Bishop Bell), not the majority, who perceive and express the divine wisdom and insight. The divine dynamic bursts out—thank God!—in the strangest places; and one of our prayers must be simply to be open to the divine dynamic wherever it may manifest itself, from whatever political party or nationality. God is a God of surprises and apparent contradictions. To those who wait upon Him He gives power from on high. He shares the divine dynamic that HE HIMSELF IS.

16

MODELS OF GOD

St Katherine's East Tilbury; 21 June 1992

I'd be surprised if most of you thought of yourselves as 'theologians', but you are; we all are. And in a few minutes' time, when I've finished what I have to say—in which I hope I shall have encouraged you to think theologically about one or two things—we shall all recite together what is called the 'Nicene' Creed: a collection of theological statements to which we say we have given our assent: we say we 'believe in' this and that. The process of giving our assent to those beliefs would in itself be sufficient to earn each one of us the title 'theologian'.

On Trinity Sunday—which was last Sunday—it has been traditional for Christians to think directly about God; but I want this first Sunday after Trinity to carry on that process for one more Sunday of unashamed theologizing.

Perhaps I might encourage you in this activity by telling you that a fortnight ago I was taking a wedding in a lovely church in Shropshire. In a side aisle of the church was a very beautiful model of the church in boxwood. The wood was golden, and it was a glorious thing in itself. But it wasn't 'the real thing': it was a scale model. When Sir George Gilbert Scott was in charge of the extensive alteration and restoration to the church a century ago, that model must have been very useful in explaining to the people what he intended; but it would have been ludicrous to imagine that the model was the church itself.

But models are very valuable and very necessary; and we have need of models in all sorts of subjects, not least in theology: we have need of models of God.

I wonder what models of God you find most helpful and satisfactory these days? I wonder what models of God we particularly need if we're to understand what God wants of us in this world today which is at last beginning to emerge from its nuclear nightmare, but only to take on a huge ecological anxiety?

You may say: 'Well, isn't Jesus good enough as that model of God?' Well, yes: He is. Jesus is Himself a model of God: the model of God; good, as a model, above all others. He, above all, enables us to see God: see God 'the Father'. He manifests in His own life and death the astounding truth that at the heart of the universe is unqualified Love, working to befriend not least the needy, the outcast and the oppressed. And this we might never have guessed about God, and often can scarcely believe; but the people Jesus sat with, at table, and told His parables to, and above all, the crucifixion itself, makes plain the Love of God at the very heart of who He is. And when the most terrible events happen to us in this life, there in Jesus is the sympathy of God: God literally suffering alongside us. There is the triumphant love of God which no deed of darkness can overcome. And as we look at Jesus' suffering, we see God the Father's suffering and sympathy.

But Jesus, the Man of God on earth, the most marvellous model of God, doesn't exhaust all that God is. Jesus, so to speak, telescopes God in this world. He's the best telescoping of God that there is or could be. But even what we see through the telescope of Jesus isn't the whole universe that God is. In this world, such a lot is hid from our eyes. 'Now we know in part.'

Each new generation needs new models of God. It needs new models for old, because the old so often betray their origins, and their origins prevent their conveying fresh insights into the manifold truth that God is: truth that God may want to be revealing and imparting to us, for instance, in this nuclear ecological age.

If, or when, you say the prayer from the 1662 Prayer Book that begins:

> O Lord, our heavenly Father,
> High and Mighty,
> King of Kings,
> Lord of Lords,
> The only Ruler of Princes,
> Who dost from thy Throne behold all the dwellers upon earth . . .

Marvellous as the language is, and the cadences, you are left in no doubt that that prayer was written in and for and by a monarchical, hierarchical, patriarchal society, which was used to cowering down before its rulers and its ruling class. Because of its origins, you might from that prayer never guess or glimpse the God who, to convey His love toward mankind, was willing to wash His disciples' feet, indeed, to have His feet wiped with a prostitute's hair; and, above all, on the first Good Friday, was willing to be nailed like a rat to a barn door. That prayer to the High and Mighty God gives no idea of the vulnerability of God: indeed, the wounds and the suffering that are in God.

'But the model of God as Father,' you may say, 'surely that is a model for all seasons, all ages, patriarchal or nuclear?!'

Well, alas . . . I could take you to many a home, to many a child, to many a young man and young woman, to whom the word 'Father' can never be a model of God without unimaginable redemptive work upon it. If 'Father' is the only model of God, they are in sore straits.

But it is not the only model. Every one of our human relationships can be ruined: Mother as much as Father. So it's never a case simply of transplanting 'Mother' as a model instead of 'Father'; but I need to record that a lot of people these days find the model of God as 'Mother' as helpful in their prayers and in their understanding of God as the model of 'Father'. If we are to convey all the care, the nurturing, the self-sacrifice, the giving birth and the creativity, the sustaining that is in God, we may need more than the model of 'Father'. 'O God, our Mother' is also an important prayer.

There is a wonderful new prayer which begins not 'Almighty God' but 'Vulnerable God'.

But this weekend, which is a week along the road from Rio, the conference at Rio, I wonder what models of God will help us most?

In St John's Gospel, it's recorded that Jesus said: 'I am the True Vine, and my Father is the husbandman.'

It's a very remarkable Greek word that John uses there in his gospel – γεωργος: My Father is the γεωργος—from which we get 'geography'. It means one who tills the soil, the earth: a farmer, a gardener, a vinedresser, a cultivator, an agriculturalist.

Maybe that's an appropriate model of God for our ecological age. O God, the γεωργος: Have mercy on us, as we wonder how to save your world—*our* world: to halt global warming; to save the rain forests, and wildlife, and face the problem of population growth; to protect endangered plants and animals, to get the right priorities in our spending so that technology will be beneficial, particularly to the poorer countries of the world, to the Tanzania I was privileged to be visiting only a few months ago.

O God, the γεωργος, the husbandman, help us to sustain your world, our world.

I suspect that here in East Tilbury, most of you have larger gardens than we have in Lambeth, where I live. I wonder whether you might not at least begin your theology in your garden, using as your model of God, the γεωργος: the Gardener.

But I don't want to suggest that only new models of God will do. You may know the hymn 'How sweet the name of Jesus sounds'—with its verse that is simply a list of models that rang true when John Newton wrote the hymn in the eighteenth century but that still ring true today:

> Jesus, my Shepherd, Husband, Friend.
>   My Prophet, Priest and King,
> My Lord, my Life, my Way, my End,
>   Accept the praise I bring.

From time to time it's worth taking seriously different models of God: God as Friend, God as Lover—and letting them occupy our minds and hearts.

Perhaps on Trinity Sunday itself the mistake has often been to let God occupy the mind but not the heart; so that we worship the God of the mathematicians and the philosophers but leave our feelings and affections arid. But in these Sundays after Trinity, we can range a little wider in our theology.

I have suggested this morning that we need to use many models of God if we are to see all that He is. In Holy Communion, we often speak of the 'Living Bread'. Perhaps this particular morning, as we receive the Wine of Communion, we should consecrate ourselves afresh to Him who calls us all to follow Him who is the Vinedresser, the Husbandman, the γεωργος: the Gardener of our souls and of our world.

But don't let anyone tell you you're not a theologian! Theology has to be taken out of the scholar's study, away from the specialist, and given back to people like you and me, who will start thinking about God in our back gardens, in sight of the oil storage tanks and the river, and with the smells of the area in our nostrils—for good and ill.

And our Creed won't only be the Nicene Creed; it will be what we have gradually—or suddenly—come to believe in our deep heart's core about God the gardener.

17
FRIENDSHIP

Beaulieu Abbey Church;
28 June 1992

Some of you, I know, were here yesterday for the wedding of Charlotte and Robert Fanshawe—as I must now call them—and will remember that they chose for one reading the passage from the Gospel according to St John in which that most memorable text occurs: 'Greater love hath no man than this that a man lay down his life for his friends.' They chose a second reading from Kahlil Gibran's *The Prophet*, and, by their choice of readings, both bride and bridegroom declared that they wanted to set self-giving, self-sacrificing friendship at the centre of their marriage.

Those who were at the wedding may remember that in the course of my address I said that friendship is all-important to me, but that when I say that, sometimes people say to me—as a priest: 'But isn't *God* more important to you than all your friends?' And I feel bound to be honest and answer 'Well: God is, as St Paul says, above all, and through all, and in all; and the fact is that it's in and through my friends, and friendship, that I think I have learnt, and still do learn, most about God, and receive most from him.'

This morning I want simply to develop a little what I said yesterday about God and friendship.

First, may I say that I never cease to be astonished that there are so few books written directly on the subject of friendship.

There was a marvellous book *The Friendship of Christ*, written by Canon Charles Smyth during the Second World War. It was a book as much about human friendship in general as about the friendship of Christ. Indeed, it was about finding the friendship of Christ in human friendship. It was a wartime book in every way (occasioned, I suspect, by the pain of the parting of friends in wartime) and has been out of print for thirty years.

I believe the time has come to make up that which is lacking now that Charles Smyth's book is not available to us. And all I shall do this morning is to sketch out the rough plan of what I believe such a book should be.

The first chapter should undoubtedly concern definitions. C. S. Lewis, who knew the love literature of antiquity and the Middle Ages as well as any other modern scholar, and could write English with a persuasive and disarming felicity, wrote in 1960 a book full of marvellous insights called *The Four Loves*—having in mind Affection, Friendship, Eros and Charity.

I think it is probable that at that time Lewis feared the erotic and thought there was something so wild and dangerous about it—which is, of course, true—that it must be strictly confined, and battened down under hatches. He feared it getting mixed up with friendship, and therefore rather desperately tried to exclude the erotic. I would want to say that if God is 'above all and through all and in all' He is above the erotic *and* works in and through the erotic, as well as in and through distilled self-giving; and there is no need, and it can do great harm, entirely to separate friendship from the erotic. In my first chapter, therefore, I would probably, with Lewis, distinguish Affection, Friendship, Eros and Charity; but I would certainly not divide them.

I'm not myself a man with a command of the Classics; but I'd want to have a chapter that tell us about Plato and Aristotle on friendship, and moves on to Cicero, because I think it is quite important to observe people valuing friendship outside the Christian tradition as well as within it. The God who is 'above all and through all and in all' works in a world much larger than the Church, and His working in friendship, the world over, is one of His chief evidences. And it would be only after I had looked at friendship in the ancient Classical world that I would want to move on to the Bible.

In the Old Testament there are Proverbs on friendship, and purple passages like David's lament for Jonathan; and the record of that friendship of David and Jonathan is clearly one of the greatest stories of friendship in all literature. But it's when you steep yourself in the Gospels, in the friendships of Jesus, and particularly in the fourth Gospel, that you know you have been led near to the heart of friendship. Jesus called Lazarus 'our friend'; and there were his two sisters—'Now Jesus loved Martha, and her sister and Lazarus.' Peter called himself the friend of Jesus, and there was, of course, the 'beloved disciple'. Jesus Himself chooses to call His relationship to His disciples one of friendship: 'I have called you friends . . .', which makes all His life with His disciples a kind of commentary on the nature of friendship. 'Ye are my friends,' He says, 'if . . .' And I have already referred to that memorable text used yesterday, 'Greater love hath no man than this, that a man lay down his life for his friends. . . .' So the cross itself is to be seen as the supreme example of friendship.

There's a good deal also in St Paul on friendship, from his personal experience. And really, there's a book to be written, not simply a chapter, on 'The Bible and Friendship'.

It would not be long in any book that I wrote before I came to one of my heroes where friendship is concerned, Aelred of Rievaulx, whose book *Spiritual Friendship* is undoubtedly one of the great Christian classics, yet eminently readable. It is a kind of Christianized version of Cicero's *De Amicitia*.

Aelred was born into the family of a Saxon priest at Hexham, and spent much of his early years at the court of King David of Scotland. He became Abbot of Rievaulx in 1147, and undoubtedly had a genius for friendship. In due course, the Abbeys of Rievaulx and Beaulieu had much to do with each other.

What supremely distinguished Aelred of Rievaulx from other writers is a daring phrase in which he changes what St John had written: 'God is love', into 'God is friendship'; and he adds: 'He who abides in friendship abides in God, and God in him.'

Another important chapter on friendship would be entitled 'Shakespeare and Friendship'. Shakespeare, I have no doubt, mused often and long upon St Paul's words: 'Now remaineth faith, hope, and love, these three. And the greatest of these is love.' And his great sonnet on love, for instance, is equally a sonnet on friendship:

> Let me not to the marriage of true minds
> Admit impediments. Love is not love
> Which alters when it alteration finds,
> Or bends with the remover to remove:
> O, no! it is an ever-fixed mark,
> That looks on tempests and is never shaken;
> It is the star to every wandering bark,
> Whose worth's unknown, although his height be taken.
> Love's not Time's fool, though rosy lips and cheeks
> Within his bending sickle's compass come;
> Love alters not with his brief hours and weeks
> But bears it out even to the edge of doom.
>   If this be error, and upon me prov'd,
>   I never writ, nor no man ever lov'd.

Thirty years before Shakespeare, the French essayist Montaigne was born. I would want to see something on his superb essay on friendship. I wish I could say—particularly as Preacher to Gray's Inn—that there would also be a chapter on Francis Bacon. He was Earl of Verulam—St Albans, of which I am now an Emeritus Canon. He was one of the great men of Gray's Inn. Shakespeare lived from 1564 to 1616. Bacon was almost his contemporary. Born three years before him, he died ten years after him. But his essay 'Of Followers and Friends' says little to me of the heart of what I mean by friendship. 'There is little friendship in the world,' he writes, 'and least of all between equals.' I like his remark that 'Talk is but a tinkling cymbal where there is little love' and, of course, that 'Friendship re-doubleth joys and cutteth griefs in half.' I've no doubt Bacon was a friendly person: he erected a memorial, a summer-house, in the Walks of Gray's Inn, to the memory of his friend Jeremy Beltenham. He dedicated his book *Arguments of Law*, when Solicitor-General, 'to my loving friends and fellowes the Readers Ancients Alter-Barristers and Students of Graies Inn' and ended the book by signing himself 'Your loving friend and fellow, Francis Bacon'.

There is to be found more of depth and quality on Friendship in Bacon's near contemporary, Jeremy Taylor; born thirteen years before Bacon died, he lived until 1667. His *Discourse on the Nature and Offices of Friendship*, which he wrote ten years before he died, really makes you think about friendship. 'Some friendships are made by nature,' he writes, 'some by contract; some by interest; and some by souls.' 'Treat thy friend nobly, love to be with him, do to him all the worthiness of love and fair endearment, according to thy capacity and his ... Give him gifts and upbraid him not, and refuse not his kindnesses, and be sure never to despise the smallness or impropriety of them.' There are of course other great writers on friendship, notably Kahlil Gibran, who was quoted at length yesterday. And I would want a chapter on great friendships, like that of Boswell and Johnson. Can anyone ignore the creative power of the friendship of Benjamin Britten and Peter Pears? But I think it is significant that the most profound and penetrating descriptions of friendship are probably to be found in fiction. I think of the novels of E. M. Forster; of Lennie and George in Steinbeck's *Of Mice and Men*; of John Hilliard and David Barton in Susan Hill's *Strange Meeting*; of L. P. Hartley's story of childhood friendship, *The Shrimp and the Anemone*; and so on.

Forster is in many ways the apostle of friendship.

There is one subject which, alas, I could not omit in any realistic book on friendship. At the head of the chapter I would put a text from Zechariah: 'One shall say unto him: "What are these wounds in thine hands?" Then he shall answer: "Those with which I was wounded in the house of my friends.".' Our Lord's words to Judas: '*Friend*, wherefore art thou come?' form one of the most poignant and painful phrases in all the Scriptures—indeed, in all literature. The *betrayal* of friends and friendship is an inescapable subject where human beings are concerned. But our Lord teaches us, as no one else can teach us, how to handle that betrayal.

I think it is significant that one of the finest oblique descriptions of human friendship is told in the story of Mole, Rat, Badger and Toad in *The Wind in the Willows*. Who can forget that description of dawn on the river-bank? In the silence of the growing daylight, as Nature is flushed with colour, Rat turns and whispers to Mole, his eyes, we are told, 'shining with unutterable love'. That description of friendship as between *animals* makes it possible to describe it at all. Toad and Mole, we all know, are *not* animals. They are us!

The end of my sort of book—and the end of this sermon—would have to be about the end of Friendship: if it ends, or if it has some eternal quality—which I would maintain, if 'God is friendship', it has.

Again, it wouldn't be easy to put what I would want to say into words. And the device that was used nearly ninety years ago in *The Wind in the Willows* was used by A. A. Milne to no less brilliant effect twenty years later.

You may remember how he writes of Christopher Robin and Pooh. 'So they went off together. But wherever they go, and whatever happens to them on the way, in that enchanted Place on the top of the Forest, a little boy and his Bear will always be playing.'

Some say that is unforgivable sentimentality; some that both Kenneth Grahame and A. A. Milne represent something infantile, and immature: a wistful search for innocence, an escape from *un*friendly reality.

Well, I am persuaded that the great mysteries of life are not only scientific. How we human beings relate at all is one of the great mysteries, and friendship is a mystery within the compass of that larger mystery. Confronted by that mystery we are always, in the end, lost for words and need to resort to such imagery as A. A. Milne used of 'an enchanted Place on the top of the Forest'. It is no shame to say with the ancient Christian writer Tertullian that 'all things end in mystery'— *omnes exeunt in mysterium*; and that is true, in the end, of friendship and of all our friendships.

🏵 18

LIVING STONE

Gray's Inn Chapel; 5 July 1992

'Come to him, to the living stone which was rejected by men but chosen by God and of great worth to him. You also, as living stones, must be built up as a spiritual temple, and form a holy priesthood to offer spiritual sacrifices acceptable to God through Jesus Christ.'

1 Peter 2.4

So long as Africa exists, so long, surely, will one man live in the memory of humankind: David Livingstone.

In the last two years I have had two encounters with the memory of Livingstone.

On Easter Sunday, two years ago, I was preaching in Westminster Abbey in the afternoon. That Maundy Thursday, a friend of mine had phoned to ask whether he could bring over that evening four young men who were from South Africa, all militant members of the ANC. They had just arrived in England to study at Lancaster. They were all, of course, black; and under twenty-four. One of them had been to prison for two years for his ANC activities. Another had had his lower arm blown off by a grenade. All of them were impoverished to a degree, possessing little more than the clothes in which they stood up.

I asked them to accompany me to Westminster Abbey for the Easter Sunday afternoon service. The Dean kindly placed them in his own stall. They had never heard music like the Abbey's or seen a building like it. Immediately after the service, I asked them whether they would like to see Livingstone's grave, in the centre aisle, where he was buried in 1874. I was uncertain what their reaction might be; but they were eager and enthusiastic to do so. I pointed out to them the words that Livingstone himself had written which were cut into the stone that marks his grave: 'May heaven's rich blessing come down on everyone—American, English or Turk—who will help to heal this open sore of the world'—which was, of course, the slave-trade. We stood there for some time in silence; but when I looked at the young man whose arm had been blown off, I saw there were tears in his eyes.

My second encounter with the memory of Livingstone came last September, when I was at the end of my time in Tanzania, in the steps of Trevor Huddleston. I had to go to the little port of Mtwara, five hundred

kilometres due south of Dar-es-Salaam, which had virtually been built
for the abortive ground-nuts scheme of the late 1940s. The very good
parish priest of Mtwara, John Umila, had two parishes to look after:
Mtwara itself, and, ten kilometres along the coast, past an old slave
market, and above a Muslim stone village, what was the small port of
Minkindani. The village church, on an eminence, looked out over the
village and its palms to the lagoon beyond. As we stood there, Fr John
said to me quietly: 'This is one of the oldest Christian churches in this
part of Africa. It was set up just after Livingstone landed here in the
early 1870s.' There was nothing twentieth century within sight, and at
that moment, time fell away, and I would not have been surprised had
Livingstone himself come into view.

In the mid-70s, I read the biography of Livingstone published to
celebrate the centenary of his death.

Born in an overcrowded Glasgow slum—one room, fourteen feet by
ten, for David, his parents and the other six children—he went to work in
a cotton mill at the age of ten, working twelve and a half hours a day in
the mill, yet making time to educate himself in the evenings to qualify
eventually as a doctor. At twenty-eight he went out to Africa as a
medical missionary, and stayed for thirty years, returning home only
twice, for a total of only two years. Missionary, geographer, astronomer,
ethnologist, anthropologist, chemist and botanist, he discovered the
Victoria Falls and the source of the Congo, and made the first crossing of
the continent of Africa from coast to coast. He was hailed by the
Victorians as an explorer unrivalled since the Elizabethans. He was
revered as a near saint, epitomizing every moral virtue. He was a myth in
his own lifetime; and it was on that myth of Livingstone that I was
brought up, as, no doubt, were many of you.

But the truth of Livingstone is very different. He was a complex and
paradoxical figure: a man capable of immense self-sacrifice and of ruthless cruelty. He was dogged throughout his life by self-doubt and failure.
He failed, certainly, as a missionary, with only one convert to his credit,
who lapsed. He failed in his search for the source of the Nile. He failed,
certainly, as a leader of Europeans. He could not bear the criticism of
equals. He was a failure as a husband and as a parent. He was avidly
ambitious for popular acclaim, and was a consummate liar and cheat.
Even what looks like courage is often more probably an obsessive and
masochistic desire to push himself to the very limits of endurance.

Yet God used him. God undoubtedly used him. For the myth of
Livingstone influenced thousands of ordinary men and women to give
money, and not only money, to serve that continent to which he had
himself rendered such signal service.

It's odd, isn't it, that in the economy of God, or the Providence of
God—or, more likely, out of sheer luck and coincidence—one of the

greatest figures in Christian missionary history, in the expansion and building up of the Christian Church in the last century, should have been called 'Living Stone'—David Livingstone—in the light of that text I have taken for our thoughts today.

'Living stones': those two words form one of the most original and arresting metaphors in the whole of the Bible.

'Stone *dead*' we so often say; but '*living* stones'! When *life* and stone are brought together in sudden and violent collision to describe Christ Himself, immediately the image brings to mind one who can bring life to the dead and to all that is most inert, inanimate, unresponsive and lifeless.

Yet to us who are privileged to worship in this chapel, rebuilt after destruction, stone can never be simply an image of death. It's curious, but it's true that this very building, these stones surrounding us now, are in some way a sacrament of Him whom St Peter called by this otherwise absurd conjunction 'Living Stone'. Perhaps why we feel justified in lavishing such care on this building, perhaps ultimately the only reason why we can possibly be justified in spending what we spend on this building and others like it, against other calls upon us as Christians, is because in some inscrutable and ineffable way it is not just a building, but is in some sense a sacrament of the 'Living Stone'.

And David Livingstone: with all his mixture of motives, his failure as much as his success, and God's undeniable use of him, God's use of his history, so to speak, and his myth. What do we make of him? What has this 'Living Stone' to say to us about ourselves?

Dorothy Sayers' play *The Zeal of Thine House*, written for the Canterbury Festival of 1937, is concerned with the reconstruction of the Cathedral after the choir had been burnt down in 1174.

The climax of the play comes when Theodatus, the monk-sacristan, goes to the Prior to protest at the morals of the architect to the Cathedral, William of Sens. The Prior turns to Theodatus and says:

> Will you not let God manage his own business? My son,
> He was a carpenter, and knows His trade
> Better, perhaps, than we do, having had
> Some centuries of experience; nor will He,
> Like a bad workman, blame the tools wherewith
> He builds his City of Zion here on earth.
> For God founded His Church, not upon John,
> The loved disciple, that lay so close to his heart
> And knew his mind—not upon John, but Peter;
> Peter the liar, Peter the coward, Peter
> The rock, the common man. John was all gold,
> And gold is rare; the work might wait while God
> Ransacked the corners of the earth to find
> Another John; but Peter is the stone

> Whereof the world is made. So stands the Church,
> Stone upon stone, and Christ, the corner-stone,
> Carved of the same stuff, common flesh and blood
> With you, and me, and Peter; and He can,
> Being the alchemist's stone, the stone of Solomon,
> Turn stone to gold, and purge the gold itself
> From dross, till all is gold.

Mixed motives. When a man or woman gives up all to serve the Lord in darkest Africa, like Livingstone or Trevor Huddleston; when a person preaches in a chapel like this; whatever any of us do, there are always mixed motives. It is the human condition.

Mercifully, God does not wait till we have 'clean hands and a pure heart' before He uses us, or He'd be waiting still. What He does is to let us hear, on a July Sunday morning, surrounded by these living stones, the words of Peter: 'Come to him, to the living stone which was rejected by men but chosen by God and of great worth to him. You also, as living stones, must be built up as a spiritual temple, and form a holy priesthood to offer spiritual sacrifices acceptable to God through Jesus Christ.'

But remember: this holy priesthood is not to be lived out primarily in this temple but in the world: a world in which clean hands and a pure heart are a kind of luxury because so many decisions that have to be made are so complex and so compromising.

I do not need to remind you that Livingstone's Africa, not least South Africa—where I hope to be in less than a month—is a boiling pot at the moment, and requires both men and women of principle and the capacity to compromise; but certainly cannot wait for people of unmixed motives to serve it.

But in Africa and here at home that call is still the same: 'Come and let yourselves be built as living stones into a spiritual temple by offering yourselves to God'—in the complex and compromising situations wherever you may happen to be.

19
HE KNOWETH THE VERY SECRETS OF THE HEART

Gray's Inn Chapel; 19 July 1992

'He knoweth the very secrets of the heart.'

Psalm 44.21

There are certain sermons which seem to arrive ready-made, out-of-the-blue, in a matter of seconds. There are others which you can mull over, chew over, ruminate upon, for months and months, and still not be quite certain whether you should preach them. This morning's sermon is of the latter variety. I've been reflecting on it for over six months.

It concerns and, in a sense, is in memory of, Paul de Fortis—Paul Maurice Georges Pierre Guichot de Fortis!: a 38 year-old priest, who was found dead last Christmas Eve; whom I thought I knew well and, indeed, whom I first met all of fifteen years ago, when I was doing a *locum* in midsummer at King's Lynn. At the end of my few weeks there he asked me to be his 'spiritual director'—not a term I greatly like. I asked him to come and see me, and, after talking things over for an hour or so, I said something I'd never said to anyone before: I said I thought he needed to go and see a psychotherapist for a couple of years, and that coming to me would probably be an avoidance of the depths to which he needed to go if he was to receive real help.

It seems to me that sometimes people ask for absolution in a rather infantile way: applying for a gift from a parental figure, a kind of immediate cure-all from heaven, thus avoiding making what contribution they can to their own healing, and accepting at least some adult responsibility for their own difficulties and their resolution. I had reason to think Paul might be wanting to use confession in this infantile way, hence my suggestion that he should go to a psychotherapist for a couple of years.

If at the end of that time he still wanted me to be his 'spiritual director' I said we could, of course, discuss the question again. I gave him the name of a psychotherapist in Cambridge whom I had learnt to value and trust over the years. Two years later, Paul got in touch with me and asked me if—now that he had seen the person for the two years I had recommended—I would be his 'spiritual director'. I was impressed by the way he had taken my suggestion seriously, and I felt I ought now to do what he asked. He came to see me three or four times a year to make his confession. I always felt he was trying to be honest to God and to himself. In recent years he told me he was also seeing a psychoanalyst. I was glad about that. Paul—rightly—felt the purposes of psychotherapy and confession and 'spiritual direction' were different and did not want to cease to come to confession because he was going to a psychoanalyst.

It does not now seem thirteen years since I began seeing Paul as his 'spiritual director', but that is what it is.

He had been brought up a Roman Catholic but had become an Anglican before I met him. At one time he had expected to enter the Roman Catholic priesthood. When I first met him he was about to begin training for the priesthood of the Church of England. Had he not gone to the Cambridge psychotherapist I would have spent much time myself enquiring into his childhood. His father was a French journalist who worked in England; indeed, Paul had been born in Camberwell, South London, on the borders of the parish of which I had been vicar.

Paul was made Deacon in 1981, after gaining a degree at King's College London and going on to Ridley Hall, Cambridge, and was ordained priest in 1982. He was a curate at St Barnabas Hackney and then became assistant chaplain at the Middlesex Hospital in 1984.

Besides meeting Paul when he came for confession I would see him quite often for a meal. He was an excellent cook and a marvellous host. He always invited most interesting guests whom he wanted me to meet. These occasions afforded an opportunity for me to get to know Paul in a relaxed way.

Exactly a year ago, Paul asked me whether I would act as a referee for him for the vacant parish of St Saviour, Hampstead. I gladly did so, after having suggested we walk around the parish together and look at the church itself. When he was appointed, he was very enthusiastic about the job, although it was a tough assignment. His predecessor had been there over thirty years, and the church itself was in a state of decrepitude.

I was away in Tanzania last September, when Paul was inducted, but I was touched by the fact that he wanted me to be one of the guests at his first dinner party in his new vicarage and to use the occasion to bless the house. He did not warn me that that is what he would want; it was while we were all standing round with glasses of wine in our hands that he suddenly asked me to bless the house. I was slightly taken aback, but quickly agreed to do what he asked. (It was rumoured that his predecessor had used the vicarage for a specialized ministry of exorcism to those who said they were devil-possessed, and I was not entirely surprised and, indeed, rather glad, that Paul wanted to make a new beginning in the vicarage.)

It so happened that I had a close friend in the parish whose marriage I had conducted and whose baby I had baptized. Paul had kindly invited him and his wife to the dinner party. Within weeks the two-year-old baby was taken seriously ill with leukaemia. I learnt from them how much they appreciated Paul's ministry to them at such a time, and how much the beginning of Paul's ministry in the parish was appreciated by the congregation. He had begun his ministry with huge zest. And not only zest. I have met several parishioners who in a short time felt they owed Paul a great deal. One elderly lady, who, later, came to the inquest on Paul, said to me: 'Whatever he did, he was very loving to *me*.'

It was in fact the father of the child with leukaemia who phoned me last Christmas Day, at lunch-time, with the literally shocking news that Paul had been found dead. The news had been announced at the Communion service at the church that Christmas morning.

Paul's cousin, who loved him much, had found him hanging at the end of his four-poster bed. It was clear from the impedimenta that Paul had been experimenting with some auto-erotic act of sado-masochism that had gone tragically awry, and he had been asphyxiated. It was not suicide but accidental death: 'death by misadventure', as the inquest eventually described it. It was a death almost identical with that which occurs in Peter Barnes' play (later made a film): *The Ruling Class*. The details of Paul's death were soon in the papers, local and national. *The Sun* outshone itself.

I am, of course, in no position to speak of what Paul spoke of in confession. I can say he had never confessed or mentioned any act like the act which ended his life. Neither, I discovered, had he spoken of it to the psychoanalyst he was going to in his last years.

Since Paul's death I have tried to find out all I could about what characterizes people who practise the kind of thing that Paul practised, and one characteristic—not all that surprising, but it is very helpful to me to know it—is that they rarely seek *help* for their condition, so that, alas, such individuals, situations and practices are better known to the police, coroners and forensic pathologists than to mental health professionals, counsellors and priests. I have found that reading the literature, thanks mainly to a young doctor at the Bethlem Royal and Maudsley Hospital, has all but eradicated whatever temptation I might have had to being in any way judgemental of Paul, and made me only conscious of the tragic inner loneliness that must have been his at *not* being able to share his affliction.

On Christmas night—that's to say, a few hours after I had first heard the news—in some distress at the news, I picked up a book I do not think I have touched for nearly thirty years: T. S. Eliot's play *The Confidential Clerk*. Half a dozen pages from the beginning I read:

There's always something one's ignorant of
About anyone, however well one knows them;
And that may be something of the greatest importance.
It's when you're sure you understand a person
That you're liable to make the worst mistake about him . . .

My rule is to remember that I understand nobody,
But on the other hand never to be sure
That they don't understand me—a good deal better
Than I should care to think, perhaps.

In the weeks immediately after Paul's death, I have to admit, I found
both the fact of his death, at thirty-eight, and the way he had died, deeply
distressing. At first, I felt a considerable sense of responsibility and
failure. 'If I had only said this, or that, or done this, or that, Paul would
not now be dead' was the thought that constantly recurred in my mind.

I was hardly less distressed by the fact that Paul had not mentioned
that he was involved in the kind of thing which had killed him. I felt sure
that I must have talked in some way that had made it impossible for him
to bring himself to tell me.

It was several weeks after Paul's death that a priest-psychotherapist
friend of mine asked me: 'If Paul had told you what he did, how would
you have responded?' I immediately replied: 'I'm sure I would have put
my arms round him and said: "Poor you! Let's talk about it."' 'What are
you worrying about then?' asked my friend.

Nevertheless, it seemed to me, it must at least be conceivable that I
had at some time shown Paul the kind of pastoral severity that had made
him unable to unburden everything he needed to tell someone—
conceivable, though I do not in fact remember an occasion of such
severity. The phrase in the Prayer Book Form of Consecrating Bishops:
'Be so merciful that you be not too remiss; so minister discipline, that
you forget not mercy' has always seemed to me not only one of the
loveliest but one of the profoundest and most penetrating phrases in the
Prayer Book, difficult as it often is to put it into detailed practice.

There are two reflections on this sad event which I should particularly
like to share with you. I well remember when I first saw Paul, at King's
Lynn, how soon he seemed to me to be in need of more skilled help than
I could give him: professional psychotherapeutic help. That is in part why
I refused to be his 'spiritual director'. Two years later, it seemed to me
that he had responded so well and so quickly to such help that I do not
think it ever again entered my head that he was still in great need of such
help, though I was glad when he told me he had sought it of his own
volition.

What his death has made clear to me is just how much Paul was still in
need of skilled help; but it has also underlined for me just how difficult it
is to distinguish between seriously sick behaviour and behaviour for

which a person must be held responsible and treated as not seriously sick.
But who of us is not seriously sick?

Hamlet says:

> 'Yet have I in me something dangerous
> Which let thy wisdom fear.'

And, at first, my wisdom did fear what was in Paul, but I suspect, not for
long enough.

In *Henry IV Part II* there are three lines:

> 'I must go and meet with danger there
> Or it will seek me in another place
> And find me worse provided.'

That is what eventually happened to Paul; and I still feel that somehow I
ought to have seen that Paul was given greater help in his earlier years to
'meet with danger there'.

But this event has made me realize just how many people are into the
heightened fear, risk and excitement and grim delight of the kind of deed
that Paul got up to, couldn't refrain from. He was clearly into, and
'hooked on', some kind of addictive pattern of compulsive behaviour in
which forces took over and held him: a cycle, probably repeated over and
over again, which always had the possibility of ending in disaster—even
death—which was itself part of the attraction; and did eventually end just
there. At the inquest, it was underlined just how dangerous what Paul
was doing was—though he may not have been conscious just how
dangerous it was—though, as I say, he may have been.

And then: the more I thought on Paul's silence in confession about
those actions which eventually led to his death, the more I have found
myself confronting a subject which certainly I have never quite confronted so deeply before, and, in these weeks and months, I have come to
think of as one of the most important subjects there is. Let me simply
outline it briefly—in memory of and gratitude for Paul, and, not least, in
sympathy for his relatives and those others who mourn his loss.

The subject I shall simply call 'Secrets'.

I'm sure it is true that we all have secrets. Some of them we will carry
with us to our grave. Maybe we shouldn't retain them, but they may be
too difficult for any of us to share—to share with anyone, however loving
they may be. It is not their fault that we cannot share our secrets with
them. Sometimes the secrets we have within us are so tied to our very
identity that they are inseparable from our identity; and that identity is,
in part, a mystery even to ourselves.

Sometimes people utter too easily John Donne's words: 'No man is an
island entire of itself.' We need to reflect as often on the other side of that
truth: that everyone *is* an island, created utterly unique in his or her

identity, and beside that unique identity—but not separate from it—we construct, probably in our earliest years a kind of defensive cage within which we exist.

Besides doing everything possible to enable people to unburden themselves, to share themselves, I feel now that there must be an equal reverence for the *in*capacity of people to share their secret. Indeed, 'incapacity', because it is a negative, gives no hint of any positive aspect there might be. It was Keats who talked of 'negative capability'. There is, and sometimes has to be, a courage in the facing of one's own secret identity, a courage in sharing that secret identity; but there has also to be a reverence which allows people their secret. To force people to 'come out' is sometimes a blasphemy, even though their failure to come out may have disastrous consequences to themselves.

There is another great and lovely Prayer Book phrase: 'Almighty God, unto whom all hearts be open, all desires known, and *from whom no secrets are hid . . .*'

Sometimes that phrase is put threateningly, as in those terrible plates with the words:

THOU GOD SEEST ME

that are hung on bedroom walls, with an odious All-Seeing Eye.

But the Almighty God is He who 'as his majesty is, so is his mercy'— and His love beyond compare. It is to Him, thank God, that all hearts are open and all desires known and from whom no secrets are hid.

And we can confidently leave Paul—and not only Paul—to that kind of God and to that kind of Love.

20
ENTRUSTED WITH THIS COMMISSION
The Consecration of John Austin as Bishop of Aston

St Martin's-in-the-Bull Ring, Birmingham; 3 September 1992

From the first verse of the Epistle for today, from the version in the Alternative Service Book: 'Seeing that we have been entrusted with this commission, which we owe entirely to God's mercy . . .'

2 Corinthians 4.1

It seemed appropriate, indeed, characteristic, John, that you should have asked me over a pint in a pub called The Pilgrim, alongside Kennington Oval, whether I would be willing to preach the sermon at your consecration. As is evident, when the actual invitation came from on high, I accepted with alacrity, out of much affection, and with a huge sense of privilege, honour and joy.

It was not long before I seized my Greek Testament and looked up the text that lies behind the translation of the appointed New Testament reading.

But a shock awaited me. Those first words: 'Seeing that we have been entrusted with this *commission*'. It never occurred to me that the Greek word translated there 'commission' is *diakonia*, which could, of course, simply be translated 'diaconate'.

How odd, how paradoxical, I thought, that for the consecration of a *bishop* the scripture should be appointed that says you have been entrusted with 'this *diaconate*'.

97

Then, suddenly, a phrase came into my mind that had been spoken to me nearly fifty years ago, when I was training for the ministry at King's College, London. My friend and mentor, Eric Abbott, then Dean of King's, later Dean of Westminster, said to me one day: 'Always remember, boy, the diaconate is never discarded.'

And that evoked a second memory. You will know that it was when you were in your diaconate, John, at St John's, East Dulwich, that we first met. You were in the much-loved Derek Tasker's post-ordination group, and I was giving some lectures in the Cathedral Chapter House at Southwark on 'The Roots of the Liturgy'. That was, of course, in those far off, much despised, sixties. (Those lectures became *Prism Pamphlet No.1!*)

And then, John, I thought of you again, but upon another shore and in a greater light. It was still the sixties; but you had crossed the Atlantic to Chicago, where, based on the Episcopal Cathedral, you were receiving some training in community work after the method and model of Saul Alinsky. I had been invited to the Cathedral to conduct the Three Hours on Good Friday and to preach on Easter Sunday morning. I had hoped for a quiet Easter Sunday afternoon; but you insisted on taking me to a huge assembly of a local community which had all the razzmatazz of American politics. Stretched out above us was a banner with a strange device in glorious technicolour which said TOWARDS A BETTER AUSTIN. I was somewhat surprised that they had divined your innermost needs so accurately and so soon; but you hastened to inform me that Austin was, in fact, the name of that particular neighbourhood.

That year's experience of community work, combined with a post-graduate course at the National Institute of Social Work Training and work with the Urban Ministry Project, greatly enlarged your understanding of diaconate, which you were soon able to put into practice as Warden of Pembroke House in Walworth. And where but at Walworth could you have got the Mums' Club to sing at the Offertory at the Eucharist on your wedding day:

> My old man said follow the van
> And don't dilly dally on the way!

And how much, and how marvellously, your marriage to Rosemary and, in due course, the birth of Thomas, Naomi and Jacob, has shaped your diaconate and ministry.

It was in 1976 that Robert Runcie, then Bishop of St Albans, invited you to be his Social Responsibility Adviser, which led on, after eight arduous years alongside the voluntary and statutory services of Hertfordshire and Bedfordshire, to the last years as Director of Social Responsibility for the Diocese of London. And what a responsibility! And what opportunity, for *diaconate*, for ministry, and to help give people a vision for London.

No one will need much persuading, John, that you have never discarded your diaconate, or that you have found more meaning in it, and filled it with more meaning, each year since you were ordained; so that, now, in God's mercy, you have been entrusted with *this* diaconate.

To say that someone has 'never discarded their diaconate' might, I suppose, be regarded in some circumstances almost as an accusation—like accusing Peter Pan of never growing up. What Eric Abbott meant by the phrase, and certainly what I mean here and now, is something very different. Diaconate has remained an outstanding and permanent part of your ministry, John. You have kept contact with people by very down to earth service and by a sacrificial humility; and, through that, your priesthood has reached people, and spoken to them, and come alive. Human beings on the whole don't care all that much for people who go around proclaiming that they are priests, or, for that matter, for bishops who proclaim that they are bishops, but they do care for those who selflessly serve them, like good primary school teachers and nurses—and clergy, if and when they *evidently* serve: if they are not simply a voice *for* the voiceless but a voice which speaks from *alongside* the voiceless.

A sermon, even on the day of a friend's consecration as a bishop, should never sound simply like a reference or a testimonial—much less like a script for *This Is Your life*. The heart of a sermon ought always to speak of our Lord Himself.

Well: 'the diaconate is never discarded'. I wonder could that ever have been more true than in the life of our Lord? Many great biblical words are attached to our Lord Jesus Christ: Prophet, Priest, King, Mediator, Intercessor, Redeemer, Saviour, Advocate, Master and Lord. But the word St Luke tells us by which Jesus described Himself was 'Deacon'. 'I am amongst you' (Gk. ὡs διακονων) 'as a deacon, as a servant, as a slave'—at a time of slavery. Jesus never discarded the diaconate.

The diaconate of Jesus brought His power, His judgement and His mercy to us through His humility. He emptied Himself and took the form of a servant. He took the towel of humility and girded Himself and washed the disciples' feet. Such was the humility of Jesus, the deacon, who became obedient, 'obedient unto death, even the death of the cross', who embraced humility in and through humiliation.

Jesus, amongst us as one who serves, appeals to the best in us and evokes the best from us and from others, both judging our self-love and motivating our humanity. There is little so humanly appealing as service done with humanity and grace. It is the power of contact between one human being and another. Jesus, washing Peter's feet, went straight to his heart. 'You ought to wash one another's feet' said Jesus. And His final service, His final act as a deacon, was the cross itself.

John, when I sat down to write this sermon, I had with me a 'Profile of Poverty in Birmingham' and *A Fresh Start*, the Report by the Birmingham Diocesan Structures Review Commission, and I imagined that I would need to speak a good deal about that Report which had recommended that a new *Suffragan* Bishop of Aston should be appointed. But then I thought: 'A Fresh Start' . . .

Could it be, John, that as you are consecrated to be a bishop, you are being called to rediscover your diaconate in this multi-cultural society: to rediscover the Lord's diaconate in you? that all the bishops of the Church are being called to rediscover their diaconate? Could it be that the priests of the Diocese of Birmingham and from beyond Birmingham are being called, as 'a fresh start', to rediscover their diaconate? Yes—and the laity: for the laity know they do not have to be 'made deacons' to be amongst people as those who serve. Could it be that the marginalized Jesus—marginalized as a slave: ὡς διακονων—is calling us all to rediscover His diaconate?

Hans Küng has written recently:

> Is it possible for there to be among the followers of Jesus any kind of office which is based on law and power, which corresponds to the office of secular potentates . . . Or can there be among the followers of Jesus any kind of office which is based on knowledge and dignity and corresponds to the office of scribe . . .? It is not law or power, knowledge or dignity but *service* which is the basis of discipleship.

Timothy Radcliffe, the new Master of the Dominicans, reviewing a recent book, which is simply called *Diakonia*, by John N. Collins, wrote:

> Need hierarchical structures be necessarily experienced as oppressive? . . .
> What is needed is a more radical transformation so that hierarchy is experienced as not just a class within the Church but an expression of the common life of the whole Church. Rather than marking off those who have power from those who do not, it should be experienced as opening out the large open spaces of God's many-roomed house in which we can all matter in different ways.

Leonardo Boff, in his resignation letter as a priest—and perhaps someone being consecrated a bishop today needs to read rather carefully such a letter—Leonardo Boff wrote: 'We are not against a hierarchy. But it must always be, according to sound theological reasoning, a hierarchy of service.'

John, I have already mentioned several spheres of service, of diaconate, which have been yours since you were ordained. I could have mentioned many more: your founding chairmanship of Church Action on Poverty and all the support you have given as a member of the Council of Christian Action. It did not surprise me that when I asked you what you would like Christian Action Council to give you as a token of all you have been to us, you should say: 'As simple a shepherd's crook as you can find'.

'Seeing you have been entrusted with this diaconate . . .'

May I say, finally, that I last heard this particular passage of scripture less than a month ago, on 6 August, the Feast of the Transfiguration, in the Chapel of the Community of the Resurrection, in their Priory in Johannesburg, during the week of mass action called by the ANC when, that very week, I was privileged to be visiting people like Oliver Tambo and Helen Joseph, who had been in prison for what they believed.

Hearing this particular passage that particular day, in that particular situation, filled me—as I trust it will always fill you, John—with hope. But may it also remind you that this diaconate with which you have been entrusted does not only make John *Austin* John *Aston*, it makes you a bishop not only in Birmingham, but in the whole state of Christ's Church—militant here in earth. John *Austin*—that ancient abbreviation of *Augustine*—is called to be a bishop of the Church in Africa as well as of Aston, in Chicago as well as in Canterbury. You have been entrusted with this ministry in the Church of God. And from all of us there wells up today a huge volume of love and support, as we see you here being entrusted with this commission, this ministry, this diaconate, this episcopate. Our prayers go with you, as God, in His mercy, gives you this ministry as a bishop: to be amongst us as one who serves.

21

IN MEMORIAM: EDWIN LAND, INVENTOR OF 'POLAROID'

To the Worshipful Company of Scientific Instrument Makers St Margaret's Lothbury, EC2; 22 September 1992

I want this evening to memorialize someone whose passing I believe should have received more commemorative notice in this country than it has, and whose contribution to this world is probably more aptly and appropriately commemorated by your Worshipful Company than by any other Company of this great City.

I want to commemorate Edwin Herbert Land. And if his name does not immediately strike a chord of recognition in your mind, let me say one other word, and I'm sure it will: *Polaroid.*

Edwin Land, whose invention of an instant camera changed the picture-taking habits of millions of people around the world, died last year. He was a physicist and—one must use an old-fashioned word—an inventor. When he died, he held patents for more than five hundred and thirty inventions.

Yet I doubt whether I would be preaching to you about him had I not met him personally. It was my privilege, many years ago, to marry Jennifer, Dr Land's first daughter, to one of my closest friends, when I was Chaplain of Trinity College, Cambridge, an American, Dr Philip du Bois, who had been Captain of the Cambridge Boat, and whom I prepared for confirmation; and then, a few years later, I conducted the marriage of Dr Land's second daughter, Valerie. It was these two weddings that introduced me to Edwin Land: to a man who was undoubtedly an enigma; who was obsessively private; who never allowed anyone to interview him at length, and never wrote an autobiography or participated in the writing of his biography by anyone else. But, to my surprise, he immediately shared very personal thoughts and convictions with me. It was as though anyone whom his daughters—and future sons-in-law—trusted, he was willing to trust.

All of us are unique, but some of us are more unique than others. Edwin Land was, I believe, in a class of his own.

He was born in Connecticut in 1909, the son of a man who ran a scrap metal and salvage business. He entered Harvard in 1926, at the age of seventeen, but soon dropped out—and returned—but dropped out again, for good. It was decades later that Harvard honoured him with an honorary doctorate. He was the recipient of many honours, including the Presidential Medal of Freedom and the National Medal of Science. He was a trustee of the Ford Foundation from 1967 to 1975 and President of the American Academy of Arts and Sciences from 1951 to 1953.

I am not a scientist, and it would undoubtedly require a scientist to do full justice to such a scientist as Edwin Land. But I am here not only to biographize him. 'The proper study of mankind is man', and I think it is proper for us to reflect, here and now, on the significance of such a man.

Land was undoubtedly a precocious physicist. On a visit to New York, while a freshman at Harvard, he had a kind of vision. He was walking in Times Square and was troubled by the glare of the lights, especially the lights of the cars and the buses, and decided to do something about it: to invent a way of controlling the glare; and to this end he dropped out of Harvard. But Land was no ordinary drop-out. He was a drop-out who worked! And within three years he had invented his first polarizing material. The secret was to use microscopic grains of needle-shaped crystals, which polarize light, and embed them in a lacquer.

It wasn't long before Polaroid sunglasses were on the market. But if it hadn't been for the War, what was now the Polaroid Corporation might well have gone under. Making a variety of sun-goggles for the military, and working on the design of heat-seeking missiles, enabled the company to prosper. Nothing of that had anything to do with photography. But, in December of 1943, Land had a second inspiration.

On a rare vacation with his family in New Mexico, Edwin Land spent some time with his three-year-old daughter, walking around Santa Fe, taking pictures. Jennifer—as three-year-old daughters are wont to do—was directing the picture taking. When they got back to where they were staying, Jennifer asked her father about the pictures he had taken: 'Why can't I see them *now*?'

Let me quote from Dr. Land's account of what followed:

> As I walked around that charming town, I undertook the task of solving the puzzle Jennifer had set me. Within the hour, the camera, the film, and the physical chemistry, became so clear to me that with a great sense of excitement I hurried over to the place where Donald Brown, my patent attorney, was, conveniently, staying, to describe to him in great detail a dry camera which would give a picture immediately after exposure.

It would be appropriate in a lecture but inappropriate in a sermon for me to go on to describe Edwin Land's concern with and indeed his theories of colour vision. These scientific theories of Land's are undoubtedly of great importance and there are accessible references in *The Oxford Companion to the Mind* and elsewhere. I could not possibly omit all reference to them. Land was fundamentally questioning the traditional theories of colour perception.

I haven't yet mentioned one of Dr Land's great achievements, which was to found the Polaroid corporation and to lavish creative energy upon it until his retirement in 1982. He spurred inventiveness among his colleagues, and he repeatedly led efforts to overcome the urgent technical problems that arose.

Land was an ardent advocate of the importance of research. He wrote in 1944: 'I believe quite simply that the small company of the future will be as much a research organisation as it is a manufacturing company and that this new company is the frontier for the next generation.'

After his retirement, Dr Land continued to conduct research in several scientific fields. He created and financed the Rowland Institute for Science, a research organization in Cambridge, Massachusetts, which in recent years developed microscopic lazer 'tweezer' beams able to manipulate single-cell organisms as small as bacteria. He founded the Institute in 1980 with a multi-million-dollar gift from his considerable fortune. You will probably remember that in a patent infringement case, Polaroid versus Eastman-Kodak, Kodak was ordered to pay Polaroid over 800 million dollars.

So far, what I have said might mostly be found in the obituary columns of, say, the *New York Times*. I want briefly now, unashamedly, to turn an obituary into a sermon.

Edwin Land was an intense man. I particularly remember the intensity of his eyes. In the hours surrounding his daughters' weddings, I was astonished that he wanted to talk to me about belief in God. The idea of 'wasting time' 'socializing' was, I think, to him anathema. He even wrote to me from the United States before the wedding service about the implications of his first daughter's wedding: about the implications for him of attending the service and the implications for his daughter of making such promises in a church of the Church of England. (The wedding was to take place, appropriately for a Captain of the Cambridge Boat, at Bix, not far from Henley.) It seemed to me, Dr Land was as fascinated by the nature of human relating as by relations in chemistry and physics—which I have not found to be true of *all* scientists. When he heard I was going out to South Africa I was surprised to find him questioning me as to whether I thought Polaroid ought to be operating in South Africa while the South African Government maintained its policy of apartheid. I was even more surprised that he treated my answers seriously.

In 1970, Dr Land gave a lecture on 'Addiction', to which he had addressed himself as a *scientist*, but not only as a scientist.

The first paragraph of his lecture is a very human introduction to the subject.

> Last Christmas, [he said] while riding through London, I found that in spite of my delight in the galleries, libraries, and concerts, there was within me a deep and insatiable need. I found myself saying to our driver 'Green, did you know that I am an addict?' He is of the old school so that he did not turn his head. 'No, sir,' he said 'I did not know that'. 'I am addicted to at least one good experiment a day' I replied. 'Sometimes I can arrange it by telephone. When I cannot, the world goes out of focus, becomes unreal.' Possibly somewhat disappointed, but clearly relieved, Green simply said: 'I see, sir'.

As he develops his theme, Land quotes again from his own experience as a scientist. He describes an alternation that was familiar to him:

> between the one mood and attitude of feeling part of the race as a whole, part of the family, part of the neighbourhood; the mood of being in love with friends, women, men, people all over the world; the mood of being in love with what is great in music and art—all that on the one hand, and then, quite suddenly, a separateness from all that: a separateness that comes during the preoccupation with a particular scientific task. There is a need, a transient need, a violent need for being just yourself, restating, recreating, talking in your own terms about what you have learned from all the cultures, scientific and non-scientific, before you and around you. During that period you want to be almost alone, with just a few friends. You want to be undisturbed. You want to be free to think not for an hour at a time, or three hours at a time, but for two days or two weeks, if possible, without interruption. You don't want to drive the family car or go to parties. You wish people would just go away and leave you alone while you get something straight. Then, you get it straight and you embody it, and during that period of embodiment you have a feeling of almost divine guidance. Then it is done, and, suddenly, you are alone, and you have a need to go back to your friends and the world around you, and to all history, to be refreshed, to feel alive and human once again. It is this interplay between all that is richly human and this special concentrated, uninterrupted mental effort that seems to me to be the source, not only of science, but also of everything that is worthwhile in life.

Land examines this 'alternation': these two different modes of relationship, the social and the solitary moods, and later says that everyone of us is both multiple-man and singular-man and unless we learn what it is to be both we are in trouble. And he goes on:

> The need for the transition to singular-man from multiple-man, social man, is so great that if an individual has been unfortunate enough not to learn *bona fide* healthy techniques for the transition, if he has not been able to find objectives in the real world to which he can relate in his mode of living then he will seek escape from permanent entrapment in the mode of multiple-man—he will seek to escape from multiple-man to singular-man through artificial means such as drugs.

The use of drugs, he says, is a 'short cut which is also a blind alley. Drugs serve not as an escape from oneself but rather as an escape to oneself—escape from multiple-man to singular-man.'

His final paragraph in this revealing lecture is particularly significant. He says:

> It occurs to me as we explore, there are indeed many lonely souls trapped in the second mode, the mode of singular-man. I suspect that alcohol enables many of them to make the transition to the first mode of multiple-man. In the few days during which these ideas have been crystallizing, I have found them very useful in understanding the mysteries of the Iagos and the Judases; the astonishing number of small betrayals by men of honor; the eternal paradox of the politician as a man of honor at one moment and of low credibility at the next; the deadly conclusions of decent souls when they gather together to make decisions; the alternations between inspired insight and unbelievable stupidity of a handful of brilliant scientists en masse; the magnificent elation that we can feel together; the kind of transcendency that we can achieve when we are a group, and the evil that we can perpetuate—all this is an antithesis not between God and the devil, but between singular-man and multiple-man, both of which we are and between which we must learn early in life to migrate skilfully.

Now you may not agree with what Edwin Land has to say in that lecture, but I think you will understand why I say I am glad to have met him and am grateful to have known him; not least because he was never content to be simply a scientific instrument maker: however high a regard he had for the task and however much he excelled in it. He knew that the making of scientific instruments for him involved vision and inspiration from beyond himself. He was thrilled by technical achievement but was never deluded into thinking that man is the master and measure of all mysteries. For all his knowledge and skill, he seemed to me a very human and humane man, a man, in the end, of reverence and humility; a man from whom I believe in our age and generation we all have much to learn.

22
DIVES AND LAZARUS

St Saviour's South Hampstead;
27 September 1992

Dives and Lazarus was a familiar folk-tale in Jesus' time. There's a first-century Egyptian manuscript which tells a similar story, and ends with Osiris ordering that the grave-clothes of the rich man should be given to the poor man.

But however ancient its origins, the parable still has power today to play upon that nerve in each of us which is unnerved when confronted by, say, a contemporary Lazarus on Hungerford Bridge, the cause of whose poverty we are probably in no position either to ascertain or evaluate.

The question how a Christian should relate his or her riches to the poverty of others is inescapable, and important, but complex, and has been for two thousand years and more. But the nature of the world's poverty and our perception of it has changed over the centuries.

In this 'One World' today—in what with reason we now call the 'global village'—we are the first generation to hear the cry of the poor from every quarter of the globe. We cannot shut our ears to it. What previous generations did not and could not know, they had no responsibility for. We have no such excuse. Which raises the important question: what common understanding and concern can hold together a world which is now inescapably economically one?

I think it's important never to claim too much for our Christian social ethic. The parable of Dives and Lazarus clearly does not provide us with detailed conclusions to complex economic questions. The most we can claim is that the Christian faith is a reinforcement of motivators to action, not a blueprint for it. It reinforces motivators by narratives and parables and aphorisms, especially those of Jesus Himself, and those concerning His mission and message. It calls forth worship which fosters faith, hope and love in working out a more detailed response. It provides a noble view of the nature and destiny of man which is not blind to his corruptions but looks beyond them, so that it can hope against hope when human affairs are recalcitrant, and not give up. But none of this avails if Christians are not alert to the actual situations which are the context of their social decisions.

I have just come back from a month in South Africa where one Sunday I went to a village church dominated by a platinum mine. The village was about ten miles from the mining town of Rustenberg which makes most of its money from the rich deposits of gold, diamonds and platinum in its vicinity. But in that village of Imfdikwe there was only one tap for the two thousand villagers. And that fact seemed of small importance or concern to the people—indeed, to the church-goers—of Rustenberg.

But, as I've already suggested, the problem of riches and poverty is not peculiar to South Africa. The contrast between riches and poverty is certainly to be seen where I live in Kennington. And the dilemma with which it confronts us is both local and global.

Since I got back to England, my desk at the charity where I work has been swamped with appeals from Somalia and similar places of massive and horrific distress, but also from individuals—students, medical and musical, and so on—who in some cases do not know where their next fees are coming from, and in others do not know where their next food is coming from. And, relatively speaking, I happen to be Dives to their Lazarus.

So I rather welcome the opportunity that today's Gospel presents, to reflect again upon what Dives today should do about Lazarus today.

Professor R. H. Tawney, in his classic, *Religion and the Rise of Capitalism*, makes two remarks which I think can goad us to thought on the subject.

He says, as an aside: 'The social teaching of the Church had ceased to count because the Church itself had ceased to think.'

A hundred pages later he says: 'Compromise is as impossible between the Church of Christ and the idolatry of wealth, which is the practical religion of capitalist societies, as it was between the Church and the state idolatry of the Roman Empire.'

Tawney is still a good guide to the Christian who really wants to take seriously what Dives should do about Lazarus. He makes it clear that the subject has two important parts. There's what we do personally and privately about our riches; and there's what we do through the public and political response of Dives to Lazarus.

These last twelve days, after what the journalists called Wobbly Wednesday, will surely have reminded us, if we needed reminding, that there are public and political aspects to poverty as well as private and personal ones; that corporate ethics are as important as personal ethics. There are now a lot of people who are fearful for the future. It may be all right for Dives who made a quick buck or two at the beginning of the crisis but it is a bleak look-out for Lazarus.

The story of Dives and Lazarus proclaims that what we do with our money matters. Money is a means of exchange between people and says a lot about how we treat other people. Behind the economic crisis there is therefore a moral crisis.

Put it another way: Lazarus, in our British society at the moment, is likely to have a large family; to be sick or disabled; old or unemployed; will lack political clout and will need someone else to give voice to his or her need. Probably, Lazarus is a computerized statistic rather than a person. It's astonishing how easily we have come to tolerate what in earlier years would have been intolerable: three million people unemployed. The unemployed can so easily become just a statistic—if you're not unemployed yourself.

There's a moral as well as economic question behind our policies on employment and unemployment, our policies which result in employment and unemployment: it's a moral aspect of the public and political response of Dives to Lazarus.

Whenever one uses the word 'moral' in relation to economics some people are apt to think one lives in cloud-cuckoo-land. It was fifty years ago this year since Archbishop William Temple, the school-friend of Tawney at Rugby, wrote: 'A statesman who supposes that a mass of citizens can be governed without appealing to their self-interest is living in a dream-land and is a public menace. The art of Government is in fact the art of ordering public life so that self-interest prompts what justice demands.'

Professor Ronald Preston, in his Maurice Lectures for 1977, with their Tawney-like title, *Religion and the Persistence of Capitalism*, wrote:

> Self-interest is a powerful and necessary element in human life which must be allowed for and harnessed, but it is also a dangerous element which has to be handled with care. The free market, which depends on it, is for certain social and economic purposes the most useful instrument yet devised by man, but it needs to be set within a strong social framework; to turn its basis into an overall ideological basis for society is precisely the wrong way to move. Human beings are capable of universalism and altruism as well as a concern for self-interest. The latter is usually the stronger and more immediate attitude, so the former needs more encouragement. It is degrading to their humanity for men and women to be involved in institutions which foster only the stronger motive and deny the weaker. They need to live in overall structures which call upon both, but foster the weaker.

What is clear is that there can be no neat borderline between the two worlds of personal and private response and public and political response to the relating of Dives and Lazarus. But, before I pass on to the personal and private, let me remind you that it was nearly twenty years ago that Robert McNamara, then President of the World Bank, referred starkly to the 900 million people suffering from absolute poverty, in the sense of squalor, hunger, hopelessness and low life-expectancy. I believe that the real victims of the last ten days of economic and political crisis are probably not the people of Britain or even of Europe, but the millions in, for instance, Africa and other parts of what we nowadays call the Third World.

When we come to consider our personal and private response as Dives to Lazarus, I want to suggest it is best seen first as a question of Christian discipline—a word which should never be separated from discipleship.

If Christians as a matter of discipline regularly address their minds to the subject of Dives and Lazarus, half the battle is won. I repeat that phrase of Tawney: 'The Church itself had ceased to think.'

A thinking Christian cannot fail to be concerned for the poor and underprivileged. Such a concern is fundamental to the whole Jewish-Christian tradition.

A thinking Christian cannot escape the fundamental Christian belief in the basic equality of all human beings in the sight of God. The belief that Christ died for us all is more fundamental than the things in which we are unequal. A corporate sense of human togetherness and belonging is also fundamental to our Christian faith.

If we begin with discipline of the mind it will not fail to result in discipline of the pocket and the purse. The mind and heart of love will bear fruit.

I do not in any way deny the complexity of the subject: how much should we give to different sorts of Lazarus—I am myself confronted with that complexity every day. But, frankly, that is not the central or the urgent problem. The world is not full of rich people writhing in agony over the question to which Lazarus they should give the help that is in them to give.

I have told you that I spent all August in South Africa. One of my tasks was to interview individually about forty people, all of whom had one thing in common: that they knew Bishop Trevor Huddleston when he was in South Africa between 1943 and 1955. In almost every case they testified—almost all of them black teenagers at that time—to what the individual care of Trevor Huddleston had done to transform their life.

But Trevor Huddleston was then a monk. He had no great riches of his own—financial riches. He was in touch with rich people in Johannesburg and he served as a go-between. But my August might well be described as a study of how Dives was enabled to minister to Lazarus in a particular place at a particular time.

The dangers of giving are evident in that study: the creation of dependency, the possibility of paternalism, and so on. The limitations of individual charity are also evident: charity as an evasion of a more fundamental provision.

But I returned from Africa refreshed in my belief that men and women are meant to live in communities of giving and receiving: some of us at one time doing more of the one and, at another, more of the other.

And I am particularly thankful for the privilege of preaching to you on this subject at a service of Holy Communion, in which we are reminded that we are all dependent on God's mercy and God's grace. I love the phrase of St Paul: 'What hast thou which thou hast not received?'

I am only here this morning because I have received rich friendship from your last and lamented parish priest, Paul,* and from several of you who have been sustained at the altar here. And when I leave St Saviour's this morning, my motivation for giving, for being Dives to Lazarus, having been strengthened and refreshed, I shall, I know, again find myself saying thankfully: 'What hast thou which thou hast not received?' For here in church we are all both Dives and Lazarus.

*See chapter 19, p.92

23

FAITH AND MUSIC

The Chapel of Haddo House,
near Aberdeen; 11 October 1992
Memorial to Tom Michie

When I learned of the special nature of this service—a memorial to one who has served you so faithfully as your organist—I wondered what message I—a near stranger—could best give you. I decided to talk very personally about what music has meant to me as part of what I will call my 'religious life' in the hope that it will in some way help you to articulate what music means to you.

I became an organist at quite a young age—fourteen—and when I think how and why I became one, I immediately think of my grandfather, John Morgan James, who was James-the-Choir at a Presbyterian church behind King's Cross, at the turn of the century. And very quickly I find myself recalling my own earliest years, and on Sunday evenings my mother at the piano, and father singing sacred songs and solos. I can even remember myself, too young to join in, lying on the sofa, and listening while my older brother and sisters and my parents all sang hymns together. Later my mother taught me my first notes on the piano.

So: many of my first and happiest memories are of music, and hymns, and home: hymns which I don't think are in most hymn-books today, because this was about sixty years ago, and we were by that time Methodists, as there was no Presbyterian church within range.

I remember, for instance, singing:

> Jesus, high in glory,
>   Lend a listening ear;
> When we bow before thee
>   Children's praises hear.
>
> Though thou art so holy—
>   Heaven's almighty king—
> Thou wilt stoop to listen
>   When thy praise we sing.

I've no doubt those earliest hymns fashioned my outlook on life a good deal. So I find myself very thankful for that beginning in music; because

I've never really been able to separate *faith and music*. Those first hymns said something to me about home, and the world, and God.

I was taken along to join our local Church of England choir when the Methodist Church closed down. I was very young—probably too young; and here I have a rather weird incident to relate. After the first choir practice I was so frightened by all those strange tenors and basses and the other choirboys—much older and much larger—that I knew I could never go back there again. But I couldn't (I thought) tell my parents. So for several winter weeks I wandered round the back of our town, carrying with me my own hymn-book (a Presbyterian hymn-book though I was now going to the C of E!), learning under lamp-posts a hymn each choir-practice night, so that when I got home and my mother said: 'What have you learnt tonight?' I could tell her, and sing it through to her. Of course, eventually I was found out. And 'I bear in my body the marks'!

So my earliest days as a choirboy were, frankly, days of terror. And I learnt then that other human beings, not least people in 'choirs and places where they sing', are often very frightening, not least because you think they may reject you—and they may—and because you think that they may hurt you—and sometimes they do.

As I grew up, I learnt a little how to cope: certainly how to *pretend* that I wasn't frightened. But I began to learn in those first choirboy days that all people are to some extent frightened people: frightened of each other; and that all people are to some extent damaged people; and that all people are damageable people—and certainly musicians as much, if not more, than others, because musicians (most of them) are themselves 'violin strings'; and violin strings snap. It's only suet puddings that don't.

If my earliest days as a choirboy were painful, it wasn't long before they were also days of joy; and I'm sure that the joy was the joy of friendship as much as the joy of music: most of my friends—most of my first experience of friendship—came through the choir; and I must confess that friendship has remained the centre of my life since those earliest beginnings. It never surprises me that David—who, we're told, was expert on the harp, and who, we're told, 'danced merrily'—was also one of the world's greatest friends, and an exemplar of friendship. You only have to say 'David and Jonathan . . .'

I ought to say that I was lucky to go to the one grammar school in Dagenham in Essex that there was then for the 130,000 people of that huge council estate; and I was fortunate that there was a wonderful music teacher, Dora Williams, who taught me the bamboo pipe and conducted the school choir, and on Saturday mornings would take me up to London to the Robert Mayer Children's Concerts, to hear, for instance, Roy Henderson and Astra Desmond sing excerpts from *The Magic Flute* and to be entranced by Malcolm Sargent's conducting. (I ought also to say in brackets that I am very angry these days because so much is being done to destroy the provision of music in our inner-city schools. I am angry, because I know how privileged I was, and it is not right that music should be only for a few privileged people like me.)

It was when I was still a boy that I began to learn the organ at my local church, and the day the Second World War broke out I played for my first service and became part-time organist and choir master, as I say, at fourteen. My mentor, another teacher, Selwyn Carlton Lowe, had suddenly been called up. The siren went in the middle of Mattins on that first Sunday in September 1939, and I sought such cover as there might be under the organ stool.

Those wartime years were unforgettable. If choirs are places of friendship, they are therefore often places of pain. Two of my choirboy friends were killed in 1941 by a land-mine on their houses close by our local church; and of the dozen choirboys with whom I played cricket on the green behind the church, with a garden-roller for a wicket, on the Saturday in September 1939 before the war broke out, three more were dead by 1945, in the RAF. And only the gospel I had heard as a choirboy, and the music I had sung—'Since by man came death: by man came also the resurrection from the dead'—could interpret, at any depth, and begin to cope with, those agonizing bereavements.

It so happened that on 10 May 1941, when I was sixteen, I went to the Queen's Hall to hear for the first time that afternoon *The Dream of Gerontius* conducted by Dr Malcolm Sargent with the Royal Choral Society, with Webster Booth as Gerontius and Muriel Brunskill as the Angel and Ronald Stear as the Angel of the Agony. The night was moonlit. The sirens went early, just as I got home; and for five hours, wave upon wave of bombers showered incendiaries and high explosives on London. Queen's Hall was completely destroyed. Where the organ had stood there were only stumps and lumps of melted lead from the organ pipes. Where I then worked was also destroyed by fire that night.

I doubt whether there were better interpreters of that event than Newman and Elgar:

> Learn that the flame of the Everlasting Love
> Doth burn ere it transform.

In 1939 I had gone out to work at a riverside wharf on the Thames and a few hundred yards along the river was Southwark Cathedral. There I became an Organ Scholar under Dr E. T. Cook who had been deputy to Sir Ivor Atkins at Worcester Cathedral in Elgar's time. Billy Reed (W. H. Reed), who did the bowings for the Elgar Violin Concerto and who died in 1942, was the leader of our Cathedral orchestra; and I soon found myself caught up in a company of musicians who introduced me virtually to Elgar himself. Dr Cook taught me to play the Elgar Organ Sonata and Elgar himself had coached him; but there were live—living—musicians who enthralled me. Vaughan Williams came to conduct his *Dona Nobis Pacem*. Eric Greene was the Evangelist in the St Matthew Passion. The young Kathleen Ferrier sang like an angel.

Since I was ordained, forty years ago, I have spent twenty-three years as a cathedral canon—for nine of them I was back at Southwark Cathedral as Canon Precentor, with responsibility for the music. My job was not only to be concerned with the Cathedral choir but often with the choirs of a very urban diocese; with school choirs as well as church choirs.

One thing I first learnt as a choirboy is that God takes and uses in this life things which *we* might, if *we* were God, despise.

Dr Erik Routley, for whom I have the greatest admiration, has written:

> That much maligned—and very justly maligned—work, Stainer's *Crucifixion*, which will afflict many congregations even in the Passiontide of this year, is a notable example of the ease with which a clutter of incongruous sentimentality can be set down on paper by an able composer who is inspired to it by a libretto of inconceivable religious squalor.

There is probably *something* in that. And in any case I must have great sympathy with anyone like Erik Routley who so obviously enjoys the intoxication of words! I can only say that at *one* time Stainer's *Crucifixion* meant a very great deal to me. God used it for me, as I know he has used it for others. It's rather like the stable at Bethlehem. I can imagine many deans of cathedrals—or directors of music—or even inferior clergy— saying that 'really this stable isn't fit for God's incarnation'. But, while they've gone off in a huff searching for a cathedral in which he might be born, God has slipped into the little town of Bethlehem by way of the manger. The woman who touched the hem of Christ's garment brought nine parts of superstition to one part of faith, but Christ honoured and blessed her.

Let's never give less than our best to God—as choir or congregation or cleric. But let's not think our choir and our gifts are the only ones God will receive.

Fifteen years ago, when I was a Canon at St Albans, I had to help interview candidates for the post of Master of the Music. There were finally two candidates. I asked the same question of both. 'It is Easter Monday' I said. 'There are a couple of thousand young people in the Abbey packing it from end to end. They have many of them walked ten miles. It has been raining cats and dogs. What would you do with and for them?'

The first said 'I haven't a clue. I don't think cathedral musicians have much of a place in that scene.'

The other said: 'I think I'd compose an instant opera and give one theme to those in the south transept, another to those in the north, and another to those in the nave, and I'd conduct from the bridge and get them all to make a joyful noise to the glory of God.'

He got the job. They tell me that even now, by the waters of Isis, he sits down and weeps when he remembers the happiness of his years at St Albans.

Choirboys' voices break, so people who go to church should never need reminding that death isn't something that happens only at the end of our life. It happens every day in some way or other. But death is a part of growth, part of life. For the Christian that's the heart of the gospel: 'Dying, and behold, we live'.

I felt very privileged in 1967 to have a seat in the Dean's Pew at Westminster Abbey for Malcolm Sargent's memorial service. As I've suggested, Malcolm Sargent meant much to me: The Robert Mayer Children's Concerts, *Hiawatha*, *Messiah*, *Elijah*, Brahms' *Requiem*, *Gerontius*. I shall not forget the Elgar *Serenade for Strings* at that service, or the *Walk to the Paradise Garden*, incomparably played, or the Abbey Choir singing W. H. Harris's 'Bring us, O Lord, at our last awakening'. It was marvellous how on that occasion music gathered up Malcolm Sargent's whole life. The sermon was superfluous. Music spoke for Malcolm Sargent: choirboy, organist, conductor, living and departed.

I would liked to have ended what I have to say this evening with some music. It would have been Sir Hubert Parry's setting of Henry Vaughan's poem 'My soul there is a country'. But you must make do with the words. It's no wonder that they provoked Parry to set them to sublime music.

> My soul, there is a country—
>   Far beyond the stars,
> Where stands a wingèd sentry
>   All skilful in the wars:
>
> There above noise, and danger,
>   Sweet Peace sits crowned with smiles,
> And one born in a manger
>   Commands the beauteous files.
>
> He is thy gracious friend,
>   And—O my soul, awake!
> Did in pure love descend,—
>   To die here for thy sake.
>
> If thou canst get but thither,
>   There grows the flower of peace,
> The Rose that cannot wither,
>   Thy fortress and thy ease.
>
> Leave then thy foolish ranges,
>   For none can thee secure,
> But One, who never changes,
>   Thy God, thy life, thy cure.

24

O MAN GREATLY BELOVED

Sermon in Christ Church Cathedral, Dublin, at the dedication of the memorial to George Otto Simms: Archbishop of Armagh (formerly Bishop of Cork and Archbishop of Dublin); 25 October 1992

The phrase from the Book of Daniel—chapter 10, verse 19—that is echoed in the inscription of the memorial just dedicated:

O man greatly beloved.

I count it a huge privilege to be invited to preach to you here and now.

I first met George Otto Simms on the very eve of his consecration as Bishop of Cork: the eve of the Feast of St Simon and St Jude, 1952, all but forty years ago. I had myself barely been ordained priest a month, but George Simms was always exceptionally kind to the younger clergy. I was then twenty-seven, and my friend and mentor, Eric Abbott, then Dean of King's College, London—later, Dean of Westminster—who was to preach the sermon at the consecration the next day, had asked me to accompany him to Cork, since he had that year suffered a serious heart attack, and his doctors were still very anxious for him.

It was my first visit to Ireland: the first of many, thanks to Bishop Simms. It was a memorable visit from the very moment we touched down on the tarmac at Dublin. A sprightly 54 year-old Canon Raymond Jenkins* was awaiting our arrival. He drove us to Cork by way of Leighlin, Eric Abbott sitting in the back of the car. Canon Jenkins *en route* evinced a considerable skill at providing us with a commentary on

---

*The 94 year-old Archdeacon Raymond Jenkins read the Second Lesson at the dedication of the memorial to George Otto Simms in Christ Church Cathedral, Dublin.

the history of Ireland, and on its natural delights, without seemingly needing to look at the road ahead—a gift I later found to be possessed by many Irish clergy.

The greeting that George Simms and Mercy gave us at the Deanery at Cork, at the end of our journey, was unforgettable and unforgotten. It was the directness of the look of the 42-year-old Dean of Cork that was so memorable; and, ever after, I knew that when I met him as bishop and archbishop there would be that same directness; the lively eyes and the same so welcoming smile.

George and Mercy were, of course, that day very concerned for Eric Abbott. Eric had been Warden of Lincoln Theological College, the Scholae Cancellarii, and, for two all too brief years, 1938 and 1939, George, at William Temple's instigation, had been Chaplain at Lincoln. It was, by all accounts, a wonderful partnership in ministry. Eric Abbott had a unique gift of friendship, and was undoubtedly a formative influence on the young George Simms, who in his letters to me in later years would often refer to Eric Abbott's 'blessed company' at Cork at the time of his consecration. At all events, there was no doubt in George's mind who he wanted to preach at his consecration; and Eric Abbott delivered in St Fin Barre's Cathedral a sermon which none who heard could ever forget. Let me read you just a paragraph or two from it.

His text was from the 12th chapter of the Gospel according to St Luke, the 32nd verse: 'Fear not, little flock; for it is your Father's good pleasure to give you the Kingdom.'

> St Luke tells us [he began] that these words were spoken by Jesus to his disciples. These are words to His intimates, not to the multitudes, and His intimates were a little flock. In a certain sense, which I leave you to judge, our Lord's intimates are still a little flock. All of us who are the grateful friends of George Simms, grateful to God for him, believe him to be one of the intimates of Jesus Christ.

Eric Abbott then went on to speak of the fight in our souls between fear and faith; and he related that fight particularly to the Church of Ireland.

> If all Ireland were yours [he asked] then would your fear cease? Perhaps it would. But clearly that is not what God has given you for your vocation. God has permitted you to be a little flock, and because you are a little flock He has permitted you to be tempted by fear. Because you are a little flock, therefore, there is only one possible response—which must be made by every bishop, every priest, every deacon, every lay man and woman; the only possible response is *faith*. And you, my dear George, as the Father-in-God and the Chief Shepherd of this particular flock, you must also be chief in Faith. You must be the embodiment of faith. And standing alone, for a Bishop *is* in a lonely position, you must typify the ability which God Himself gives those who have a vocation, to remain men of faith.
>
> After all, [Eric continued] a minority is always in a state of peculiar

temptation; it swings between pride and despair; it is prone to too much introspection. A majority also has temptations, and God must save us all. But if a minority is to avoid the temptation to be too self-concerned and too self-regarding, it has to turn its eyes to the Cross of Jesus Christ not only for consolation in its solitary faithfulness, but also for strength in its outgoing power. Jesus Christ, the Shepherd and Bishop of our souls, hung on that Cross alone, but its outgoing power into all the world is *Almighty Love*. We must be that kind of minority, and the Bishop must have the secret of *being* the little flock and of *leading* the little flock with all the *power* of the solitary Christ upon the Cross.

Eric Abbott ended his sermon with a paragraph on unity:

Though you are a minority, the whole of Christendom must be in your heart . . .
   The first biography of an Irish Christian which I ever read [said Eric] was the life of William Doyle. I remember how in the 1914—18 War, when he bent over a dying soldier in No Man's Land to minister to him, the soldier said 'I don't belong to your Church.' 'No,' said Willie Doyle, 'but you belong to my God.'
   I venture to prophesy [Eric continued] that something like this will be true of George, your new Bishop. It will happen both ways. Many who do not belong to the Church of Ireland will recognise that he, George, belongs to their God. And he in his turn, as he moves about the diocese, carrying the whole Church, and not simply part of the Church, in his person, will show to many who do not belong to his Church that they belong to his God. And this will be because his secret is not only Faith but Faith working through Love.
   'Fear not, little flock; for it is your Father's good pleasure to give you the Kingdom.'

After the service and the reception, I wonder if you can guess what happened?
   Well, let me tell you: we played hide-and-seek! George took us to the as yet unoccupied Bishop's Palace; and there—in the crypt—we played hide-and-seek!—the Bishop, Mercy, the young family, Eric Abbott and I, and, if I remember rightly, the agile Canon Jenkins. It was a wonderful place for hide-and-seek; but I had never before played hide-and-seek with a bishop—with a bishop in gaiters. I have to say they seemed on that occasion the perfect garb for the game. The Bishop stood behind the pillars with the youngest of the children. That visit for me—and not least that game—was the foundation of a forty-year friendship. From that day forward I knew that the Bishop's holiness was set in his humanity.
   In the next years, that friendship was refreshed, so to speak, by visits to George and Mercy when, for instance, I took on various locums in the Diocese of Cork—in places like Bantry and Roaring Water Bay.
   One incident at Bantry seemed to spring straight from that Consecration Sermon. I took a film into a shop to get it developed. In the window I spotted a fine photograph of the Bishop in his episcopal robes—given

pride of place. I said to the lady behind the counter: 'I see that you have a photograph of the Bishop of Cork in your window. Does that mean that you are Church of Ireland?' 'Oh, no' she replied 'But we all think of him as "*our* Bishop".'

One of the books I most treasure is a *Church Hymnal*—music edition—which is signed 'George Dublin'. The Archbishop had asked me to conduct a Quiet Day for the clergy here in this Cathedral, in September 1962. I treasure the book not least because it carries with it several memories.

I had flown over to Dublin the evening before. Nicholas Simms had kindly come to collect me at the airport, and in the car on the way to the See House said to me: 'My father will probably ask you whether you'd like to go to the Abbey Theatre tonight.' '*We* know', he said, 'that he'd much prefer to show you his slides of the Book of Kells—and *we* would like that very much as well.' At dinner, the predicted moment came, and I answered the Archbishop's enquiry as Nicholas had coached me to do. I can remember the surprise and delight that filled the Archbishop's being—and the incredulity that filled his voice: 'Would you *really*?' he asked, and, moments later, 'Oh well . . .'; and we had a remarkable evening.

It was remarkable in several ways. There was the shared delight of the family. There was the truly remarkable combination of the erudition of the scholar, the simplicity of the really great teacher, and the humility of the man who is reverent before the greatness of his subject. I learnt that evening many reasons why George Simms was a man so greatly beloved.

The next day it interested me that I was not just left to conduct the Quiet Day by myself. I have conducted a good many Quiet Days for the clergy of different dioceses; but I cannot ever remember the bishop himself attending and staying all day. In fact, that day I was able to observe the Archbishop as pastor; for he used the occasion to talk with one priest after another.

There was one aspect of the day which gave me much amusement. 'Give them plenty of silence', the Archbishop had instructed me. 'Not all the clergy of the Church of Ireland are used to silence', he added; and then said: 'I think we will all have lunch together in silence.' But at lunchtime, as the Archbishop and I walked over to the Synod Hall together, the roof was nearly being lifted off by the volume of voices that came from within. 'Perhaps it was not such a good idea to have lunch in silence,' said the Archbishop, with an understanding smile. 'They have so few opportunities to meet with their friends.' George Otto Simms was ever the soul of charity.

At the end of the day, George said 'Let us just walk to the APCK bookshop.' He told me he particularly wanted me to have my own copy of the *Revised Hymnal*. He wrote an inscription in the book as we stood in the shop, and pointed out some of the hymns that were his special delight, including that lovely old Irish hymn, versified by Eleanor Hull:

> It were my soul's desire
> To see the face of God
> It were my soul's desire
> To rest in his abode.
>
> It were my soul's desire
> When heaven's gate is won
> To find my soul's desire
> Clear shining like the sun.

Later, the Archbishop was to write of that particular hymn:

> It were my soul's desire
> To see the face of God

takes us to the heart of prayer and the core of faith. This vision of God will be granted to the clear-eyed, the pure in heart, who will see him as he is. It involves looking in the right direction, facing up to him with penitence and courage.

I only once visited the Archbishop in Armagh. He gave me that day, in April 1975, a copy of his little book *Christ Within Me*. It was at his instigation that I had brought with me from London a delegation from the charity Christian Action. The Archbishop wanted me to talk with community workers, church leaders and representatives of the United Nations Association. At that time, in the Ardoyne, unemployment was over fifty per cent, and the Archbishop hoped that Christian Action might be able to finance the purchase of machinery which would provide work for a small factory set up with an ecumenical management. That day I was struck with the Archbishop's personal concern for the unemployed and for human rights in Northern Ireland. His encouragement enabled our visit to achieve a success it would not otherwise have had; and I noted the way the Archbishop dealt with politically sensitive subjects. It was not the way of the politician but of the practical pastor: dealing as best he could with those who were at risk in society.

It was in his retirement here in Dublin that I felt I could ask the Bishop to come over to St Albans, where I was Canon Missioner, to conduct the annual retreat for the clergy. His retreat addresses were expanded and published later as the book *In My Understanding*. He used each clause of 'God be in my head' to provide an address for the retreat. The clergy of St Albans knew they had been given a feast.

It is ten years since the book was published. I have little doubt that it is one of the best books of spiritual reading published in the last decade and for many more years. I read it again as a kind of remote preparation for this address:

There are some famous examples from spiritual history for us to follow [wrote the Bishop] as we search for a better understanding of God. Prayer in the experience of the prophet Daniel was seen as an opening of the mind. This openness is an attitude for us to *practise*. It encourages receptiveness; it involves listening; it removes narrowness, tight tensions, proud prejudices and dull indifference from the mind. Daniel, while in exile in far-off Babylon, 'had windows in his upper chamber open towards Jerusalem, and got down upon his knees three times a day, prayed and gave thanks to God.' With this open view, and a wide panorama stretching out before him, the prophet concentrated his gaze in one consistent direction and commented: 'When I, Daniel, had seen the vision, I sought to understand it'. He had made a fresh start.

Daniel was a 'man greatly beloved'; so, too, was George Otto Simms, who was called to be—had to dare to be—a Daniel, in and for Ireland.

O man greatly beloved.

All this August I have had to be in South Africa. At the invitation of Bishop Trevor Huddleston, I am writing his biography. I saw forty or so individuals all of whom had one thing in common: that they knew Bishop Huddleston when he was Father Huddleston in Sophiatown from 1943 to 1955. One such person I interviewed was Archbishop Desmond Tutu. It wasn't long in our conversation before the name of George Simms cropped up. I told Archbishop Desmond I had been invited to preach here today, and how honoured I felt. His face lit up: 'Please, please, take a message of love and thanksgiving to them from me for all that George Simms meant to me and to so many.' Desmond Tutu then explained how in the 1978 Lambeth Conference he was chairman of one of the main three sections of the Conference, and Dr Simms was vice-chairman of it. He, Desmond Tutu, was at the time an assistant bishop of only two years standing in the Province of South Africa and had recently been appointed General Secretary of the South African Council of Churches. He came to the conference overburdened with the weight of South Africa's problems and with the burden of the church there. Desmond Tutu said: 'Any good that may have come out of that section of the conference which might be thought to be due to my leadership must be attributed to George Simms.'

He was such a tremendous help and support for such a maverick as me, utterly inexperienced, not knowing from one moment to the next what I was supposed to be doing, and he would be there by my side, an encouraging presence and influence. I am enormously grateful for what I have learned from my association with him. He did not speak a great deal, but whenever he did he spoke quietly, unobtrusively and unassumingly. I am wonderfully enriched, truly blessed to have been touched by him.

I had no idea when I went out to South Africa of the bond between Desmond Tutu and George Otto Simms. In 1978 they were *both* ambassadors in *bonds*. They 'bore one another's burdens and so fulfilled the law of Christ'. I suspect that bearing the problems of South Africa and the problems of Ireland bound them both together.

It was thus that George Simms became 'a man greatly beloved'.

* * *

In my beginning is my end.

I have earlier spoken of Eric Abbott's sermon at the consecration of George Otto Simms as Bishop of Cork. I have not told you that what I also most remember from that service is the singing of the Breastplate of St Patrick by that great congregation.

It was not simply that we sang that day such ancient Irish words to such an ancient Irish melody. There seemed even in the few hours that I had known the Bishop, an intimate connection between that hymn and him whose consecration as bishop we had been privileged to witness that day. The words of the hymn seemed to be the words of George Otto Simms and never in the succeeding years could I separate him from them.

On 28 October 1952—yes; they were true then—but whenever I met with him, George seemed to be saying

> I bind unto myself today
> The power of God to hold and lead,
> His eye to watch, his might to stay,
> His ear to hearken to my need.
> The wisdom of my God to teach,
> His hand to guide, his shield to ward;
> The word of God to give me speed,
> His heavenly host to be my guard.

And he taught us all, by his example, to make the words our own.

And that above all is why, surely, George Otto Simms was a man so greatly beloved.

25

DECLINE AND FALL?

Gray's Inn Chapel;
Remembrance Day
8 November 1992

Each Remembrance Day is slightly different. Perhaps some event in the year that is past, or some anniversary, alters a little what we are doing that particular Remembrance Day; alters the way we are remembering.

I wonder what shapes and makes your remembrance this Remembrance Day?

For the older ones amongst us it may be the anniversary of Alamein, or the memory of the V2.

I wonder would I be wrong in thinking that all of us find much that is happening around Sarajevo and Bosnia, but also in other parts of the world at the moment, so sickening that there is little but dejection and dismay within us when we think of 'man, at war with man' again, and in so many places? This year in particular it has sometimes seemed to me that that doom-laden title to Gibbon's great work on the Roman Empire *Decline and Fall* says it all: not about our country, or our country alone, but about the world.

It's not difficult on this Remembrance Day to side with Gibbon's pessimistic definition of history as 'little more than the register of the crimes, follies and misfortunes of mankind'.

Yet in our saner moments we know that isn't all. However justified our cynicism, we know that history is more—much more—than Gibbon allowed. Another great student of history, G. M. Trevelyan, whose biography by David Cannadine appeared earlier this year, said in 1955, on the occasion of the publication of his *English Social History*: 'When I first read those words of Gibbon as a Harrow boy in 1889, I thought they were untrue. I think so less now, I fear; but we must add that history is also the register of the splendour of man, and of his occasional good fortune, of which our island has had more than its share.'

When I ruminate on war: when I try to remember 'the truth, the whole truth and nothing but the truth' about war, I turn more often to the poets than to the politicians—or the preachers: for the poets, where war is concerned, are most often our priests and prophets and pastors.

As you will well know, a month ago was the centenary of the death of

124

Tennyson; and I found myself reading Tennyson for the first time as a war poet. I suspect that some of you had to learn as a child 'The Charge of the Light Brigade', but may therefore have dismissed it as a poem of power and perception about war. But this Remembrance Day I think it could say something to us all about the very nature of war: its good and its evil:

> Half a league, half a league,
>   Half a league onward,
> All in the valley of Death
>   Rode the six hundred.
> 'Forward, the Light Brigade!
> Charge for the guns!' he said:
> Into the valley of Death
>   Rode the six hundred.
>
> 'Forward, the Light Brigade!'
> Was there a man dismay'd?
> Not tho' the soldier knew
>   Some one had blunder'd:
> Their's not to make reply,
> Their's not to reason why,
> Their's but to do and die:
> Into the valley of Death
>   Rode the six hundred.
>
> Cannon to right of them,
> Cannon to left of them,
> Cannon in front of them
>   Volley'd and thunder'd;
> Storm'd at with shot and shell
> Boldly they rode and well,
> Into the jaws of Death,
> Into the mouth of Hell
>   Rode the six hundred.
>
> Flash'd all their sabres bare,
> Flash'd as they turn'd in air
> Sabring the gunners there,
> Charging an army, while
>   All the world wonder'd:
> Plunged in the battery-smoke
> Right thro' the line they broke;
> Cossack and Russian
> Reel'd from the sabre-stroke
>   Shatter'd and sunder'd.
> Then they rode back, but not
> Not the six hundred.
>
> Cannon to right of them,
> Cannon to left of them,
> Cannon behind them

Volley'd and thunder'd;
Storm'd at with shot and shell,
While horse and hero fell,
They that had fought so well
Came thro' the jaws of Death,
Back from the mouth of Hell,
All that was left of them,
   Left of six hundred.

When can their glory fade?
O the wild charge they made!
   All the world wonder'd.
Honour the charge they made!
Honour the Light Brigade,
   Noble six hundred!

Those of you who have read that remarkable book *The Reason Why*, by Cecil Woodham-Smith, will know why that charge was made: why it was as much a record of human blunder and folly as of misfortune, and of shame and sin as of glory. But that is war.

The record of Cardigan, Lucan and Raglan—the whole mess of the Crimea—requires us to say something like *Kyrie eleison* when the full tale is told: when we remember. But not only when we remember the Crimean War.

Twelve weeks ago, in August, I went to another place which is now only history; I went to Mafeking. In my childhood, Mafeking was a place-name often on my parents' lips. The relief of Mafeking had been unforgettable to their childhood memories. The hysteria of Mafeking night in 1900 had caused a new word to enter the English vocabulary: to 'maffick'. The relief of the garrison was in every sense hysterical euphoric relief: relief from the nightmare of national humiliation. Colonel Baden-Powell, the commander of the garrison, was also ever after a household name. It was he who had enabled the British Empire to escape a crushing psychological defeat: a devastating blow to its self-confidence. But read Thomas Pakenham's *The Boer War* and you will wonder how human beings could ever have conjured up that terrible war.

As I said, three months ago I stood before the memorial in the middle of Mafeking, and read each name of those who had been slaughtered there. But I read it in the midst of a thronging black population with hardly a white face to be seen; for Mafeking, for the last thirty years or more, has been an area in which only black people may live. Until the sixties it was a white town with a black native location. But since the sixties a total of about five million black people have been removed and relocated in South Africa.

That terrible removal of races to other areas for 'separate development', so-called, was in fact the fruit of a policy which had had its origins in earlier years. Lord Milner, the great British imperialist High Commissioner, contributed more than most to apartheid: 'One of the strongest arguments why the white man must rule', he said, 'is because that is the only possible means of raising the black man, not to our level of civilization—which is doubtful whether he would ever attain—but to a much higher level than that which he at present occupies.'

Thomas Pakenham tells us the truth about Mafeking: how the white defenders, to hold out, took part of the rations of their black comrades, who were accordingly given the choice of starving to death in the town or running the gauntlet of the Boers.

Baden-Powell prevented some of the Africans from starving by feeding them part of the horses' rations. The members of the white garrison who could not afford to buy rations out of their own pockets were provided with rations on credit. The Africans were made to pay, and pay handsomely, for their food, including food commandeered from their own stocks. The white Army Service Corps sergeant-major in charge of rations was found to be running his own 'black market' in food for whites. But B-P's ingenious solution to the problem of conserving food in a beleaguered town was to say to that part of the garrison that was 'expendable', namely the natives, leave here or starve here. Using one method or another, he reduced the garrison by a quarter. What was happening did not escape the eagle eye of the correspondent of *The Times*: 'There can be no doubt that the drastic principles of economy which Colonel Baden-Powell has been practising' he wrote 'are opposed to the dignity and liberalism which we profess and which enter so much into the settlement of native questions in South Africa.' The correspondent of the *Pall Mall Gazette* gave a graphic description of the plight of the Africans fortunate enough to be allowed rations by B-P. 'I saw them fall down on the veldt and lie where they had fallen, too weak to go on their way. Hunger had them in its grip, and many of them were black spectres and living skeletons, their ribs literally breaking their shrivelled skins.' When relief came, no thanks were given to the African. A relief fund was raised in England to put Mafeking back on its feet. None of it went to Africans, thousands of whose farms had been looted or burnt. It was considered a white man's country and a white man's war. The Africans were only there to be useful to the white men and, if they were no longer useful, they had to pay, like the animals, a most terrible price.

On the Mafeking Memorial no mention is made of those who were black and lost their lives; though, strange to relate, there is an addition to the memorial which ironically records the gallantry of the Black Watch.

Remembrance Day, if it is to be worth anything at all, requires a rigorous honesty of remembrance: of the Crimea; of Mafeking; of the Somme; of Alamein; of Dresden and Coventry; of Hiroshima; of Viet Nam, of the Falklands; of Iraq; of 'ethnic cleansing' yesterday and today.

But is the story only gloom and doom? Surely 'The Charge of the Light Brigade' makes clear that each war will also have its glory and honour to record; and its story of human hopes fulfilled.

Some of you may have heard what I had to say on BBC when I returned from South Africa. I spoke of how I was privileged to see in Johannesburg the production of a new play by the great South African playwright Athol Fugard.

It's called *Playland*, and it's set in a travelling amusement park encamped on the outskirts of a South African town. The play's a powerful parable. The time is as important as the place. It's New Year's Eve, 1989.

Two men, a young white ex-serviceman from the war against SWAPO, on the South African border, and a black night-watchman, who looks after the amusement park, meet accidentally and, as the eighties become the nineties, confront and work through their differences, and through the nightmare of guilt which they find they both share. They both have, for different reasons, blood on their hands. The ex-serviceman's guilt has brought him to the point of breakdown; but both characters, in their distress, shout out truths which in calmer moments they would keep to themselves.

'You've got to speak up in this bloody world' says Gideon, the white man. 'It's the only way to put an end to all the nonsense that's going on.'

Gideon is aware not only of his guilt but of his mortality. Like a good many soldiers, he says he's aware of having swapped jokes with his buddies one moment only to be praying for them the next.

It had been his job to throw the bodies of some of his men into a hole, like rotten cabbages—but, suddenly, he found himself realizing that one of those cabbages was some mother's son.

So far, the story may sound fairly depressing. But it's more than that: it's a secular story about repentance, forgiveness and reconciliation, at a time when, of course, South Africa has desperate need of such things; but, like all great plays, it's not only about one country at one time, or about only those two people. It's a play about hope—not naïve optimism, but hope that is born of facing up to the realities of existence.

Fugard gave an address to some university students in South Africa in 1991 when he said:

> I was on the brink of being a pessimist, but the Fugard that is talking to you now has a hell of a lot more hope and optimism. Not naïvely so. I am aware of how precarious our movement towards a new reality, a new dispensation in our society is—but I would be dishonest with you if I did not say that I am one of those people who believe that we are going to win through—in the end.

I ended my BBC broadcast by reminding people that that week-end had seen the start of the Jewish New Year. I said: 'As a Christian, I have hope; but hope isn't the monopoly of Christians: you find it in the Psalms and in many a Jewish story—yes; and in plays like this play of the agnostic Athol Fugard: because Hope is an inexhaustible gift of God, our Creator, which I believe is available to us all.'

I want to add this Remembrance Day just a sentence or two more.

I have a very aged friend: Alan Ecclestone, a priest of eighty-eight years of age, living in retirement. Recently, he had a slight stroke. Not so long ago, his wife died after a very long illness. He looked after her until she was taken into care and then each day he'd make the long journey to the hospital and back. After his wife's death, his son died, in early middle age. I was privileged to preach at his memorial service. The aged father cast the soil on the coffin of his son. The father is a very remarkable man. He talks even now of having the courage to begin again. He uses the phrase of many things in life: of being prepared at his age and in his condition to try and take a walk up the grassy track behind his cottage in the Lakeland hills. He uses it of prayer: beginning again. He uses it of relationships which have been broken for one reason and another: of reading a new book or reading again a Shakespeare play that he's read a hundred times. And after the funeral of a loved one. Beginning again.

To hope is important in this life—I note that the President-elect of the United States was born in 'a place called Hope'. But hope is not enough. In this life we need to begin again and again—not least to begin peacemaking again and again. It's in our beginning again that the creative power of God is most revealed—as it was the first Christmas and the first Easter, and as it is in the life of my aged friend. That creative power is specially needed at any time of decline and fall.

I noticed that Governor Clinton, on the night of his election, said the American people have 'voted to make a new beginning'. As we think of him and pray for him, let us pray also for ourselves, that we may have the courage, whatever our age or situation, in ways small and great, to begin again.

26

THE CREATIVE SIGNIFICANCE OF THE FEMININE

Gray's Inn Chapel and Westminster Abbey; 15 November 1992

All of you will know that during this last week the General Synod of the Church of England decided that women shall be ordained to its ministry.

I do not want to preach directly on that subject today, but it seemed right to preach on a subject intimately connected with it; and I thought it might be helpful were we all simply to think together about the creative significance of the feminine. That subject, in my judgement, concerns us all: men *and* women; and is fairly closely related to this week's historic vote.

You can't be a priest these days and not know how important a vocation motherhood is. But you know it perhaps most of all because you meet in your ministry so many whose relation with their mother has 'gone wrong' in some way, by damage, or by virtual breakdown—or 'gone too right', so to speak, with over-attachment.

In this world of uncertainties there can be little doubt that there is no one more important in anyone's life than their mother. The relationship of the mother to the child is fundamental in a way that the father's probably is not. The very sense of 'being', as opposed to having to fight for your very existence; having to prove your existence; 'being' as opposed to being uncertain about your very existence—the very sense of 'being' is largely the gift of a good mother.

Fundamental truths like this are often illustrated and clarified for me by works of art; and I think that Michelangelo has most marvellously portrayed this relationship between 'being' and motherhood.

Between the years 1503 and 1506, Michelangelo, for reasons best known to him, produced four Madonnas. (Perhaps he was reflecting on his own 'failed' mothering, for his mother died when he was six.)

The first, the Doni Madonna, is a painting of Mary, Joseph and Jesus: an intensely active group.

Then Michelangelo began to explore what lay behind that capacity for activity: what that capacity for activity sprang from, and he produced a

130

marble statue—the Bruges Madonna—and two marble reliefs—what are called the Pitti Tondo, and the Taddei Tondo.(The second is in the Royal Academy.)

The Bruges statue portrays simply the Madonna and Child, in a state of complete composure. The Madonna is sitting quite still, with an expression of calm and peace on her face which expresses perfectly, I think, just 'being': this gift of being, which, as I've said, a mother—including, presumably, the Mother of our Lord—has unique power to give.

The Child stands motionless at her knee in the same state of composure. They are not looking at each other, but are simply 'at one' and together in a way which expresses, as well as anything I know has ever expressed, the most complete and absolute security: the experience of identification and 'sharing-in-being' of mother and child. In this statue of Mother and Child is portrayed the true starting point for the growth of the human being to a capacity for confident and vital activity: that activity which is developed in the other three works of Michelangelo.

In the Pitti Tondo relief, the Child turns towards his Mother. It is a much more active sculpting.

In the Taddei Tondo relief—the one on show at the Royal Academy—the Child has sprung into action, and a third figure, the boy John the Baptist, is included. He holds out a goldfinch (an ancient symbol of the Passion) to Jesus, who, moved by curiosity, has started forward to see what it is; but he's not quite certain what to make of it. Mary sits there, calm and undisturbed, holding out a protective arm to her Son, but with a reassuring expression towards the boy, John the Baptist.

The painting, the Doni Madonna, which is often reproduced, on, for instance, Mothers' Union baptism cards, is a scene of full and unrestrained healthy activity on the part of the Child. Jesus, a strong and muscular little boy, is vigorously climbing on His mother's shoulder, while Mary, a woman of strong physique, though retaining her basic mothering quality, is holding Him up there, and Joseph is lending a helping hand to support the vigorous young Child; but Joseph's expression contains—to me—something of motherhood too.

If, today, I wanted to celebrate in art the great gift of motherhood, and of the motherhood of our Lord, I would want to exhibit those four Madonnas of Michelangelo.

But, as I've said, the importance of motherhood for me is underlined, paradoxically and painfully, because I meet so many whose relationship with their mother has 'gone wrong'—by over-attachment, damage or virtual breakage.

Sometimes it has 'gone wrong' for culpable, blameworthy reasons; sometimes what has happened has been quite unavoidable. The child may have lacked a real mother because his mother has refused the breast, or been all too often cross, impatient and punishing; or, maybe, has been absent temporarily, or for a longer period, through illness or, permanently, through death; or has, for one reason and another, in the child's earliest weeks and months, been emotionally detached, aloof and unresponsive.

The result, from the receiving end, has seemed the same: mother has seemed to cease to love. The child has felt deserted. I think one also needs to speak of the 'enveloping' mother—with a virtually absent father—and the damage through that.

At all events, I could not speak honestly just about the glories of motherhood and the Mother of our Lord without also speaking of the tremendous, the almost terrifying responsibilities of motherhood.

You will know well how many of our hospital beds are still occupied by the mentally ill. I suppose it is as certain as anything can be that a very large proportion of such people are those whose mothering has 'gone wrong'. But, of course, most of the mentally ill are nowadays seldom 'in-patients' in hospitals. They are to be found, if I may say so, on Cathedral Chapters, in Cabinets and Shadow Cabinets, on the Bench, and on Parochial Church Councils, and so on: in the world at large.

And so to delinquency. What has so often been dealt with by Christians from a moral standpoint, assuming an individual strong enough to respond to the appeal of moral values—not least Victorian values—we now very often have to see as concerning someone who will only be healed if they can have back their lost motherhood and their lost childhood. The rebirth, regrowth and healing of the lost, living heart of the child in all of us is very often of paramount importance, if we are to be strong enough to respond to the appeal of moral values.

There are certainly thousands of people about, who, having been faced with too early and too intense a fear and anxiety, with an environment with which they could not cope, have begun and continued a retreat from outer reality, in one way or another. As infants we cannot take literal flight, so we begin the flights of fancy and fantasy which prevent our ever being the adults we were meant to be.

'I feel so exhausted that I just want to lie down flat and never wake up' said someone to me the other day. I had little doubt this was not something of that moment, or even a reaction to life that had begun in adult life. There was good evidence it had begun in infancy, in damaged mothering. You don't need me to tell you that when many of us from time to time say that we 'want to die', or when we show signs of what people loosely call 'depression', we are revealing a desire to 'withdraw' that often had its beginnings in infancy. There is also a compulsive activity and dominance which is only a thinly disguised inability to 'be': to be like the Child Jesus in that Michelangelo Bruges statue.

Again, when nowadays I am asked for help by people with disordered sexual or aggressive drives, I rarely find it in my heart to say first—whatever they have done, or want to do, or feel impelled to do—'Thou shalt not'. If the object is their healing, then first I most often find myself wanting to hear all they have to say about their earliest relations with their mother.

So, when these days I am asked, say, to thank God for Mary, the Mother of our Lord, and for all good mothers and good mothering, I find myself also thankful that the damage done in infancy—often with the best intentions—is seldom wholly irreparable, and that here 'Mother Church' has, I believe, a tremendous potential vocation.

Many of us, bearing with us still some damage, some wounds, have much mothering within the Church for which to be thankful. But within the Church we find ourselves looking out not for miraculous cures but for ways of helping others—and ourselves—towards continuous personal development, step by step, towards growth, towards personal strength and maturity.

For the Church really to be 'Mother Church' demands that we should all be schooled in compassion, in tenderness, and in patience. In patience, because once an individual has developed a certain organized pattern of personality, he or she is able to retain it with a high degree of persistence.

Disturbed patterns persist as stubbornly as more harmonious ones. They are not simply discarded at will. To be tender with the tenderness of Christ means that we learn that spiritual and physical strength-in-gentleness which gave the touch of Christ its healing power. To be sensitive and schooled in compassion certainly means that we cease to be naïvely censorious, judgemental and gossipy. It means that we give the sympathy that strengthens, not the sympathy that weakens. But I'd be the first to say that most of the mothering that we need is supplied outside the Church.

One of my heroes is a man whom some of you will have heard of: C. F. Andrews, a very great Anglican priest who, after a time in South London, went out to India and became Gandhi's greatest friend. He figured a lot in the film of Gandhi's life. Gandhi once wrote to Andrews: 'I have missed you every moment today. Oh your love.' C. F. Andrews—not long ago I visited his grave in Calcutta—once wrote to the great Indian poet, Rabindranath Tagore—Gurudev, as he called him—in a birthday letter to him:

> There 'has' been (as I have often told you and still delight to tell you) this mother instinct in me (and there is no stronger instinct in my nature than this) which somehow,—by dear illusion or by dear reality, I care not which—has become so wrapped up in you in this way of love as to bring back, when I am with you, all the joy I had with my mother when I was a child. And there has

been equally strongly in me towards you the sense of being a child, and needing something of that tender love from you, which I have instinctively been giving you, just as we used to change the parts together so often, my mother and I, in the play of love, when I was mother and she was child.

I do not think this is all unintelligible to you [Andrews says] and I feel I can write it all down without further explanation, though if I were ever to hint at such things to anyone else, I should be called a fool; and I should be made to feel so utterly foolish that I could not even hint, or write at all. But with you it is different.

I suppose the truth is there,—that this mother instinct and this mother love has always been by far the strongest factor in my life, far stronger than I ever dreamed; and that the time of childhood—which I spent entirely with my mother—has been by far the happiest in my life, far happier than I ever knew or dreamed.—And in this new awakening which you have brought me, my whole nature has gone back to its truest source, and expressed itself over again in the old, old way, through this new love.

And in you,—it was—shall I dare to say it?—the mother in you that was drawing me all the while; even when I felt most the mother in me going out to you;—that was the play of love, the inter-change of love:—and, while it has always been true, absolutely and entirely true, that your whole glorious manhood roused me, stirred me, impelled me forward, urged me, wakened me, with a trumpet call: yet it has been all the while the mother in you which has quickened in me this love, this love.

And what Dadu said yesterday about 'the woman in one' responding to the worship of God in religion—may that not be true also of human love? And may not divine love (which we call religion) and human love be somehow ultimately the same? . . .

. . . simple unlettered Dadu was right—it is the woman in one, in the very heart of manhood when it is fullest and strongest and best, that is deepest of all and goes back to God himself.

What a letter! Some people, particularly Western people, will immediately resist, and may even lash out at the idea that as 'males' they have any mothering to do—maybe because their own mothering has 'gone wrong'. But I like the saying of Lao-Tse, the founder of Taoism, that 'he who understands the masculine and keeps to the feminine shall become the whole world's channel'.

What I have, of course, been saying by implication is that ordination—priesthood—gives to many of us—however barren we may otherwise be!—a part in the ministry of Mother Church for which we can only rejoice and be deeply thankful.

But, as I've said, the thought of Mother Church and of priesthood does not exhaust the work of mothering—not if you include within the Church, as I believe we should include in it potentially, all humanity. Certainly the ordained priesthood does not exhaust the work of mothering. In every nurse, married or unmarried, male or female; in every doctor, man or woman, in every physician of the soul and mind, lay or ordained, skilled or unskilled, and in every friend, there is I think something of the mother. When some women feel called to the priesthood, I myself have little doubt it is to exercise the gift of mothering to which some of us men feel called by ordination, that they, too, feel called.

I used to know well in South London, when I was living next to Guy's Hospital, Dr Stafford-Clark, the Physician-in-Charge there of Psychological Medicine and Director of the York Clinic. He has written of the death in the Second World War of a friend of his, when he was twenty-six and his friend about twenty-two, when his friend's aircraft crashed on take-off, with a full bomb load, and caught fire, and his friend was dragged from the wreckage.

Dr Stafford-Clark's views of organized religion and mine are widely different, so, too, I suspect, are his views on the masculine/feminine relationship. But to end what I have to say, I would simply like to read you what he has written—as a tribute to that motherhood-after-infancy which I believe goes on through so many people, male and female, married and unmarried, and in which I think we should be devoutly thankful that we are so wonderfully included by our baptism—and some of us by ordination—in Christ's Church; yes, but also by God's gift to us in our very creation.

Graham was badly injured and terribly badly burned. One of his legs was charred right down to the bone of the femur, and the other was baked so that what remained of the flesh had split open. The whole of the lower half of his body had the terrible sickening smell of burning flesh.

As he lay on the grass at the side of the runway, I gave him the contents of three ampoules of morphia, which was all I had immediately available. I put each one of them straight into one of the veins of his arm, fairly confident that this would produce a sleep from which he would not awaken. It was quite obvious that he could not possibly survive the severity of those appalling injuries. But whereas I was right in my judgement, I was wrong about the immediate effects of this very large quantity of morphia, given intravenously to a man in such terrible shock and pain. Its immediate effect was to kill the pain virtually instantly but to leave him clear-headed and, apart from his awareness that his burns must be severe and his injuries possibly fatal, feeling no longer shocked or shattered.

We lifted him on to a stretcher, and took him gently back in the ambulance to sick quarters, where we put him on to a bed in the emergency theatre while I prepared to set up a saline drip.

He followed these preparations with interest, though I think we both knew they were essentially a formality.

'What are you going to do now, Doc?' he said.

'Well,' I said, 'we've got you over the worst of your shock. Now I'm going to put some fluid into you.'

He looked at me steadily for a moment, and then said: 'Come and stand beside me, Doc.'

I did so.

'Tell me the truth,' he said ... 'The truth is I'm never going to leave this room alive, am I?'

I looked back at him. I think there were tears in my eyes; but if there were, neither of us cared about that.

'No, Graham,' I said. 'I don't think you will leave this room alive.'

'Well, then, tell me, Doc, how long do you think it's going to take me to die—and is it going to hurt?'

'I'll see it doesn't hurt, Graham,' I said. 'We've finished with pain as far as you're concerned; and as far as time goes, I should say it will take about half an hour to an hour. You see, your vitality's pretty low, and although we can kill the pain with morphia, there's so much damaged tissue fluid in your circulation that it will kill you quite painlessly without your knowing much about it. If there was anything else I could do, I would do it. You know that.'

'Yes,' he said, 'I know that. Everything seems very clear at the moment. I think there's just one thing I want to ask you.'

'Yes, Graham, what is it?'

'Doc, I want you to stand beside me, and talk to me about everything we think to talk to each other about. The things I'd like to talk about in my life, about the future I won't have, and maybe there are some things you might want to say to me—and, of course, there are some things I want you to tell my parents about me after I'm dead. But let's just talk together like two friends . . . And I want you to do something else for me.' He bit his lip for a moment. The well-established British reserve was making its last appearance.

'I'll do anything you ask, Graham,' I said.

'Well, I just want you to hold my hand, David,' he said—using my Christian name for the first time. 'And don't let go of my hand until I let go of yours.'

'Alright,' I said. 'I'll do that. And I won't let you go until you do.'

About twenty minutes later, earlier perhaps than either of us had expected, he became finally unconscious, and a little while after that, he was dead.

As we thank God today for the Mother of our Lord, let us also thank God for that gift of femininity that is in us all, and pray that it may be appropriately recognized and used.

27

PROFIT WITHOUT HONOUR?

Gray's Inn Chapel and Westminster Abbey; 22 November 1992

The Archbishop of York is recognized to be one of the wisest heads in Christendom today.

He provided recently a four-paragraph foreword for a Report which was published for the Council on Christian Approaches to Defence and Disarmament. And there could be no better introduction to what I want to say today than those four paragraphs.

The Archbishop wrote:

> The voice of the churches in public affairs is frequently unheard or disregarded—and sometimes with good reason. Surveying their dismal record in the economic sphere R. H. Tawney commented 'the Church ceased to count because she ceased to think'.
>
> The same charge could not, I believe, be levied in relation to war and the weapons of war. There is a long and distinguished tradition of Christian thought on these matters, no doubt because they are so inextricably bound up with moral and religious commitments, and can arouse such deep passions. Political and military leaders who failed to reflect on the morality of war would be guilty of a shocking abdication of duty. Furthermore such reflection needs to be continuous, because the moral judgements made have to bear a proper relation to the actual complexity of the political and military scene. Christian thinking, therefore, cannot afford to stand still if it is to be part of this continuing process.
>
> Since the end of the Cold War, and in the aftermath of the Kuwait War, questions about the international control of arms transfers have moved centre stage. It seemed to me that a well-informed Christian study of this issue would thus be timely. I was delighted when the Council on Christian Approaches to Defence and Disarmament agreed to undertake it, when the former Archbishop of Canterbury agreed to fund it, and when Dr Roger Williamson agreed to do the bulk of the work. The result is a report which is wide in its scope, well researched, easy to read, and which manages to combine a high degree of political realism with some profound theology.
>
> I am sure it will be a valuable resource in informing and shaping Christian opinion. I hope it will also be read carefully by those who may not immediately warm to its Christian basis, but who need the moral and religious perspectives which such a study can bring to this enormously difficult issue.

That Report, entitled *Profit Without Honour? Ethics and the Arms*

Trade, was published this summer, and at the time the subject of arms to Iraq had hardly surfaced. But now the Report is what I can only call 'burningly relevant'.

It is a superb document but it is inevitably complex. Few will question that its subject is of the utmost importance.

Amongst other things, the Report tries to restate for our time the main theological, moral and political criteria that should govern our evaluation of arms sales—primarily concerning what are nowadays somewhat euphemistically called conventional arms: that's to say, it assumes that the proliferation of nuclear, chemical and biological weapons is a separate subject.

The Report also considers whether and why, in the aftermath of the Iran–Iraq and Iraq–Kuwait wars, we should think of the present time as a particularly opportune moment for thought and action concerning the arms trade.

The Report attempts to make the subject—which is, of course, in part highly technical—something which, let us say, the Intelligent Person in the Pew can confront.

For instance: its second chapter is entitled 'The Arms Trade: What Should We Pray For?'

Let me read you just a few of its paragraphs:

> It is necessary to address the problem of the arms trade from the point of view of Christian concern and to ask why Christians and the churches should take up this issue and whether there is anything particular which Christians can contribute to the discussion.
>
> To Christians, the spiritual resources of prayer and the challenge to act for the good of one's neighbours go back to the life and teaching of Jesus. The term 'neighbour' should be understood as embracing anyone in the 'global village' whom we are able to help, if one accepts a broad application of the parable of the Good Samaritan.
>
> What should Christians do and pray for when confronted with the arms trade? The pacifist can pray for the arms trade to end. Others can pray that the weapons we export may be used only in good causes—either for deterrence or for just wars of defence, which do not infringe the just war criteria, in which no civilians are directly targeted, and so on. Many of us probably look at the complexity with less clarity of vision, unsure that clear lines can be drawn and with less faith that there is a simple prayer to utter or obvious actions to be taken which will hasten an end to, or responsible limitation of, the arms trade.
>
> Nor can we simply sell our consciences to the government by assuming that the government knows best, and that whatever arms deals our government allows are consonant with financial advantage, political wisdom and morality. The will of God on arms sales and the exports for which permission is granted do not necessarily coincide.
>
> All Christians, in their spiritual life, are confronted with the figure of Jesus. If one begins with the testimony of the Beatitudes and the Lord's Prayer (which almost all accept as recording the teaching of Jesus in an authentic manner), we observe that close to the core of Jesus' faith were the call to be peacemakers, the need to love our enemies, and the prayer that God's will

should be done 'on earth as it is in heaven'. All who seek, in whatever way they can, to be true to the Christian faith face a problem in reconciling this message with the reality of our world. It is a message of peace in a world of violence.

The pacifist maintains that it is incompatible with the message of Jesus to use violence or to support others when they do so. But how, in a world in which the innocent are menaced by those with weapons, can people be defended with exclusively non-violent strategies? The effectiveness of the many techniques of non-violence is often under-estimated by those who pride themselves on being realists. But the cost of such techniques, well recognized by Gandhi, is often under-estimated by pacifists.

On the other hand, those who believe in the efficacy of force, whether they are conservative or revolutionary (e.g. upholding Mao's belief that power proceeds 'from the barrel of a gun'), face the difficulty of explaining how their approach to the questions of power and violence can be related to the historical example and teaching of Jesus.

Those who uphold the legitimacy of the just war position would argue that the driving impulse of that tradition (at its best) is to limit the use of violence in a world in which it cannot be wholly eradicated.

Gradually, that chapter moves towards the heart of the matter: arms sales today:

To refuse arms sales may lead to the deaths of innocent people.

The production of weapons is deeply ambivalent—some weapons, in some hands, can ensure that access to goods and wealth is reasonably fair, and that innocent people are defended against predatory neighbour states. But weapons in the wrong hands, and too many weapons in any hands, are a danger to the life and security of people. In addition, it is obvious that the resources used for arms production cannot be used for the production of food and medicine.

How then do we pray about arms transfers? Prayer should, at the very least, provide a deeper understanding of our reality. It should help those who pray to see that there are no easy answers and no escape from being caught in unjust and unpeaceful structures. It should make us more honest as well— since the insight is inescapable that a prayer like 'O God, please make a world in which no arms are necessary' has more to do with infantile wish-fulfilment than the mature acceptance of responsibility. So, as well as praying as best we can, Christians also need to talk and think with one another, since there are genuine disagreements on this issue. The splits run through the churches. The issues of war and peace seem to confront each generation afresh, with agonizing choices requiring responsible decisions.

It can be argued, though, that most people, including most Christians, do not know what is happening in the arms trade or what its consequences are. The average citizen or church member has plenty of other matters to attend to without trying to find out what weapons are sold to whom and whether that is a good idea. Most people in Britain have no detailed knowledge of the arms trade or the procedures whereby decisions are reached as to what can and what cannot be exported.

Faced with the daily toll of suffering, we cannot afford to discuss and discuss until there is consensus, since that too costs lives. Even careful talk costs lives.

One prayer which is useful in such circumstances is the prayer to be kept from despair.

The idea that Jesus, in a sense a victim of the Pax Romana, and his message of peace, can be well served by even responsible arms transfers is one which surely carries the burden of proof with it. The stronger assumption must surely be that the world needs fewer weapons, not more; that it needs more environmental protection, not more military expenditure. It is not enough simply to discuss whether conflicts create the need for arms or whether the acquisition of arms creates conflicts.

True prayer is not running from reality, it is seeking the strength to bear more reality than we could otherwise bear.

Well: that is enough quotation from the Report to go on with.

I was grateful to those who produced the Report for going over some of the previous reports on the subject. We do not need always to 'reinvent the wheel' and a lot of thinking has gone into this subject over the years. In 1977, the same Council on Christian Approaches to Defence and Disarmament produced a report entitled *The Sale and Transfer of Conventional Arms, Arms Systems and Related Technology*.

This latest Report has a very fascinating and creative chapter which parallels the arms trade with the slave trade and compares and contrasts the problem of getting rid of both trades. It then compares and contrasts the arms trade with the drugs trade.

After that, there is a detailed study of the *pattern* of arms exports: the main *suppliers* around the world and the pattern that arms *control* has been taking—through, for instance, the United Nations and the World Bank—and attention is given to arms industries as part of a country's political aspirations: there is evidently a kind of *psychology* of armaments; you acquire arms to enhance your *status* as well as your *security*.

And who can in fact prevent nations getting the arms they want?

Of course, other major reports—like the Brandt Report and the Palme Report—made their contribution to the subject, and a kind of theoretical consensus has been growing that the arms trade is a threat to world development, to world security and to the environment of the world.

The former Secretary of the Methodist Conference, Dr Kenneth Greet, has termed the arms trade 'the most cynical and unprincipled trade the world has ever seen'.

Some people say the arms trade is unstoppable—and they may be right. But Christians cannot be content with that sort of statement. And they haven't been: the World Council of Churches has worked hard at the question, so too has the Roman Catholic Church.

Cardinal Hume, addressing the mass Lobby of Parliament on Fighting World Poverty, in 1985, outlined the extent of arms spending and said: 'I can find no better witness to cite than General Dwight D. Eisenhower who once said: "Every gun that is made, every warship launched, every rocket fired, signifies in a final sense a theft from those who hunger and are not fed."'

Soon after the Kuwait War, Cardinal Hume wrote to *The Times*:

> One of the lessons of the Gulf War is that international arms sales should never be governed solely by commercial considerations. The consequences of ignoring the moral dimension of arms transfers are now all too obvious.
>
> Of course the world arms trade is as much a symptom of international tension as a cause of it. But even if curbing arms sales is no panacea, it is still an objective to be pursued, in conjunction with diplomatic efforts to build trust and confidence in highly unstable areas such as the Gulf, through regional security agreements and guarantees.
>
> If we are to escape from the intolerable mess which allows the poorest of our world to suffer unspeakably whilst global spending on arms grows inexorably, we must begin to create a moral climate in which the sale of arms is generally unacceptable. Any substantial transfer of arms should have to be justified in terms of helping to meet a genuine need for self-defence, and without creating real social deprivation to pay the cost. There should also be compulsory registration of all such transfers at the United Nations, and an effective procedure for ensuring that, once sold, arms cannot be used with impunity for the internal repression of civilians.
>
> There is a tendency to assume that the principles of morality apply only to individuals and not to international relations. Here economic self-interest and political opportunism too often prevail. And yet these have repeatedly failed, even on their own terms.

The chapter in the Report on the 'Theology of the State and the Arms Trade' is important, but it is perhaps the most complex and I shall not attempt to include it in what I have to say today.

Nevertheless I think it is important to say that part of that chapter is simply about sin. 'A deep understanding of how we are entrapped in sin has to be applied', it says, 'to the issue of arms transfers.'

There is a valuable section of the Report on the Arms Trade and the 'signs of the times'. It says that:

> One of the gravest charges Jesus brought against his contemporaries was that though they could read the signs of the weather, they could not discern the signs of the times.
>
> Jesus used a particular word to refer to a special time when decisions have to be made that are likely to have far-reaching consequences: when a new set of possibilities is offered to us which we have either to accept or refuse.

The Report suggests 'that the effects of the Arms Trade in the Middle East—above all surrounding Saddam Hussein—have made this a crucial time for facing the truth about the Trade'.

There is one quotation in the Report which moved me particularly. Sheila Cassidy, herself a victim of torture and prisoner of conscience in Pinochet's Chile, in a sermon during the Human Rights Day Service in Westminster Abbey in 1980, said:

Christ's reaction to the by-standers at his Passion was 'terrifying'; he said, 'Weep not for me, weep rather for yourselves and for your children.' Rather than weeping for the victims of torture, we should weep for ourselves as guilty by-standers. Often our complicity is unwitting, but it is nonetheless real. We can no longer be unaware of the 'spiral of violence' caused by poverty and oppression, which leads to revolt, followed by renewed oppression. There is now clear analysis of the economic interdependence of the world and the mechanism whereby the rich get richer and the poor get poorer. Christians in Britain 'have been educated to give to the poor but not to refuse a good business deal because the merchandise might be misused', as is the case with arms sales. 'By accepting injustice tranquilly, we are guilty of complicity. If our government is trading with dictators and torturers, we must confront it, and make it clear that we would rather be poor than a party to repression.'

The Report comments on Sheila Cassidy's words:

This is quite clearly not a platform on which any contemporary British political party could get elected. There is not a consensus of that kind—even against arms sales to highly questionable governments. One task facing the churches is thus the creation of a moral climate in which there is a strong presumption against arms sales unless a legitimate need for their transfer can be proven. Cardinal Hume has argued, and the Church of England report states, that Britain should take a position whereby 'arms sales are by and large forbidden, except where there are important policy objectives'.

In the concluding section of the Report, there is a play on the Latin motto 'If you want peace prepare for war'. That motto is revised: '*Si vis pacem, para pacem*'.

The shock of the 'Saddam factor', the end of the Cold War, fears about proliferation and the inability of many Third World countries to pay for arms imports mean that there are sound economic and political reasons to believe that a more restrictive policy is possible. Within the churches, there are many points which can now be accepted by both pacifists and adherents of the just war teaching. In short, with determination and commitment, there is a great deal of possible common ground between pragmatic politics and principle, between secular concern and Christian faith on the need to subordinate arms transfers to ethical criteria.

There can surely be few more important subjects for intelligent Christians to form a Christian judgement upon than this subject of the arms trade today.

But there is no reason for Christians to stand alone. Only this week, in a letter to *The Times*, the former Chief Rabbi Lord Jakobovits wrote:

The unscrupulous supply of military material, sometimes to utterly evil regimes or terror groups, is unconscionable. The trade in conventional arms has caused and sustained some 170 wars since 1945, killing tens of millions of innocent people (whilst nuclear weapons, without a single casualty since the Second World War, have preserved the peace of Europe).

If the United Nations were to secure an international agreement to enforce a complete ban on all arms sales and shipments to countries not producing them, confiscating them when found, with heavy penalties or sanctions, the oxygen of violence would soon run out to starve the wars in Bosnia and Angola, relieve the famine in vast stretches in Africa ravaged by civil war, and maybe help to end the terror in Ulster and the Middle East.

The arms trade is undoubtedly profitable for governments and dealers. It also provides employment and helps to maintain the industry for self-defence. But all this does not morally justify helping to kill others. It is wrong to save your own life at the cost of someone else's, unless it threatens you.

It should not be beyond human resourcefulness to transfer the capital and labour invested in arms production to constructive ends—building houses, hospitals, schools and high-tech crime detection devices for a start.

I commend the words of Lord Jakobovits to you and I commend the Report *Profit Without Honour? Ethics and the Arms Trade* to you—in the name of the Father and of the Son and of the Holy Spirit.

28

RECEIVE YE ONE ANOTHER

St John's East Dulwich;
6 December 1992

From the Epistle for today: Romans 15.7: 'Receive ye one
another, as Christ also received us, to the glory of God.'

I have returned recently from as privileged a month as I have ever spent
in my life.

I was in South Africa for the whole of August, following in the
footsteps of Bishop Trevor Huddleston, who was born eighty years ago
next June, and who was Bishop of Stepney from 1968 to 1978. I interviewed about forty people who had one thing in common: that Trevor
Huddleston looked after them thirty to fifty years ago.

Trevor Huddleston spent a dozen years working amid the slums and
shanties of Sophiatown, Johannesburg, from 1943 to 1955. Five years ago
I began to write his biography, at his request, and I knew that some time
I must go out and see for myself where he had worked.

As it happened, I was in South Africa at a crucial time this August: at a
time of general strike and of what was called 'mass action', but also of
tragic conflict between the ANC and Inkatha. Nevertheless, while I was
there I managed to see, as I say, about forty individuals who knew
Bishop Trevor in the 40s and 50s: some of whom, like him, have now
risen to eminence: people like Archbishop Desmond Tutu, Oliver
Tambo and Walter Sisulu.

It was a unique opportunity to see things, in church and state, at first
hand.

I wish this morning I could transport you to, for instance, a church in
Soweto where I was one Sunday in August. Let me read you just a few
paragraphs from my diary for that day: Sunday 23 August:

At 8.30 this morning, Stephen Montjane came to collect me and take me to
his church in Soweto: St Andrew's, Pimville. It was a very memorable service.
The church was packed, with over three hundred people. In fact, people were
coming in the whole time, not just individuals but groups. Young men went
out to fetch in more pews, and the children sat on the floor of the sanctuary.
They were all ordinary Soweto people. I was the only white face in the church.
The singing was superb: sometimes like a South Wales chapel; sometimes like

144

an Eastern Orthodox liturgy; sometimes like a charismatic church, the singing turning into a kind of dance with clapping. There was an ideal mix of joyous celebration; of ritual that was well done; of reverence and of informality; of noise and silence. Stephen's preaching, with a translator, was clearly that of a poet: there was rhyme and rhythm to it. He used his hands and face most expressively, and people laughed easily. Children and adults wore clothes which were not expensive but which had been washed and ironed beautifully, so that the white shirts looked very white and the colours very colourful. The hymns were announced in five languages: Tswana, Zulu, Xhosa, Tsotho and English, but the tunes, English with African harmonies, were so loved that the fact that we were singing five different sets of words simultaneously didn't matter at all. I was asked to get up and introduce myself, and the mention of Bishop Huddleston provoked a round of vigorous applause.

Let me repeat one sentence in that entry in my diary:

The hymns were announced in five languages:

Tswana
Zulu
Xhosa
Tsotho
and English

But the tunes, English, with African harmonies, were so loved that the fact that we were singing five different sets of words simultaneously did not matter at all.

Couple that sentence with our Lord's words: 'When you pray, say "Our Father".' And couple it with St Paul's words in the Epistle to the Ephesians: 'I bow my knees before the Father, from whom every family in heaven and on earth is named.'

Tswana—Zulu—Xhosa—Tsotho—or English; it simply doesn't matter. We all have one Heavenly Father, whatever our race, or tribe or colour.

I have to say: I have never been in a congregation which had so many races in it or used so many languages, in all my forty years of ordained ministry; but that congregation was so clearly a unity. We knew we had one Father, no matter how many and how different were our languages.

But now let me tell you a little about the parish priest of that church in Soweto: Stephen Montjane. Stephen was born in 1933, the second of four sons. He was ten when Trevor Huddleston arrived in South Africa. Trevor saw Stephen's potential and got him into St Peter's School, Rosettenville, Johannesburg. In was in 1952 that Stephen's mother was diagnosed as having cancer of the gullet. Trevor Huddleston saw her out of this world and saw the family through their bereavement. Stephen matriculated that same year. Trevor Huddleston arranged that he should come to England: to Leeds University and to the College of the Resurrection, Mirfield, Yorkshire, to train for the priesthood. Stephen did four and a half years in England. Trevor Huddleston virtually clothed him, because he had no money of his own. Stephen remembered going to Aberdeen with Trevor in 1956 when Trevor received an honorary doctorate at the University there.

Although Stephen valued Leeds and Mirfield and his stay in England, he was also homesick there, and left Mirfield after only a term and got a secular job back in Johannesburg for a few years.

He was eventually ordained deacon in 1976, to the Cathedral in Johannesburg. He has been Rector of Pimville, Soweto, since 1981, and has been Archdeacon of Soweto since 1990. Stephen said some important things to me about Trevor Huddleston. 'You know' he said 'Trevor, by what he has done for us, has saved a lot of white people from our hate.' 'They say some times Trevor's a politician. But I've never met anyone who prays as he does.'

'Receive ye one another, as Christ also received us, to the glory of God the Father.' Trevor received the black people of Johannesburg as Christ received him to the glory of God.

Stephen's wife, Henrietta, whom Trevor helped to train as a nurse, described to me what it was like to be the wife of a husband like Stephen when he was 'detained' in prison for three months, for marching in a march of protest with other black priests, just after Steve Biko had died under similar circumstances of detention in prison. She wondered each day whether a message would come from the prison to say that Stephen had been found dead.

In those four weeks of August I came to know what a good many of my fellow Christians and my fellow priests have suffered because of the present government of South Africa's policies: the policies of white people who call themselves Christians.

I have known for a long while that no Christian should ever have anything to do with apartheid. But those four weeks in August refreshed my determination. We have to 'Receive one another, as Christ also received us, to the glory of God'.

I've told you a little about St Andrew's, Pimville, in Soweto, which I went to on 23 August. Let me tell you now a little about the church I went to only a week later, in Alexandra, to the north of Johannesburg. Again, let me read you a few paragraphs from my diary, for Sunday 30 August.

Deane Yates was a white headmaster in Johannesburg when I first met him, thirty years ago, here in England, in Cambridge. Deane—that's his Christian name—had promised to take me to St Michael's, Alexandra, and introduce me to some of the problems of that township. Deane helps at St Michael's, which was as refreshing an experience of worship as was St Andrew's, Pimville, Soweto, the previous Sunday. And just as Stephen Montjane had an extraordinary story to tell, so had the young vicar of St Michael's, Samson Makhalemele. He had experienced being beaten up at the hands of Inkatha.

I sat with Deane's wife, Dot, in the congregation, and greatly enjoyed the worship, and gave a brief talk from the lectern on +Trevor Huddleston and his message and significance for us all.

Then, after church, began an hour with Deane, going round the township, which exceeded my worst imaginings. Alexandra has a population of 350,000 people, about a sixth of the size of Soweto, but many of its problems are even more serious. It is largely a shanty town, but the fighting between Inkatha and the ANC has left part of the township like a battlefield or an area that has just been blitzed. Inkatha has taken over what was ANC ground, and the people have had to take refuge wherever they could find it. There were twenty-six families in one hall I visited: they have been there since last March. Outside the hall, the children gathered round me much as they did for +Trevor Huddleston in Sophiatown. 'What will *become* of them?' I thought. The mothers were cooking inside the divided hall, amid all their remaining belongings: beds and wardrobes, like a second-hand furniture store. There were vast brick hostels, like barracks, for migrant workers. Deane and Dot work tirelessly in Alexandra. Having begun as a school master, Deane has ended up, at seventy, as a kind of voluntary social worker: a skilled community reconciler. He introduced me to the Inkatha leader, who has many killings to his account. 'Divide in order to rule' is the aim of the Government. Deane spends much time dragging people together to talk to one another and be reconciled.

Eventually, having spent some four hours in Alexandra, Deane and Dot took me to their own home.

What impressed me that Sunday morning was that outside the church most Zulus were in the Inkatha movement and violently anti-ANC. But in the church, belonging to the Church, tribal barriers were forgotten. Zulu, Tswana, Xhosa, Tsotho were all one in church—one in Christ. I felt thankful for the Church which could say OUR Father.

But I have to remind myself that it's Christians, white Christians, churchgoers, who have caused much of the trouble in South Africa through the policy of apartheid.

Apartheid is no longer the official policy of the Government, but its effects are going to last for a very long time. And what people do about the continuing situation will continue to be important. Change will come only when people want it to.

The political situation has changed, but not changed enough, because politicians are playing literally a cynical political game, like a game of chess, waiting for the other party to move, and make a false move. Meanwhile, people suffer and suffer greatly. But the ANC enjoys the major support of black South Africans, and the country at large knows its only hope—in the end—is in negotiation with the ANC.

I was also in Cape Town for a couple of days in August. I stayed with a white Anglican Anglo-Catholic priest: a friend of mine, David, whom I hadn't seen for twenty years. He drove me to the Cathedral and then to the coast road immediately opposite Robben Island, where Nelson Mandela was in prison. I asked him 'Did you ever think, when you drove along here, of the prisoners on the island?' 'Candidly, no' he replied. 'No one ever did. If we did, I suppose we thought of them as law-breakers.'

'Receive ye one another, as Christ also received us, to the glory of God.'

In South Africa, I came across a prayer which Fr Timothy Stanton, erstwhile curate of St George's, Camberwell, wrote. He was in prison only three years ago for not being willing to betray someone to the police. He is eighty years old and a member of the Community of the Resurrection. Let me read that prayer to you now:

O Lord, thank you for South Africa:
> for its beauty, its resources, and for its variety of
> > people of all races:
> for their courage, their love, and their joy.
Thank you for all who want to live and work together for the
> coming of your kingdom there.

But there is much that is wrong:
> avarice, injustice, exploitation, cruelty,
> above all, racism.

So we pray for all the people of South Africa:
> for Whites:
> > those who have the power to change things but don't
> > use it, for fear of losing their power and
> > privileged position—or just through laziness.
> for Blacks:
> > for those who have worked with the system, and are
> > now well off, and don't want to change things;
> > for those who are trying to change things, both from
> > inside and outside the country;
> > and for those who have lost hope of changing things
> > except by violence.
> for Coloureds and Indians and other races, torn between
> > their desire to share white power and privilege,
> > and their duty to share with Blacks in the
> > Liberation Struggle.

O Lord, save us and help us all.
> Things won't come right without repentance.
> Help us to recognise our sins and grant us true
> repentance.

Grant us your Holy Spirit:
> that we may see how to bring about change in the
> best way,
> and with as little violence as possible.

May we each do what we can in the situation we are in,
> and with the gifts we have, to create peace and
> harmony;
> that all the people of our countries may live fully
> human lives, in right relationship with you, with
> each other, and with all your creation;
And so may your Kingdom come in all its fulness,
> > > Amen.

For those who prefer something shorter there is a prayer written by Trevor Huddleston himself:

> God bless Africa,
> Guard her children,
> Guide her leaders,
> Give her peace.

But I don't want my sermon this morning to be thought to be only about South Africa. So I want to go back to the Lord's Prayer, Our Father, which we shall be saying later this morning.

I want you all to bow your knees before the Father from whom every family on earth is named:

> Tswana
> Zulu
> Irish
> Italian
> Polish
> Bosnian
> Somali
> Xhosa
> Caribbean
> Tsotho
> White South African
> Afrikaaner
> English

and remember: we must 'Receive one another as Christ also has received us, to the glory of God'.

29

CHRISTIAN IDENTITY AND CHRISTIAN VOCATION

St Peter's Vauxhall;
Farewell Eucharist to the
Community of St John the Divine;
9 January 1993 ·

In the twentieth chapter of St John's Gospel, Mary Magdalene stands outside the tomb, weeping; she turns round, and Jesus is standing there, but she doesn't recognize him. And then, in the sixteenth verse of that chapter, there is the most marvellous fragment of dialogue:

> Jesus saith unto her, Mary.
> She turned herself, and saith unto him, Rabboni; which is to say, Master.

I believe that that fragment of dialogue lies at the heart of every Christian vocation.

Jesus calls every one of us by our own name. He speaks to our deep heart's core. He understands our true identity—in a way which we do not understand it ourselves; and he says to us:

> Mary—Monica, Teresa, Iona, Christine, Peter, James, Andrew, John.

And he waits for our individual 'Rabboni'—'Master', which may take us a lifetime.

We each of us have to give our answer in a particular context and setting, and with our individual temperament, background and history. And our history is caught up with the history of others; indeed, it is caught up with history.

Most of you will know that the history of the Community of St John the Divine has made a not insignificant contribution to the whole history of nursing.

Most often, lately, in the Church, the discussion of gender and sex

150

roles has been related to ordination to the priesthood. But it's worth reminding ourselves, here and now, the important part that nursing has played in the emancipation of women. That history is also fairly painful: with, for instance, conflicts between nurses on the one side and doctors and administrators on the other. *The Lancet* of 1880 carried a statement: 'Nursing is not a craft: still less can it be regarded as a profession.' Brian Abel-Smith, commenting on nursing at that time, has written: 'Many of the new nurses were of a higher social class than the doctors working in the same hospitals . . . and the doctors feared that these educated women would undermine their authority.' The problems of authority, class and gender, have all played their part in the relatively recent history of nursing, which is not least why it was important that the Christian religious orders should have closely related to nursing. If, in 1850, Jesus had said to someone, 'Mary', her response would not have enabled her to be the kind of nurse, the kind of midwife, the kind of Sister, which, later, the Community of St John the Divine has enabled the Sisters to be. Sarah Gamp, and other literary examples of drunken and illiterate nurses remind us of some important changes that have occurred in the history of nursing!

Quite a lot is owed, of course, to pioneers, to leaders, like Florence Nightingale. But the trouble with such people as the Lady with the Lamp is that their light tends to put in shadow the large number of people who are their accomplices in the reforms with which they are concerned. What is needed is what will evoke the best from each one of us: will bring to light our identity and true vocation.

So that the structures of support for each of us in our vocation are of huge importance, especially at a time of change like this. Sometimes that structure will take the form of an actual community, like the Community of St John the Divine. Sometimes the support is simply the local church, or a marriage, or a partnership, or some special support group. We are all looking forward in faith and hope to the Community at St Katharine's. We all know something of CARA, and the London Lighthouse, which are structures of care and support appropriate to our time, called forth by our particular bit of history: at a time when AIDS has demanded a special response of care and support. At all events, it is safe to say that none of us can discover by ourselves, our response, our identity, when the Lord calls us by name.

I said that each of us has to give our vocational response in a particular context and setting, and I suggested that it is caught up in a particular history. A house like 308 Kennington Lane, St Peter's House, reminds us we are also caught up in a particular locality: a particular geography.

I was reading recently what Charles Booth, the Victorian social scientist and ship owner, in his *Life and Labour in London*, had to say about this particular locality and its church at the turn of the century, July 1899. You may like to hear what he wrote:

The vicar of St. Peter's [it says] is emphatic on the need of the most definite doctrines and observances and on the futility of even moderate High Church lines. At this church nothing in the teaching is 'watered down'. The doctrinal training begins with the schools, and it is hoped, that the impress made may remain. It is an individualistic system. Every child who attends the day school learns thoroughly the doctrines which are regarded as of such vital importance; and the fact that no child is ever withdrawn from this teaching raises a hope (not I think likely to be realized) that through the children the parents also may be reached.

On Sunday those who attend the Sunday school are 'swept into church' for a celebration, and so brought to 'worship God in the only way they can understand'. Once a month there is a 'pomp with banners etc.'. Beyond this 'formalism' very great stress is laid on the essential importance of confession. The work employs four clergy and ten Sisters. Every effort is made to hold as well as to teach, and great hopes are entertained for the future, but as regards adults and the present, the success is very limited.

At the principal service, the Choral Mass, there may be perhaps one hundred women and fifty men. The numbers at evensong are rather greater. Those who come appear to be middle-and lower-middle-class people. The congregation is, however, said to be entirely parochial. The church has considerable architectural beauty, but lacks decoration, and there is nothing attractive in the music. Almost all who attend are communicants, and many, it is said, come to the early celebrations but not again. This small congregation of middle-class communicants is the result of many years of devoted work by the present incumbent's predecessor.

I am myself very thankful for these last years in which the Sisters have occupied what was the Vicarage of St Peter's, and Christian Action has been below stairs. We have very greatly valued their friendship and hospitality—and I have particularly appreciated being able to celebrate the Holy Communion with and for the Sisters and those in the House most Thursdays. It was G. K. Chesterton who said: 'For anything to be real it must be local.'

It has been good in these last years to be in this locality: part of it. I doubt whether any of us have done much for it, but we've received a lot from it. I'm very glad that, thanks to the Church here, Christian Action is going to be able to remain within this locality; and one of our prayers for the Royal Foundation of St Katharine which the sisters are joining, is that it will be *real* in and to its surrounding locality in Stepney.

When I was a child, we had a large framed sepia print in our sitting-room—which was the room we hardly ever went in. It was kept for Sundays, for guests, and for the piano. The print was called 'The Sister of Mercy'. There was a fraught-looking mother with a small child in her arms. They were within the home, looking out. The front door was open, and at the door stood a Sister of Mercy. She was tall and seraphic. I can remember my mother one day pointing to the little child in his mother's arms and saying to me—then in *her* arms: 'There's a little child—like you.' You will not be surprised to hear that child was also seraphic. But I discovered early on that Eric was not seraphic. Yet for quite a long while I lived under the illusion that all Sisters of Mercy—all Sisters of all religious communities—were seraphic: long after I'd begun to stay with Communities of Sisters at, say, St David's or West Malling. I now know differently. I now know that *sometimes* Sisters are seraphic!

And now I know that each one of us, as we come to know our identity, has a tough time. I always reckon that I've learnt more about myself in my last five years than in all the previous years put together; but that suggests that in my first sixty-two years people had to put up with quite a lot: And I reckon that's true for most of us!

Most of us, as we learn to answer what is involved in responding with our 'Rabboni' when Jesus calls us by our name, have quite a tough time.

Recently, a book has been published called *Ignatius of Loyola: the psychology of a saint*. It's by Dr W. W. Meissner. You can either call him Dr Meissner or Father Meissner. He's a Jesuit of very considerable psychoanalytical experience and skill.

The reviewer in *The Tablet* said the average reader would need to have a warning label attached to the book: 'Caution: This book may challenge your previous understanding of holiness in general and of St Ignatius in particular.' But he adds 'This book is a labour of love, and a significant contribution to the soldier-saint who founded the Society of Jesus.' And he ends his review with these two paragraphs:

> As a spiritual theologian, I found myself at times murmuring: 'There may be more things in heaven and earth, doctor, than are dreamt of in your psychology.' I like to describe saints as superconductors of divine love, who offer so little resistance to God that he is able to fill their hearts to overflowing with his presence, power, and love. Through the hands and hearts of saints God reaches out to help the poor and hungry, the confused and hopeless. A saint has so intimate a communion with God at the deepest level of the soul as to be able to walk and work with him in a way that dazzles our eyes, accustomed as we are to the ordinary. Nothing is impossible to divine love.
>
> This book was the most demanding I read last year, the five-hundredth anniversary of Ignatius' birth. It was also the most rewarding, perhaps because I have been reading Meissner for thirty years. As I have already indicated, this partial portrait does not detract from the sanctity or spirituality of Ignatius; rather, as an inquiry, it adds new lustre to God's handiwork. It reveals Ignatius as a truly marvellous example of divine grace elevating and perfecting frail human nature. I think St Ignatius himself is viewing it with bemused wonderment, though possibly with an enigmatic smile.

> Jesus saith unto him, Ignatius.
> He turned himself and said unto him, Rabboni; which is to say, Master.

When we turn ourselves to answer with our 'Rabboni', the turning, the conversion, may take a long while—as I've already suggested. It will involve being willing to go on learning and receiving from others, in various ways: psychological, spiritual, intellectual, with all that we are as persons, and in various situations, historical and geographical. Here and now it is perhaps worth reflecting that the Sister who stood outside the door, in the sepia print in our sitting-room, would now be standing in a very different world, wherever she stands—Stepney, Vauxhall, the Dagenham of my childhood or Birmingham. Romantic dress may be appropriate for the Sisters of today on ceremonial occasions—as, indeed, it is for the Yeomen of the Guard; but the true symbols of our dedication and commitment today need to speak of the rigour with which we are responding to God's call to be and to do—amidst the realities of his world.

In my beginning is my end: that fragment of dialogue still lies at the very heart of every Christian vocation and is the most important dialogue in the life of us all.

Jesus saith unto her, Mary.
She turned herself, and saith unto him, Rabboni; which is to say, Master.

✣ 30
THE CITY NEW YEAR SERVICE

St Michael's Cornhill; 12 January 1993

'And having done all, to stand.'

Ephesians 6.14

The invitation to preach the sermon at this City New Year Service, here in St Michael's, has stirred all sorts of memories in me, which I have unashamedly allowed to shape what I have to say to you today.

I started work, here in the City, as a boy of fourteen, over fifty years ago, in the autumn of 1939, just after the outbreak of the Second World War. I worked for a few months as an office boy at a Norwegian shipping firm in Mark Lane. I can still remember the name of one of the ship's captains, Einar Tvedt, whom it was my job to take to the Customs and to Adelaide House on London Bridge. But the invasion of Norway, in April 1940, brought all that to an abrupt end, and I started work at a firm which owned riverside wharves, by London Bridge and across Southwark Bridge. But alas, after only five more months, the wharves this side of the river—Commercial Wharf and Old Swan Wharf—were destroyed by fire, the first night of the blitz, in September 1940. I can remember standing amid the hoses, the morning after that night of destruction, and seeing the flames leaping high. I sometimes think I can still smell the burning embers of those wharves.

But already, in that first traumatic year in the City, I learned to love and value the City churches. I came here often to St Michael's, to listen to Dr Harold Darke, who had been organist here for a quarter of a century—since 1916. As a fledgling organist myself, learning the organ, over the bridge at Southwark Cathedral, I had been learning also, when so much was being destroyed, the indestructibility of beauty—not least the beauty of Bach—from people like Harold Darke. His weekly organ recitals here were a source of spiritual strength in those dark days. It was here that I first heard Bach's *St John Passion* sung by the St Michael's Singers.

155

Let me add that, in 1940, I bought, at Alfred Wilson's bookshop in Gracechurch Street, the second of T. S. Eliot's *Four Quartets, East Coker*, which first appeared that very September. I doubt whether at fifteen, as a boy who had not long left school, in Dagenham, I greatly understood that poem with my *intellect*, but I had already learnt the importance of understanding things at a level deeper than the intellect.

I read, that September—as I say, at fifteen, undoubtedly hurt by the blitz, not physically but mentally—I read, in that first edition of *East Coker*, which I still proudly possess:

> In order to arrive at what you do not know
> > You must go by a way which is the way of ignorance.
> In order to possess what you do not possess
> > You must go by the way of dispossession.
> In order to arrive at what you are not
> > You must go through the way in which you are not.
> And what you do not know is the only thing you know
> And what you own is what you do not own
> And where you are is where you are not.

There were, of course, many City churches destroyed or severely damaged in 1940 and 1941, but those that carried on ministered marvellously at that terrible time. Often, the Archbishop of Canterbury himself, William Temple, would preach, here in the City. He was Archbishop only from April 1942 to October 1944, and he was only 63 when he died; but his leadership had been remarkable. I heard him preach in St Paul's on the text I have chosen for my sermon today: 'And having done all, to stand'. It was a great text to preach on, when part of St Paul's itself had crashed to the ground; and the rest stood amid a huge wilderness of ruin. That sermon challenged me to think: when *I* had done all, what would *I* really stand for? I heard the Archbishop also preach in St Mary Woolnoth. It was a sermon on the complexity of Christian discipleship and decision-making. I can hear him asking: 'Which is more loving, to take up arms against an enemy, like Nazi Germany, to try to save the lives of thousands in concentration camps, or to keep your powder dry?' Christian decisions, Temple said, are rarely between black and white. In this world they are most often between different shades of grey. Temple in those days showed himself to be a man greater even than his great office.

It was one day in October 1944 that I arrived to begin the day at my wharf office—by then on Bankside on the South Bank of the Thames opposite St Paul's. There was already a queue of horses and carts waiting for deliveries from the wharf. I switched on the eight o'clock news—as I did first thing every day, to get the latest news of the war. The first item of that news—26 October 1944—was the sudden death of the Archbishop. I had to dry my eyes before I could face my wharf foreman. I knew Temple's death was a calamity for the Church.

The last public engagement of William Temple in London had been to stand among the ruins of the bombed City, outside the Mansion House, opposite St Stephen's Walbrook, to preach at a lunch-hour service.

I have no doubt that I learnt from Temple in those days that it was possible even for an archbishop to be, and to remain, a prophet whom no one could silence. In those days the pundits of Threadneedle and Throgmorton Streets presumed that they alone knew the mysteries of the City of London, but Temple—theologian, leader, philosopher, pastor and prophet—was not afraid to take them on.

When the War was over, I forsook the world of the wharf, and, in 1946, went to King's College, in the Strand, to train for ordination. In 1951 I was ordained, in St Paul's Cathedral, which still clearly bore its battle wounds and scars: the choir and the sanctuary were still closed to the public; but I was proud to be ordained in St Paul's.

After four years as a curate in Westminster, I went up to Cambridge, to be Chaplain of Trinity College. Cambridge was a place virtually unknown to me, and at first it seemed a world far removed from London and the City; but, looking back upon those days, I realize now that in some ways Cambridge bound me closer to London. When you are a Chaplain of a college like Trinity, you are Chaplain to a thousand young men who are already at the College, and each year you are there another three hundred or so fresh faces—and often friendships—are added to you. It was nearly two thousand young men that I got to know in Cambridge, between 1955 and 1959, many of whom eventually came to work in London, and many of those to work here in the City. I think of people like John Nott—Sir John, as I must now remember to call him—who became Chairman of Lazard's, and Garry Runciman, now Viscount Runciman, Chairman of the Royal Commission on the Criminal Justice System, who has spent most of his working life in Leadenhall Street—and many others who have reached less dizzy heights.

As the years go by, you get invited into the later lives of former undergraduates, to share in their domestic events: birth, marriage, suffering, bereavement, some sudden collapse of employment, or even some fall from grace. (Trinity men are not wholly immune to the Seven Deadly Sins.) You get to know not only what makes the warp and woof of their individual lives but what builds those lives into the life and power structure of the City. With them, from time to time, you may be called to reflect on the purpose of it all: what should shape and guide life? What is true and false ambition? Where and how any power and influence they have achieved in the City can and should best be exercised—and where it all ends.

My former undergraduates are all beginning now to approach retirement—like me—and Journey's End is beginning to stare us all in the face.

After I left Cambridge, all the jobs I have done in the succeeding years I have judged to *some* extent by how that particular job would enable me to keep in touch with those whom I had got to know in earlier years. I left Cambridge to become vicar of a parish in Camberwell which for nearly a century had been called the 'Trinity College Mission'. It was obviously ideal for keeping in touch with Trinity men. So, too, was a Canonry at Southwark Cathedral, on London Bridge, and so was a Canonry in St Albans—which isn't far from London.

But in all those years one subject has continued to worry me more than any other: the gap between rich and poor. Put more personally: to be brought up and educated in Dagenham, a housing estate then of 130,000 people—many of them Ford's workers—makes you familiar with one side of life. During the War, along the riverside, I got to know, from the inside, the homes and lives of Bermondsey dockers. In my curacy in Westminster there was a huge difference between the north of the parish—service flats for admirals, generals, MPs, civil servants and civil engineers—and the south of the parish: the rehoused slums of Millbank. In Cambridge I was often shocked by the ignorance of the so-called intelligent, educated most often at public schools but most of them abysmally ignorant of how the other half lived. In my parish in Camberwell, homelessness and bad housing was undoubtedly the chief social evil.

After the Brixton Riots of 1981, I decided to write a letter to *The Times*, suggesting the immediate appointment of an Archbishop's Commission on the problem of our inner cities. It was published on 27 May 1981, and I sent a copy to the Archbishop of Canterbury, Robert Runcie. He and I had been close friends ever since we worked together in Cambridge, and he had made me his Canon Missioner when he was Bishop of St Albans. As a result, I found myself arguing my case before all the inner-city bishops of the land, and by June 1983 the Archbishop's Commission was set up: a broad-based representative commission.

As a Commission, we visited thirty-two towns and cities outside London and nine areas of London. After two years' work, our Report *Faith in the City* made thirty-eight recommendations to the Church and twenty-three to the nation. Perhaps the most significant two sentences were: first: 'It is our considered view that the nation is confronted by a grave and fundamental injustice in the UPA's. The facts are officially recognized but the situation continues to deteriorate and requires urgent action. No adequate response is being made by government, nation or church.' Second: 'Somewhere along the road which we have travelled in the past two years, each of us has faced a personal challenge to our lives and life-styles: a call to change our thinking and action in such a way as to help us to stand more closely alongside the risen Christ with those who are poor and powerless. We have found faith in the city.'

It was of huge significance that the Report was unanimous.

The Financial Times said of the Report: 'These are not revolutionary proposals from a Church of militants, but sober suggestions mainly within the Government's own terms of reference. They deserve a thoughtful hearing.'

Many in the City, I am glad to say, did give the Report a thoughtful hearing. A group of what I will call top City men, met regularly under the chairmanship of the then Dean of St Paul's, first in the Chapter House of St Paul's, and then in the cinema below *The Financial Times*—by the kindness of *The Financial Times*—to thrash out their response.

It is now seven years since that Report was published—seven lean years, even if the Church Urban Fund, set up as a result of the Report, has achieved its target of raising £18 million. Over two hundred local projects have been funded.

But . . . and it is a huge 'but'. But I have no doubt that whatever Church and State have done, that 'grave and fundamental injustice in the UPA's' remains; indeed, the situation *continues* to deteriorate. I believe it is true to say that in the inner city, in almost every major respect, the situation is worse than it was. The nation—and the City—have, by and large, failed to confront the fundamental injustice.

*   *   *

'And having done all, to stand'.

I have felt it right to be autobiographical today in this City Sermon. I am very thankful for my last fifty years that began here in the City. I can myself do little *more*—but no *less*—than, having done what I have been able to do, to *stand*; and to continue to challenge people to *respond* to the challenge to remove the grave and fundamental injustice of our inner cities and UPAs which still confronts us.

If anyone wants to respond to the challenge of that 'fundamental injustice' there are a thousand ways of doing so—if anyone *wants* to. For instance, there is a marvellous organization called *Church Action on Poverty*, to which they can give their fullest support. *Business in the Community* has attempted and has made a significant response. But it is the *will*, above all, that is needed: the will to respond to the challenge, and to remove the 'grave and fundamental injustice of our inner cities'.

'And having done all, to *stand*.'

31
WHERE SHALL WISDOM BE FOUND?

Gray's Inn Chapel; 24 January 1993

'Where shall wisdom be found?'
Job 28.12

Each year we gather here in chapel, in the season of Epiphany, to celebrate the journey of the Wise Men, mythical as it may be; to acknowledge, nevertheless, that the symbol has something significant, even sacred, to say to each one of us about our own journey. No time of the year, and no place, surely, could be more appropriate to welcome a new Treasurer to the highest office of this Inn; for institutions as well as individuals have a life of their own and are on a journey. We are all conscious this year that we meet also in the shadow of the death of Edmund Davies, erstwhile Treasurer and Dean of Chapel of the Inn, one of the best-beloved members of our Society and undeniably one of the wisest of men. On such a morning it seemed to me appropriate that we should reflect together on Job's heartfelt question and cry: 'Where shall wisdom be found?'

If I had my way, I would not be preaching to you on the subject but presiding over a kind of *Question Time*, because I would much like to hear what every one of you has to say about where in your judgement wisdom shall be found. But it was you who in your wisdom—question mark!—appointed me to be your Preacher; and I have many reasons to be grateful—not least that Lord Edmund-Davies was the first of the three Deans of Chapel under whom I have been privileged to serve.

I haven't as yet many biographies or autobiographies of judges on my shelves, but one I have, which I often take down and dip into for five minutes: Montgomery Hyde's biography of Norman Birkett, Lord Birkett of Ulverston, as he became. There is no more fascinating passage in that biography than the account of his television interview with John Freeman, in 1959, in the first of his series of interviews entitled *Face to Face*. One of the central passages of that interview is this:

'What sort of upbringing did you have in childhood? I mean, were your family puritanical and stern?'

'Well, my father and mother, they were Wesleyan Methodists,' Birkett answered, 'and I suppose one would say they were very, very devoted people. I shall always be grateful for my home life and for the chapel life to which they led me. My knowledge of the Authorized Version and the hymns of Wesley and Watts are certainly some of my very greatest possessions, and at the most formative period of my life I shall never cease to be grateful for the training I had in religious things.'

'Do you still hold these beliefs yourself?'

'No. You know, as one grows older one rather grows out of certain ideas, and, although I have my own very strong views about the conduct of life and the qualities which are necessary for the conduct of life, the great doctrinal things rather perplex me and trouble me.'

Mr Freeman now posed a most pertinent question:

'Would you in fact describe yourself as a Christian, or not?'

Birkett paused for a moment or two before replying. 'I would call myself a Christian,' he said, 'but, of course, as it was once said, you've got to define your terms. If you mean, do I believe in what are called *Christian* qualities, I most certainly do.'

'But not perhaps in the Thirty-Nine Articles?'

'I sometimes would like to say that I called myself a Christian agnostic,' said Birkett to this question, 'but I don't know whether that term is permissible.'

Well, to my mind it *is* permissible to use such a term; indeed, it may itself be a sign of wisdom; and I have little doubt, after hearing that answer and reading that biography, that Lord Birkett was a wise man: a wise man whose life had involved a spiritual journey.

What convinces me of that? His self-knowledge; the fact that as a Lancastrian, from one of the least accessible parts of Lancashire—Furness—he was drawn to the Lakeland poets and to the Lakes themselves, where he could take time to pause and reflect. As William Blake succinctly said: 'Great things are done when men and mountains meet, That are not done by jostling in the street.'

Birkett loved his books; he was humane; he was a liberal in politics—with a small 'l'; he was unassuming; he was considerate.

There's an important chapter in his biography entitled 'Justice at Nuremberg'. It is an engrossing chapter for many reasons. There are a good many quotations from Birkett's diary:

4 December 1945: Shawcross made a good opening speech at the trial. He came to dinner at night. I think Shawcross is marked out for high distinction.

7 December: Griffith-Jones and Elwyn Jones were good. Biddle said that Elwyn Jones was always relevant and lucid, and was of great assistance to the Tribunal. He said to me that it was the best presentation we have yet heard.

The Master Race in the dock [Birkett wrote] seems singularly like the dregs of humanity.

Birkett reflected on the evil manifested in Nazism, but he saw that evil first in the abrogation of the rule of law: that led, in his judgement, to the advent of the secret police and the concentration camp and the reign of fear and terror. Birkett did not isolate evil in the Nazi prisoners who sat in front of him. He saw it as something which permeated a generation like a bacillus or like some poison gas that gradually filled every nook and cranny.

It is often part of the unwisdom of liberals to ignore the existence of evil, and its extent, its power and reality. Birkett was not that kind of liberal. If he was a wise man, one of the marks of his wisdom was that he took seriously the mystery of iniquity.

I have admitted that I haven't many biographies of judges on my shelves. They are, understandably, stocked rather more with the biographies of bishops. I do not want to mention by name the living; but I am aware that some bishops are more shrewd than wise. Some are too conscious of what the papers say—not least, about *them*. Some have the kind of wisdom which results only in caution, and lacks the courage that needs to complement that wisdom. Some have love, but love without wisdom, without judgement. All their geese are swans. Ecclesiastics—of different forms of churchmanship—have often a pious wisdom, a rather enclosed wisdom, a wisdom which, for instance, is always quoting scripture as though the Bible could be treated like a rule-book for every decision in the world. I myself prefer the wisdom of Birkett's Christian agnostic.

My hero—some of you will know—is Bishop John Robinson. He was a brilliant philosopher, a gifted Classical scholar, an outstanding New Testament theologian. He knew a great deal about the other major religions. He was loving—to a fault. He was as loyal a friend as one could ever hope to have. But the word 'wise' does not immediately come to my mind when I think of him. Perhaps he was too impetuous on too many occasions to be thought wise. He lacked that caution with which I have already suggested many of his fellow members of the episcopate were all too liberally endowed. John had more intellectual and moral courage than wisdom.

Yet there was one facet of wisdom which John Robinson displayed which I think is important. If he was a Christian agnostic—and he would have been happy to have that title applied to a good many areas of his thought—he was not agnostic in one aspect of his life, and he wrote of it best, in my judgement, in the prologue to his book *Exploration into God*.

All my deepest concerns both in thought and action [John wrote]—and I cannot separate the theological, the pastoral and the political—find their centre in a single continuing quest. This is to give expression, embodiment, to the overmastering, yet elusive, conviction of the 'Thou' at the heart of everything. It is a quest for the form of the personal as the ultimate reality in life, as the deepest truth about all one's relationships and commitments. How can one give shape to the conviction that the personal is the controlling category for the interpretation of everything, both conceptually and in action? That it *is* this is one of those basic acts of trust which it is impossible to say whether it comes from one's Christian commitment or whether Christianity authenticates itself because it provides its definition and vindication. At any rate it is, as near as I can determine it, my central concern, that which chiefly decides what rings a bell, what I respond to as meaningful, significant, stimulating . . .

And I think the phrase 'respond to' is the key. What I have in mind is that which makes one say, 'Yes, that's true, that's real—for me.' There are so many things one could have thought up or even expressed, but when one hears them or sees them one says 'Yes'. There is the sense that what is most deeply real is there before one: one is simply catching up on it, entering into it. Pascal's remark has always haunted me: 'Thou wouldst not be seeking me if thou hadst not already found me' . . . life is response—and hence responsibility—to something that encounters one, as it seems, with the claim of a 'Thou'. This is the mystery that lies at its heart.

John Robinson's faith in the 'personal', in the 'Thou' at the heart of everything, provided him with a spiritual security from which he could launch out into the deep, questioning the unquestioned in a way which was the envy of some but the alarm of others. To some it was just the spiritual wisdom which they desperately needed to hear. And it was the wisdom which John himself needed to have and to hold in his last weeks and months when he learned that he had cancer of the pancreas.

Talking of John Robinson has rather naturally brought me to the subject of the 'End of the journey'.

Wisdom and concern for truth and for beauty—and for the mystery of iniquity; yes, but part of wisdom is to know how to face the end of the journey.

> Journey's end in Lover's Meeting
> Every Wise Man's son doth know.

At the moment I am having to attend or assist at five memorial services in the space of ten days, two of them of bishops: both close friends. The good memorial service is as good a service to attend as any I know because *Memento mori* lies at the heart of a good deal of wisdom.

Oliver Tomkins, latterly Bishop of Bristol—a lovely man—had set at the end of his Memorial Service sheet last Thursday four lines from his favourite John Donne sonnet:

> Batter my heart, three person'd God; for, you
> As yet but knocke, breathe, shine, and seeke to mend;
> That I may rise, and stand, o'erthrow mee, and bend
> Your force, to breake, blowe, burn, and make me new.

That's quite a wise prayer, surely, to place at the end of a memorial service.

Frank Woods, my predecessor as Chaplain of Trinity 1933-1936, Arch-bishop of Melbourne from 1957 to 1977, another beautiful man in so many ways, asked that the last prayer of his memorial service—at St Paul's Cathedral last Friday—should be:

> We beseech thee, O God, the God of truth,
> That what we know not of things we ought to know
> Thou wilt teach us.
>
> That what we know of truth Thou wilt keep us therein.
>
> That what we are mistaken in, as men must be,
>   Thou wilt correct.
>
> That at whatsoever truths we stumble,
>   Thou wilt yet establish us.
>
> And from all things that are false
> And from all knowledge that would be hurtful,
> Thou wilt evermore deliver us.

That too, is, surely, a prayer for wisdom. It has the humility of the wise man about it; and Frank Woods was a wise and good—even great—Archbishop of Melbourne: a wise human being.

'Where shall wisdom be found?' In some ways it is a by-product. It arrives when you're not looking for it, when your goal is some other thing—certainly when you're looking away from yourself—at 'yonder shining light': at the beacon of the life and love of Jesus; at the City set on a hill; at the twin lamps of truth and beauty.

The prayer I shall want at my funeral is not a direct prayer for wisdom—it will be all but too late to pray for wisdom then. But it is my favourite prayer now, and it is to the 'fountain of all wisdom':

> Almighty God, the fountain of all wisdom, who knowest our necessities before we ask, and our ignorance in asking: We beseech thee to have compassion upon our infirmities; and those things, which for our unworthiness we dare not, and for our blindness we cannot ask, vouchsafe to give us for the worthiness of thy Son Jesus Christ our Lord. Amen.

✺ 32
REJOICE IN
THE LORD ALWAY

Gray's Inn Chapel;
7 February 1993

> The Epistle of Paul to the Philippians: chapter 4, verse 4:
> 'Rejoice in the Lord alway: and again I say, Rejoice. Let your
> moderation be known unto all men.'

The 'Bell' anthem, so-called, by Purcell, which sets those sentences to
music, is one of the loveliest in all English church music. Purcell was
astonishingly gifted: composing songs at the age of eight, a chorister of
the Chapel Royal, then organist of Westminster Abbey, he composed
anthems for the coronation of James II in 1685 and for the funeral of
Queen Mary in 1694. Alas, he himself died, at only thirty-six years of
age, in 1695.

But I have to say, sadly, that familiar passage of scripture—'Rejoice in
the Lord alway: and again I say, Rejoice. Let your moderation be known
unto all men ... ': that much loved passage of scripture is probably a
rather misleading translation which has been misleading us for 600 years
since William Tyndale.

The word which is translated 'Rejoice!' is nothing more nor less than
the word which is usually used in leave-taking. Χαιρετε means literally
'Fare-thee-well', or 'Good-bye'—'God be with you'.

And immediately that verse is over and done, we come upon the
second puzzling piece of translation: 'Let your *moderation* be known
unto all men.'

Whatever does that mean?

Well, it certainly has nothing to do with wine or women: 'Abstinence is
easier than *moderation*' ... 'The Bishop's wife is *moderately* chaste.'

The Greek word translated 'moderation' is a wonderful word: ἐπιεικης
it's wonderful, but not easy to translate with precision. 'Kindliness' is
near to it, but not quite robust and vigorous enough. It's closer to
'magnanimity': magnanimity which includes courtesy, kindness, con-
sideration, caring, forbearance, thoughtfulness.

Paul is saying: 'Everyone should recognize this quality of life among
you, among Christian believers, even though they may hate you for it,

and rage against the gospel that creates and sustains this spirit among you. Everyone should know you for your ἐπιεικης.' 'Let your *magnanimity* be known to all.'

I think our word 'tolerance' has a good deal of the flavour of the word, though that, too, can easily be weakened.

Some of you may know a rather fine book that's thirty years old now called *The Spirit of Tolerance*. It's edited and arranged by Katharine Moore; and Victor Gollancz, who published it, wrote a memorable preface to it, in the course of which he said:

> The spirit of tolerance is the spirit of respect for personality, the social value of values . . . In spite of *accidental* differences, and very wide ones, in spiritual development—the difference, for instance, between St Francis at one end of the scale and Herr Hitler at the other; in spite, too, of greatly varying levels of capacity and intellect: respect for personality recognizes the *essential* spiritual equality of all human beings, including ourselves, and perhaps every living thing . . .

Gollancz continues:

> I remember reading as a boy something written by Oscar Wilde—I think it is in *De Profundis*—which made a profound impression on me. Wilde had been tried and sentenced: and as he left the dock for prison, when everywhere around him was an atmosphere of hostility and contempt, a bearded stranger, whom he was never to see again (I believe it was Bernard Shaw), raised his hat in salutation. He did this, I like to think, not because he sympathized with Wilde's practices, nor because he disapproved of the sentence, but as a simple act of respect to a fellow human being in torment.
>
> Only one person on earth, so far as the records go, has shown a respect for personality utter and without reservation. Christ consorted with harlots and sinners neither in condescension nor without recognition of their sins: he thought of them quite naturally, quite as a matter of course, one might say, as fellow human beings, and therefore, to him as a man, essentially and beyond their sins his equals. 'Why callest thou me good?' he asked: 'There is none good but one, that is, God.' And he preached respect for personality in words of a beauty and conviction that never have been and never can be surpassed . . .

Later in his preface, Gollancz, who was, of course, a Jew, asks:

> But *why* should we respect personality—not this or that personality, but personality as such? What is the sanction? There are many answers: one, and an obvious one, would be given by pantheism, and others by various systems of eastern wisdom and western philosophy. But there are two answers, I think, that come naturally to people trained in the European tradition; and they are not, as will be seen, mutually exclusive. They may be loosely called the religious and the non-religious. In western religious thought, respect for personality is demanded by three interrelated religious doctrines: that God created all men in His own image, that God is the Father of all men, and that all men are therefore brothers. Both before and after the birth of Christianity,

Judaism insisted on this Fatherhood of God and brotherhood of men. But it was Christ who was to experience the universality of God's Fatherhood with a directness and immediacy never approached before or since. Or if that is too bold a claim, for no one can know what is in other men's hearts, it is at least true to say that he alone has had the power to communicate some measure of this experience to countless others. 'Are not two sparrows,' he asked, 'sold for a farthing? and one of them shall not fall on the ground without your Father . . .' In the injunction to love our enemies respect for personality finds its ultimate expression. And we are immediately told *why* we should love our enemies: 'That ye may be the children of your Father which is in heaven: for he maketh his sun to rise on the evil and on the good, and sendeth rain on the just and on the unjust.' These few words, so rebuking to the self-righteous, are the greatest of all Christ's gifts—the greatest of all the gifts, I would dare to say, of Hebrew prophecy—to the religion of the western world.

I have reminded you that Victor Gollancz was a Jew, and few more than he did more to remind us in Britain of the realities of places like Auschwitz and of the Holocaust. So it is no 'magnanimity-in-*moderation*' that Gollancz has in mind. And I believe that all that Gollancz has included and encompassed within the 'spirit of tolerance', Paul has in mind when he says: 'Let your magnanimity—your vigorous tolerance— your ἐπιεικης be known unto all.' It won't do simply to say 'Rejoice in the Lord alway . . .' when faced with the Holocaust and with all the evils of 'ethnic cleansing'; but a costly magnanimity, that may well be required of each one of us at some stage.

When I was Chaplain of Trinity, in the late fifties, one of the more elderly Fellows was Professor A. V. Hill, a renowned physiologist. He had been awarded a Nobel prize before I was born—way back in 1923. He had done a great deal of pioneer work on nerves and muscles. During the Second World War he was an Independent MP for Cambridge; he also did much for the initiation of radar—and to defend fellow scientists driven out of Germany. He was as humane a man as one could wish to meet, and was always wrestling with the philosophical questions which modern science provokes. The year after I left Trinity, 1960, his book *The Ethical Dilemmas of Science* was published—which we had talked over from time to time at table.

There is a passage in his book which I think also helps to fill out what Paul had in mind:

Tolerance [he wrote] far from being indifferent, depends on the fact of difference: it is a way of meeting difference which has been clearly recognized as such; and we cannot meet difference unless we are sufficiently interested in it to feel its challenge and to wrestle with it . . . Before we ever become capable of tolerance, and before it can ever exist in any true sense, we must be shaken by the recognition that there are profound differences between ourselves and others, and that nobody can be really indifferent to the truths which imbue his whole existence. What we have to fear much more (than these differences) is that pseudo-tolerant attitude that takes neither one's own nor the other man's beliefs seriously enough to battle about them ... tolerance can become the watchword of a philosophy of life which excludes all others under the pretext that they are narrow and intolerant. This, of course, is not tolerance but budding intolerance ... Karl Jaspers makes the point that 'indifference is born ... of the arrogance of one's own truth and is the mildest form of intolerance: secret contempt—let others believe what they like, it doesn't concern me.'

It is the duty of all intelligent people continually to question, not seldom to disbelieve, what they are told ... Scepticism, however, is not a sufficient index, or the sole duty, of an intelligent person: it must be balanced by some genuine enthusiasm. Disbelief alone leads to sterility, it must be examined just as critically as belief, its emotional basis must be sought. Those who disbelieve from ignorance and meanness are as many as those who believe from stupidity. Faith is not necessarily a sign of mental infirmity. Most men are fundamentally good and kind, not a few, in some respects at least, are far-seeing and wise. The problems of life, of medicine, of politics, of international relations, of economics, lack simple solutions not merely because of the stupidity and baseness of mankind. It is safer to have faith without the evidence than to doubt without cause. Criticism is the basis of scientific advance, of social and ethical progress: it is also the cornerstone of intellectual honesty, of the conservatism which preserves as well as creates. To be uncritical, particularly of oneself and one's ideas and motives, is the first long step towards dishonesty. Much criticism, however, is mean, mean indeed in its ancient sense of wicked. It is mean to pretend that politics is necessarily a 'dirty game': to imagine that piety is always a pretence. It is mean to sneer at those who carry a heavier burden than one's own. Let us laugh at, and—by good fortune—with, those from whom we differ: let us recognize, however, that they are probably neither criminal nor insane, that we also may be wrong.

You can see why I had great respect for Archibald Vivian Hill—who died in 1977.

There is, I think, a complementary passage to what he wrote in Dr David Stafford-Clark's Robert Waley Cohen Memorial Lecture, delivered to the Council of Christians and Jews in 1960 when Stafford-Clark was Professor of Psychological Medicine at Guy's Hospital. He called his lecture 'The Psychology of Persecution and Prejudice':

We must learn to love others as ourselves [he said]. Unless we can do this; we not only doom others but are doomed ourselves. But if we can do this there is no problem of racial or any other kind of prejudice, which need overwhelm our judgement.

If we can but renounce our innate determination to regard ourselves as unique and of supreme importance, with everything else ultimately going to the wall, then we can tackle this. But unless we are capable of this renunciation of self-centredness, then we cannot tackle it at all. Love and humility are the only answer to this problem and they must be calmly and vigorously maintained in the face of prejudice, in the face of indignation; of segregation, of all arguments, all the answers about what is good and what is sound, and what is practical for society and so forth; because these answers and arguments are based ultimately on fear, hatred, insecurity and the threat of being regarded as just like other men. Humility then and acceptance, are part of love: and love alone can pay the price for the abandonment of prejudice . . . the roots of prejudice are not in the actual fact of difference; or in the supposed superiority or inferiority of one race to another; persecution arises not primarily out of bitter situations, not out of frictions of human proximity or distrust, which varies by distance, but simply out of the will of living man to think more highly of himself and less highly of others than he ought to think. The essential feature is the inescapable self-centredness, separateness, and tragic personal pride of each individual one of us; whereby we do not love others as ourselves.

When I had finished writing what I had to say to you today I was left with a lurking question: 'Are you right entirely to exclude—as you have done—'moderation' from your re-translation of the word St Paul used—ἐπιεικης—replacing it with 'magnanimity'? Isn't moderation often *part* of magnanimity—just as temperance is part of tolerance? And wouldn't the world be a better place today if people were to learn a little *moderation*? Yes, most certainly it would!

But I must make one last point.

Last week, in this 'upper room, furnished and prepared' I preached on the five words of that phrase, and I spoke of what Jesus did in the Upper Room—of, for instance, His washing His disciples' feet. But I did not say that it was in the Upper Room that Jesus was *betrayed*—betrayed to those who crucified Him. What was Jesus' response to that betrayal?

'*Friend*', He said to his betrayer, 'Wherefore art thou come?'

In the anonymous late fourteenth-century mystical treatise, the *Theologia Germanica*, the comment is:

> He said to Judas, when he betrayed Him: 'Friend, wherefore art thou come?' Just as if He had said: 'Thou hatest me, and art mine enemy, yet I love thee and am thy friend.' . . . As though God in human nature were saying: 'I am pure, simple Goodness, and therefore I cannot will or desire or rejoice in, or do or give anything but goodness. If I am to reward thee for thy evil and wickedness, I must do it with goodness, for I am and have nothing else.'

That is Jesus' magnanimity. And Jesus' magnanimity was never silenced—not even on the cross itself. 'Father, forgive them' He said. 'They know not what they do.' But when we hear Jesus crying from the Cross: 'My God, my God, why hast thou forsaken me?' there is very little trace of 'Rejoice in the Lord alway' about His words. *That* is why I am making more than a mere *translator's* point today. I am not simply 'nit-picking'. I am saying that Christ's magnanimity cost Him the cross— and that sometimes it will cost us the same. The cross is not a *moderate* remedy.

Let your magnanimity be known unto all.

Let Christ's magnanimity be known through you to all.

33
THE TRANSFIGURATION OF OUR LORD

St Giles' Camberwell; 7 March 1993

One of the books I most treasure is simply called *Ecstasy*. It was published over thirty years ago, and is sub-titled *A Study of Some Secular and Religious Experience*. In it, the writer Marghanita Laski summarizes the results of asking a large number of people several questions:

> Have you ever experienced a sensation of transcendent ecstasy?
> How would you describe it?
> What do you think has induced it in you?
> How many times in your life have you felt it?
> What is your religion or faith?
> What is your profession?

Now almost everyone Miss Laski asked said that they had had such an experience of transcendent ecstasy, and these experiences were regarded by everyone who had had them as supremely valuable. Miss Laski discusses and analyses the experiences. She finds the way people describe them very significant, but also what she calls 'the triggers' are no less significant—the things which trigger off the experience: natural scenery, sexual love, childbirth, exercise, movement, overtly religious situations, art, music, poetry, and so on. Then Miss Laski has a chapter on what she calls 'anti-triggers'—things that inhibit these experiences, for instance, the presence of other people, noise and so on.

That book of Marghanita Laski's often comes into my mind, when the Gospel for the day is the transfiguration of Jesus. I can almost see the disciples, Peter, James and John, filling in their forms for Marghanita Laski, and describing their experience of transcendent ecstasy. That experience becomes a little less out of the ordinary and a little more manageable if we can classify it with other such experiences.

Similarly, I sometimes imagine what a psychiatrist today would say to the disciples. 'I'm right in thinking that you said you'd been overcome by sleep', he might say, 'and that it was *as you were waking* that you saw the figures you thought were Moses and Elijah. Yes; well that's not at all uncommon with such experiences.'

But, in the end, I know that any attempt to *reduce* the story to what we find manageable, within the bounds of what we recognize today as 'rational', can only be achieved at some cost to the original story.

The story as it is described in Matthew, Mark and Luke, is virtually the same, and clearly comes from the same source; but Luke adds the significant detail that it was 'while he was praying' that Jesus was transfigured.

What is very significant is that the story is not mentioned at all in St John's Gospel, and yet that Gospel might well be called 'the Gospel of the transfiguration', because so often it uses words that seem to have the transfigured Christ very directly in mind. Right at the beginning of the Gospel, for instance, in what we call the Prologue, there are those memorable words: 'The Word was made flesh, and dwelt among us, (and we beheld his glory, the glory as of the only begotten of the Father).' And only a few verses before, there's that clear statement: 'In him was life and the life was the light of men'—like the transfigured Christ; and, in a later chapter there's of course that other great saying of Jesus: 'I am the Light of the World'.

Well, how should we handle this somewhat overwhelming, somewhat baffling story today?

Perhaps the Orthodox Church shows us the best way. There is hardly an Orthodox Church without its own icon of the transfiguration—indeed, there's hardly a home. I have such an icon in my own home—only a cheap reproduction of the icon by the great artist Rublev—but it shows the disciples, on the Mount of Transfiguration, being literally bowled over by the glory they encounter, emanating from the transfigured Christ; and, as you stand and look at that icon, sometimes you too cannot help being bowled over by the glory. And, surely, it's important in our rational age, our utilitarian age, just to stand from time to time and catch a glimpse of the glory of God in the face of the transfigured Christ.

Yet I believe it's also very important to keep on pressing what I will call the 'Marghanita Laski question': What experience of transcendent glory, transcendent ecstasy have *I* had?—and not to allow my own personal answer to that question and my understanding of the gospel record to be too easily separated.

Now I've said virtually all *I* want to say to you this morning—that's to say, all I want to say to you in my own words. But, to end what I have to say, I want to read you a poem: a poem which is called 'The Transfiguration'. It's by the Scottish poet Edwin Muir who was a poet of vision and faith, who was not afraid to explore in a poem his own reaction to the transfiguration of Jesus. I think it's very significant that the story of the transfiguration that we had read this morning should have evoked such a poem from such a poet. Edwin Muir writes his poem as though he was one of the disciples actually present at and witnessing the transfiguration:

> So from the ground we felt that virtue branch
> Through all our veins till we were whole, our wrists
> As fresh and pure as water from a well,
> Our hands made new to handle holy things,
> The source of all our seeing rinsed and cleansed
> Till earth and light and water entering there
> Gave back to us the clear unfallen world.
> We would have thrown our clothes away for lightness,
> But that even they, though sour and travel stained,
> Seemed, like our flesh, made of immortal substance,
> And the soiled flax and wool lay light upon us
> Like friendly wonders, flower and flock entwined
> As in a morning field. Was it a vision?
> Or did we see that day the unseeable
> One glory of the everlasting world
> Perpetually at work, though never seen
> Since Eden locked the gate that's everywhere
> And nowhere? Was the change in us alone,
> And the enormous earth still left forlorn,
> An exile or a prisoner? Yet the world
> We saw that day made this unreal, for all
> Was in its place. The painted animals
> Assembled there in gentle congregations,
> Or sought apart their leafy oratories,
> Or walked in peace, the wild and tame together,
> As if, also for them, the day had come.
> The shepherds' hovels shone, for underneath
> The soot we saw the stone clean at the heart
> As on the starting-day. The refuse heaps
> Were grained with that fine dust that made the world;
> For he had said, 'To the pure all things are pure.'
> And when we went into the town, he with us,
> The lurkers under doorways, murderers,
> With rags tied round their feet for silence, came
> Out of themselves to us and were with us,
> And those who hide within the labyrinth
> Of their own loneliness and greatness came,
> And those entangled in their own devices,
> The silent and the garrulous liars, all
> Stepped out of their own dungeons and were free.
> Reality or vision, this we have seen.
> If it had lasted but another moment
> It might have held for ever! But the world
> Rolled back into its place, and we are here,
> And all that radiant kingdom lies forlorn,
> As if it had never stirred; no human voice
> Is heard among its meadows, but it speaks

To itself alone, alone it flowers and shines
And blossoms for itself, while time runs on.

But he will come again, it's said, though not
Unwanted and unsummoned; for all things,
Beasts of the field, and woods, and rocks, and seas,
And all mankind from end to end of the earth
Will call him with one voice. In our own time,
Some say, or at a time when time is ripe.
Then he will come. Christ the uncrucified,
Christ the discrucified, his death undone,
His agony unmade, his cross dismantled—
Glad to be so—and the tormented wood
Will cure its hurt and grow into a tree
In a green springing corner of young Eden,
And Judas, damned, take his long journey backward
From darkness into light and be a child
Beside his mother's knee, and the betrayal
Be quite undone and never more be done.

34

JUST HOW DO WE REMEMBER THEM?

All Saints West Dulwich; 14 March 1993

'Just how do we remember them?' That was a headline in *The Times* last week. The question referred to two poets whose anniversaries are approaching. The centenary of the birth of one of them, Wilfred Owen, occurs next Thursday, 18 March.

I thought it might just help you to remember him if I were to 're-member' Wilfred Owen in my sermon this morning.

C. Day Lewis wrote of Owen:

> His war poems, a body of work composed between January 1917, when he was first sent to the Western Front, and November 1918, when he was killed, seem to me certainly the finest written by any English poet of the First War and probably the greatest poems about war in our literature.
>
> His fame was posthumous—he had only four poems published in his lifetime. The bulk of his best work was written or finished during a period of intense creative activity, from August 1917 (in one week of October he wrote six poems) to September 1918 . . .
>
> Under conditions so hideous that they might have been expected to maim a poet rather than make him, Owen came into his own. No gradual development brought his work to maturity. It was forced growth, a revolution in his mind which, blasting its way through all the poetic bric-a-brac, enabled him to see his subject clearly—'War, and the pity of War'. The subject made the poet: the poet made poems which radically changed our attitude towards war . . . It is Owen, I believe, whose poetry came home deepest to my own generation, so that we could never again think of war as anything but a vile, if necessary, evil.

Thus C. Day Lewis, gives us, surely, reason enough to remember Wilfred Owen.

Wilfred Edward Salter Owen was born in Oswestry, the son of a railway clerk and his wife. Wilfred was the first of four children. The family moved to Shrewsbury and then to Birkenhead. Wilfred went to the Birkenhead Institute. By the time he left school he was writing verse and dreaming of becoming a poet.

The cost of university made it out of the question for Wilfred. After a period as a pupil teacher he became the unpaid lay assistant to the Vicar of Dunsden, near Reading, in return for tuition for a scholarship. At this time Wilfred was still a Christian believer; indeed, there seemed a possibility that he might in due course get ordained. But the effect of Dunsden was the opposite of what had been anticipated. The abject poverty of the area awakened Owen's social conscience but killed his Christian faith.

In 1913 Owen gave up his work at Dunsden and got a job as an English tutor to two boys in a French Catholic family in Bordeaux.

There's one poem from that period which I love, called 'Maundy Thursday'. It was probably written when Owen had gone with his young charges in Holy Week to the local Catholic church: to the service of Veneration of the Cross:

> Between the brown hands of a server-lad
> The silver cross was offered to be kissed.
> The men came up, lugubrious, but not sad,
> And knelt reluctantly, half-prejudiced.
> (And kissing, kissed the emblem of a creed.)
> Then mourning women knelt; meek mouths they had,
> (And kissed the Body of Christ indeed.)
> Young children came, with eager lips and glad.
> (These kissed a silver doll, immensely bright.)
> Then I, too, knelt before that acolyte.
> Above the crucifix I bent my head:
> The Christ was thin, and cold, and very dead:
> And yet I bowed, yea, kissed—my lips did cling
> (I kissed the warm live hand that held the thing.)

The First World War broke out in August 1914. It was not until September 1915 that Owen returned to England. Next month he joined the Artists' Rifles and next year he was commissioned in the Manchester Regiment. In December 1916 he sailed to France on active service; after only four months he was a casualty, though he was back with his battalion after only a month to be a casualty again after another month. He was returned to England, and in June 1917 sent to Craiglockhart War Hospital, Edinburgh.

It was at Craiglockhart that Owen met a man whose poetry and whose pacifism transformed him: Siegfried Sassoon. Sassoon had been a most successful company commander but in his poems he had uncompromisingly condemned the War. Sassoon gave Owen both the technical criticism and the encouragement as a poet that he needed. It was at Craiglockhart that Owen wrote several of the poems which have become most memorable and which have spoken to our generation not least through Benjamin Britten's *War Requiem*. For instance, his poem: 'At a Calvary near the Ancre':

One ever hangs where shelled roads part.
   In this war He too lost a limb,
But His disciples hide apart;
   And now the Soldiers bear with Him.

Near Golgotha strolls many a priest,
   And in their faces there is pride
That they were flesh-marked by the Beast
   By whom the gentle Christ's denied.

The scribes on all the people shove
   And brawl allegiance to the state,
But they who love the greater love
   Lay down their life; they do not hate.

Though Owen was still estranged from the Church, he loved the old words of the Bible and of the services of the Church and often went to services. It was probably after Craiglockhart, when he was stationed at a barracks in Ripon, that he wrote the poem which so clearly reflects his biblical background: 'The Parable of the Old Man and the Young':

So Abram rose, and clave the wood, and went,
And took the fire with him, and a knife.
And as they sojourned both of them together,
Isaac the first-born spake and said, My Father,
Behold the preparations, fire and iron,
And where the lamb for this burnt-offering?
Then Abram bound the youth with belts and straps,
And builded parapets and trenches there,
And stretchèd forth the knife to slay his son.
When lo! an angel called him out of heaven,
Saying, Lay not thy hand upon the lad,
Neither do anything to him. Behold,
A ram, caught in a thicket by its horns;
Offer the Ram of Pride instead of him.
But the old man would not so, but slew his son,
And half the seed of Europe, one by one.

On 4 July 1918, when Owen was training troops in England and himself preparing to return to the front, he wrote a letter to Osbert Sitwell the prose of which is as barbed and bitter and as powerful as any of Owen's poems:

For 14 hours yesterday I was at work—teaching Christ to lift his cross by numbers, and how to adjust his crown; and not to imagine he thirst till after the last halt. I attended his Supper to see that there were no complaints; and inspected his feet that they should be worthy of the nails. I see to it that he is dumb, and stands at attention before his accusers. With a piece of silver I buy him every day, and with maps I make him familiar with the topography of Golgotha.

Thus the agnostic Owen.

At the end of August 1918 Wilfred returned to France. He was killed in action on 4 November 1918, exactly a week before the Armistice ended the War.

There is, however, a strange postscript to the life of Wilfred Owen.

On Armistice Day 1918 Wilfred's brother Harold was serving on the cruiser *Astraea*—which had been launched the day Wilfred was born. The *Astraea* at that time was lying off the Cape of Good Hope, South Africa. Harold had no idea his brother was dead. But let him describe what happened. [*Here I used the illustration which I had used before, which is printed on page 59.*]

I began what I had to say with *The Times* headline: 'Just how do we remember them?'

I'm not sure it will do simply to look back in remembrance of Wilfred Owen. 'My subject is War, and the Pity of War.' If we take Owen's subject seriously, it has implications for us now, seventy-five years on.

The Times not only contained that headline concerning Wilfred Owen. A few days earlier it published a letter from Cardinal Hume. He wrote:

> Whatever stance individuals may take over the morality of the nuclear deterrent, there must be general agreement on the aim of preventing the spread of nuclear weapons to non-nuclear states. It is clear that the renewal and the extension of the non-proliferation treaty, hopefully leading in due course to a comprehensive test ban treaty, depends crucially on the actions of existing nuclear weapons states. If the United States, Russia and France can accept a moratorium on nuclear testing, why cannot this country? If Britain took this step, other states would be more likely to sign the non-proliferation treaty.

Just how do we remember them? Our subject—as Christians *today*—must still be 'War, and the Pity of War'.

35

POVERTY AND COMPASSION

Centenary Eucharist of the Joint Council for Social Responsibility, Canterbury and Rochester Dioceses

Canterbury Cathedral; 24 April 1993

Honoured as I felt myself to be at receiving the invitation to give the address at this your Centenary Eucharist, I was at first minded to refuse it. My life, you see, began in Essex, and my ministry has been mainly in London, Cambridge, Southwark and St Albans; so what could I say—I asked myself—at a Centenary for Canterbury and Rochester?—especially as only two years ago I addressed some of you, at the Ecumenical conference of the Kent Churches' Social Responsibility Group, on 'Social Responsibility and the Decade of Evangelism'.

And then it occurred to me that in *1893* Southwark was in the Diocese of Rochester, and Randall Davidson was Bishop, therefore, of Southwark and the South Bank of the Thames, living five minutes from where I now live, in Kennington—the Bishop's Palace is now a Day Nursery for children—and I thought: 'Surely someone from *Southwark* should be present at your Centenary: that is to say *our* Centenary; and, if so, why not one of Southwark's aged, retired pensioners—like *me*?' And the more I thought about *1893* the more it had to say about *1993*.

It was, in fact, Arnold Toynbee who said, in 1894: 'It would be well if, in studying the past, we could always bear in mind the problems of the present, and go to that past to seek large views of what is of lasting importance to the human race.'

So the *subject* of my sermon this morning will be 'Poverty and Compassion in *1893*', but the *object* of it will be to provoke you to think about 'Poverty and Compassion in *1993*'.

Of course, poverty had not just been discovered in Britain in *1893*. In

1849, for instance, Henry Mayhew's *London Labour and the London Poor* was published. Mayhew's book was personal, colourful and dramatic; but undoubtedly it contributed to the volume of legislation on poverty and distress that took place in the half century *before* 1893. There's always a relation between law and public opinion.

In 1885 there was the first report of the Royal Commission on the Housing of the Working Classes. Lord Shaftesbury, who had been agitating for sanitary reforms for almost half a century, testified to that Commission how much worse the situation had been.

Compassion had meant legislation—detailed legislation. It needed more than medicine to defeat, for instance, the scourge of cholera in our Victorian cities. It needed better housing, and housing legislation—about windows, for instance. It needed legislation about hours of work, and rates of pay—for women as well as for men; and that needed strikes and Trades Unions. It needed sewers and legislation on sanitation. It needed education and the improvement of diet. But if poverty was *re*discovered in the 1890s the poor themselves did not rediscover it. *They* had never been allowed to forget it. They had had to live with it: day after day, year after year.

Yet in celebrating our centenary, one thing would be wrong: to magnify the role of the Church in 1893 where poverty and compassion were concerned.

Of course, there were the great Christian reformers, like Lord Shaftesbury and Josephine Butler. But the sheer size of the problem meant it was 'all hands on deck': Jews, Christians, atheists, agnostics, Evangelicals, Catholics. Human sympathy was required rather than sectarian sympathy. 'Social questions are the vital questions of today' wrote Beatrice Webb in her diary in 1884. 'They take the place of religion.'

On such a day as this, Rochester certainly will want to remember its famous resident Charles Dickens, and pay tribute to his contribution. 'So long as homes are hovels', Dickens had written in *Sketches by Boz*, 'gin palaces will make up for them in number and splendour.' That was in 1836; but what Dickens wrote in the early Victorian era continued to influence later Victorians.

But nearer our centenary than Dickens, in 1892, there was published something which was to be of huge significance where poverty and compassion were concerned: the first volume of Charles Booth's immense *Life and Labour of the People in London*. Eventually Booth's work reached seventeen volumes of sober and careful analysis. I notice in Randall Davidson's biography that he studied Booth's volumes as soon as they appeared. Before Booth, journalistic screeds such as *The Bitter Cry of Outcast London* had played their part as shrill sirens sounding their alarms where poverty was concerned, but now, through Charles Booth, compassion and care took a new and immensely important form.

Booth was a man of intellect and property, a successful businessman, a Liverpool merchant and shipowner. Reverence and awe were as close as he could get to belief in God. He was a lapsed Unitarian. 'I worship Humanity' he confessed. Humanity was certainly his concern; and the seventeen volumes of the *Life and Labour of the People in London* were the primary way he chose to discharge his debt to humanity.

What Booth did was carefully observe the conditions of a large part of the population of late Victorian England. He formulated slowly his ideas of social science and social investigation. Beatrice Potter, his cousin, recalled as the main lesson she learned from him in the art of social investigation:

> However accurate and comprehensive might be the description of technical detail, however vivid the picture of what was happening at the dock gates or in the sweated workshops, I was always confronted by Charles Booth's sceptical glance and critical questions: 'How many individuals are affected by the conditions you describe; are they increasing or diminishing in number?' 'What proportion do they bear to those working and living under worse or better conditions?' 'Does this so-called sweating system play any considerable part in the industrial organization of the four million inhabitants of London?'

I am not suggesting Charles Booth was the first social scientist, but I am suggesting social science and a good many other subjects—including social work itself—were never the same again after Charles Booth.

What we nowadays call 'case work', which in the past century many a Canterbury and Rochester and Southwark social worker will have practised with care and skill, first appeared as a term in the literature of the Charity Organization Society in the early 1880s. It would be foolish to suggest there was no systematic visiting before then. The venerable practice of the parish clergyman—and, indeed, the squire's wife making her rounds with baskets of food and clothing—goes back centuries. Again we might refer to Dickens: to, for instance, Mrs Pardiggle in *Bleak House*, a notable visitor who proudly said of herself: 'I am a School lady, I am a Visiting lady, I am a Reading lady, I am a distributing lady; I am on the local Linen Box Committee, and many general Committees.' (Mrs Pardiggle may best be remembered as an associate of Mrs Jellyby, the practitioner of 'telescopic philanthropy' who was so devoted to the natives of Borioboola-Gha.)

But what Charles Booth did was not only to observe and record the statistics of poverty, what he called 'the arithmetic of woe', he brought professional standards to visiting. These standards determined not only the way information was collected and recommendations were made but also the way visitors conducted themselves in relation to the poor. An eminent social worker at that time remembered some words which the inhabitants of purgatory in Dante's *Purgatorio* reply to the interrogations of visitors: 'Who are *you* who come asking about our conditions?'

The first volume of Charles Booth's seventeen volumes appeared the year before General William Booth's *In Darkest England*—actually written by W. T. Stead, the editor of the *Pall Mall Gazette* and published in 1890. This Salvation Army publication sold a quarter of a million copies in two years and raised all sorts of questions of what I will call 'procedure'. William Booth of the Salvation Army did not trouble to integrate the good word and the good works: the gospel of salvation with the gospel of sustenance. But there were not a few who found an uneasy tension between the two: 'I must assert in the most unqualified way that it is primarily and mainly for the sake of saving the soul that I seek the salvation of the body' wrote William Booth—or Stead—in *In Darkest England*; but the main thesis of the book was that the soul could not be saved without saving the body. There were critics like T. H. Huxley who said of the Salvation Army: 'Men are to be made sober and industrious, mainly, that, as washed, shorn, and docile sheep, they may be driven into the narrow theological fold which Mr Booth patronizes.' Others accused the Army of the opposite, saying it was essentially a 'philanthropic and humanitarian agency in which religion is entirely subservient to social organization'. Beatrice Webb demurred at the 'religious pressures exerted upon men and women in a weakened condition by those in a position of authority'.

Charles Booth's studies and analyses illuminated the subject of who precisely were the unemployed and soon began to shed light on the subject of unemployment itself. In hardly more than a decade William Beveridge would be writing his book *Unemployment*, with its significant sub-title *A Problem of Industry*. Beveridge saw unemployment as a problem of industry rather than—as was once thought—of the unemployed themselves. The implication for the larger problems of poverty was obvious: poverty, too, was a problem of society rather than of the poor, and thus of society rather than of the individual. Beveridge, by 1904, was sub-warden of Toynbee Hall, in Whitechapel. It's interesting and significant that the *Reverend* Samuel Barnett—who came from a prosperous family of merchants in Bristol and went to Oxford and became Vicar of St Jude's, Whitechapel, became the first Warden of Toynbee Hall in 1884. Toynbee Hall was not only non-denominational but secular, having nothing of the nature of a religious mission. The residents of Toynbee Hall and of other such settlements were neither missionaries bringing faith to the heathen nor almoners bringing money, food and clothes. They were 'settlers', people who came to live alongside the poor—'to learn as much as to teach' Barnett said; 'to receive as much as to give'. The settlers, or residents, were university men, mainly from Oxford. The university element was borne out in the ambitious education programme of the Settlement. Among the most popular lecturers was Charles Booth. Samuel Barnett's favourite philanthropy—which antedated Toynbee Hall—was the Children's Country Holiday Fund, which in 1888 sent more than 17,000 children from the East End to the country for a holiday—a good many, of course, to Kent, not least to its hop-fields. In 1903 R. H. Tawney, the great social historian, then a resident in Toynbee Hall, and contemplating a career in social work, decided to begin that career by working for the Children's Country Holiday Fund. It provided him, he said, with the perfect apprenticeship in social work.

In 1904 William Beveridge delivered a lecture as sub-warden of Toynbee Hall entitled 'The Influence of University Settlements'. Significantly, it was devoted entirely to their influence upon the residents. Beveridge described Toynbee Hall as a school of humanity in Whitechapel.

*   *   *

As I begin to draw my sermon to a close, some of you may want to say: 'But it's not really been a *sermon*, has it? It's been a talk, almost a lecture. There has been no mention of Christ and very little of God or of religion. You haven't even given us a text. And there's been precious little vision for the future.'

Well, I will gladly provide a text, if that will make anyone happy. How about 'We are members one of another'? Or: 'The poor ye have always with you'? or 'When you give alms, do not let your left hand know what your right hand is doing'? But probably those five simple words from the parable of the Good Samaritan are best: 'He had compassion on him.'

Yet perhaps I ought to tell you that not long ago I asked a congregation 'Why did the *Samaritan* cross the road?' There was quite a long silence until someone put their hand up and said: 'Well, because he was a *Christian*'. And I had to say, 'I'm terribly sorry: I think you may have missed the point. The Samaritan crossed the road because he was a *Samaritan*—who nevertheless won *Christ's* approval.'

Now concerning providing you with *vision* for the future, I have been implying that the *heart* of the matter has not changed in a century. It's how the *heart* of the matter is *applied* to our changing scene and circumstances that matters.

Let me put it this way. Last August I spent a month in South Africa. I spent much time in Soweto. I was dismayed to discover that there had been no accurate and comprehensive survey of the people of Soweto. Different authorities gave different figures for how many people there were there—and they differed by literally millions. So when you came to estimate what education or health might cost, you were completely lost. Care and compassion first mean accurate observation and analysis: but *that* probably means living closely alongside those who need our care and compassion. It means the end of every kind of apartheid.

But reading up the *history* of South Africa I was even more dismayed to find that Randall Davidson, by then Archbishop of Canterbury, on 27 July 1909, spoke in the House of Lords in favour of imposing restrictions and limitations on the rights of the black people of South Africa, because, he said, they correspond with those which we impose on our children, and the overwhelming majority of the South African population would for generations to come, he said, be quite unfit to share equal citizenship with whites. Of course, Randall Davidson had never set foot in South Africa, let alone lived alongside black people.

So apartheid had its roots not simply in South Africa but here, and in Christians here, not least in the Archbishop of Canterbury. And it was not only the analysis and observation that had not been done. That had not been done because they had got the *heart* of the matter wrong—as some of us no doubt still have.

I have been suggesting to you that if the poor are to have hope, to have the compassion of Christ in *1993* is as fundamental and important *now* as it was in *1893*—as fundamental, as important, as practical, as demanding of imagination and detailed care, and as demanding of living alongside the poor; and that it is as costly in 1993, and as rare, as it was in 1893.

36

A TRIBUTE TO OLIVER TAMBO

Gray's Inn Chapel;
25 April 1993

Until yesterday evening, when I got back from preaching at Canterbury Cathedral, I had a very different sermon prepared for you today. But the news of the death of Oliver Tambo, in Johannesburg, immediately made me feel I must throw that sermon away, and preach a sermon of tribute to his memory.

A Sunday after Easter seems peculiarly appropriate for such a sermon. Before I started to put pen to paper last evening, I found myself singing to myself:

> The strife is o'er, the battle done

and singing it with Oliver Tambo in mind.

Bishop Trevor Huddleston said to me, some years ago: 'It would be hard to find a more devoted Christian than Oliver.' Trevor had been visiting him in hospital in London in August 1989 when Oliver was at death's door after a severe stroke.

The Chapel of an Inn of Court also seems to me exactly the right place to commemorate such a person: a truly noble lawyer. Nelson Mandela and Oliver Tambo together, in 1952, opened the first all-African law firm to operate in Johannesburg.

So let me tell you something of Oliver's story. For what I know of it already, makes me quite sure that when the history of South Africa comes to be written, he will have a very special place on its role of honour; but his task has taken him far beyond the confines of his own land. He lived in London—perforce—for much of his life.

Oliver Tambo was born in 1917, in the most easterly part of the Cape, at Bizana, Pondoland, in the Transkei, six miles from the border of Natal. He came of a very poor peasant family. His father and his mother were illiterate, and both his father and his mother died when he was very young. He spoke to me of his having 'two other mothers' who enabled him to survive. He was one of seven children, four of whom died.

Oliver Tambo first came in touch with the Church through the local Methodist Mission and the Anglican Holy Cross Mission, Pondoland. He was educated at mission schools and on bursaries; and eventually graduated from Fort Hare University. Later, he taught science, mathematics and music at the prestigious St Peter's School, Rosettenville, Johannesburg. It was there, as a boy, that he first met Trevor Huddleston. I doubt whether Trevor had a closer African friend than Oliver, or Oliver a closer white friend than Trevor; and it was under Trevor's influence that Oliver took the decision to train for the priesthood. He planned to go overseas to train—probably at Mirfield, at the College of the Resurrection, run by Trevor's Community, the Community of the Resurrection. There's little doubt he would have made a wonderful priest. To the end of his days, though he *wasn't* ordained, he was a natural priest and pastor to those around him. Had he been ordained he might well have become a bishop or archbishop—like Desmond Tutu.

But in those days, getting trained as a priest depended very much on the judgement and approval of your bishop, and the Archbishop of Cape Town was Geoffrey Clayton. Oliver, a faithful worshipper at the Church of Christ the King, Sophiatown, had in 1954 just been banned, under the Suppression of Communism Act, for his activities in the ANC, and the Archbishop made it abundantly clear that he would not recommend anyone for ordination who was so committed to the ANC. Politics and priesthood had to be kept separate according to Clayton's theology— that's to say: the brand of politics of which Clayton disapproved. It was the failure of the Church—not least Clayton's failure—to respond to Tambo's banning which caused Trevor Huddleston to explode in an important article he wrote for the *Observer* which he called 'The Church Sleeps On'.

I should perhaps explain that Oliver Tambo and Nelson Mandela were student friends at Fort Hare, then the only black university college in South Africa. With people like Walter Sisulu they were founder members of the Youth League of the ANC. They drew up a radical programme of action that called for civil disobedience, strikes and boycotts. It committed the ANC to a strategy based on mass action in defiance of legalized apartheid.

We're talking, of course, of fifty years ago, and talking of people of immense, almost foolhardy courage and bravery, but intelligent and—in spite of their origins—educated; Tambo was ardent for justice for his people but he was a most uncharacteristic militant. Diana Collins, widow of Canon John Collins, wrote only last year:

> Oliver Tambo is one of the gentlest and sweetest-natured characters I have ever been lucky enough to know. But beneath that gentleness and moderation is a selfless dedication, founded upon a deep Christian faith and belief in the future of his country and his people. It is Oliver who has held the ANC to its non-racial policies.

I have to say that to me, certainly, Oliver Tambo was very clearly a gentleman, a man of peace and a man of God.

It was when in the 1950s the door to ordination was clearly closed to him that he decided to get trained as a lawyer, as the most effective means of working for black rights. He continued to teach until he became an attorney.

On 5 December 1956—the year of Suez and the Hungary uprising—in the early hours of the morning—a favourite time always for the security police—156 men and women of all races were arrested in South Africa and charged with high treason, the penalty for which was death. I do not cease to be proud that Christian Action immediately asked Ambrose Reeves, by then Bishop of Johannesburg, to brief the best available counsel, for the defence of the accused, and guaranteed that Christian Action would raise a fund to pay all legal fees, look after the accused, help rehabilitate them if and when they were released, and meanwhile care for their families and dependants. Bishop Ambrose Reeves responded immediately; he set up a corresponding Treason Trial Fund to raise money from within South Africa and got together a committee to administer the fund.

The accused were a remarkable collection of people from all over South Africa, from the most distinguished to the relatively modest. Chief Luthuli, Nelson Mandela, Walter Sisulu, Oliver Tambo—and many others.

Canon Collins was then head of Christian Action. He approached Gerald Gardiner, later Lord Gardiner, to ask if he would attend the preliminary hearings as an observer. After consultations with Justice and the Bar Council, it was agreed that Gardiner should go, representing both Christian Action and the Bar Council. On his return, early in 1957, Christian Action put on a meeting for him which packed Central Hall, Westminster. Afterwards, the speech was published as a pamphlet. It was a masterpiece of clarity and legal discretion. He drew attention to the manner in which the Nationalist government had openly packed the judiciary with judges who shared its views. 'But,' said Gardiner, 'we might still hope at least some of the appointees would put law before politics'; and over the years, some of them have. In the early days of the hearing, the accused had been put into a large cage of tubular scaffolding and wire netting upon which some wag hung the notice 'Do not feed'. Gerald Gardiner wrote:

> This is the first time in the history of the Church of England that it has openly assisted in the organization of a Fund to defend men and women charged with High Treason in a foreign land, and it is the first time in the history of the Bar Council that they have been represented at a foreign trial . . . The Church and the Bar have always been the last bulwarks for civil liberty . . . .These are matters from which no one who is interested in civil liberties can afford to dissociate himself.

That trial ended in humiliating defeat for the Crown. It was five years after its beginning—March 1961—when Tambo and the others heard the words: 'You are found not guilty and you are discharged. You may go.' But many were only free for a time.

The ANC decided that a new strategy was required: someone must be sent overseas to lead an external mission, to rouse world opinion and to persuade the nations and the United Nations to act against apartheid. They chose Oliver Tambo. Oliver escaped to London and was exiled for thirty years. It was Oliver who persuaded Canon Collins that help must be given without discrimination to all who suffered through active opposition to the policies of apartheid, and the International Defence and Aid Fund, which raised millions of pounds, was the result.

The ANC made its headquarters in Lusaka, but Oliver had to spend a great deal of time touring the capitals of the world, lobbying governments and appearing at the United Nations. He seemed each year to grow in stature and in political wisdom. There was no Mandela around for most of the time, or Sisulu. They were imprisoned on Robben Island. Oliver's task was in some ways simple, but exceedingly demanding: to hold the ANC together; to draw and hold the young revolutionaries within a disciplined force; to build it up as a body—in exile—that could command respect, yet also to keep his own integrity as a Christian.

I have seen a letter from Oliver Tambo to Canon John Collins which I think speaks volumes. Oliver is writing, as I've said, as a devout Christian.

> The best that can be said for Christianity [he wrote] is that over the years—no, over the decades and even centuries—it has gone to sleep, for if it has not, if it is wide awake, then it is for me difficult to escape the feeling that Christianity is fully implicated in the perpetration of so much of the evil that bedevils the world of our day. . . . If the Church was not busy sleeping, it would be up and fighting evil all the time at all places, and would, if need be, follow the Master to the Cross. . . . Instead, those who seek to lead the Church into action and resistance against policies and practices that can only be described as monstrous sin are ostracized, victimized and treated with official displeasure by the authorities of the Church and the Chief Priests of the Christian Faith.

Oliver first looked to Britain and the USA for support. Alas—to their shame—he looked in vain. But Oliver was a forgiving man and never lost his love for Britain; though he was bewildered by Britain's continual branding of the ANC as terrorists without criticizing South Africa's institutionalized violence.

When Oliver returned to South Africa in 1990, ten months after Mandela's release, he received a hero's welcome. Even after his stroke later that year, he did not spare himself.

My first appointment with him, last August, did not take place, because, when I got to his home, there had been a shooting incident at

Fort Hare, the University where Oliver was by then Vice-Chancellor, and he felt he must immediately fly there to be what influence for peace he could be.

When I did see him, a few days later, the effects of his stroke were still very apparent and he was exhausted. One of his arms was fairly useless and it was not easy for him to stand. His speech was slow and somewhat impeded, but he kept our appointment, because he said he so wanted to talk to me about Trevor Huddleston.

> He has been a great influence on my life [Oliver said] particularly through his involvement in our politics, for this gave me the assurance that the Church was with our people, and encouraged me to have faith in the work of the Church. . . . I thank him for his personal friendship and for his role as a priest. It has been a great thing to have Fr Huddleston as a friend because he has also been a father.

Eastertide is an appropriate time for such a person as Oliver Tambo to lay down his burden and take his rest. His life, to my mind, is a sermon in itself. For him, as I've said:

The strife is o'er, the battle done.

🎭 37

PLACE, PEOPLE
AND TIME

*Service for the Archdeaconry of
Southwark: Southwark Cathedral;
5 May 1993*

The Epistle to the Ephesians, chapter 6, verses 13 and 14: 'And
having done all, to stand. Stand therefore . . .'

The invitation to preach to you this evening would not have been given
me, I am fairly sure, had I not been inducted to a living in this Archdeaconry, to wit, St George's, Camberwell, nearly thirty-four years ago:
half my life-time.

It was suggested to me that in my address I might reflect on those
thirty-four years. Well, it's not often one is given official permission to go
on an ego-trip!

I want to begin what I have to say by making a rather simple statement: that in all our lives there are three important God-given
ingredients: place, people and time; and I want to proclaim this evening
that God works through each of these ingredients, though these three
strands are often inseparably intertwined and interwoven.

So first: I invite you in this *place*, from *this Archdeaconry*, to think of
the significance of *place* in your life—in the providence of God.

Let me say that I am particularly glad to be preaching here this
evening: in this Cathedral: in this particular place.

I well remember how in 1939 I first entered this place, and as a boy of
fourteen was accepted as an Organ Scholar by Dr E. T. Cook, the then
Organist and Master of the Music. At first, I was rather in awe of him.
But I owe him a very great deal. And this *place*, for over fifty years, has
meant much to me—*fifty years*: *there* is the significance of *time* as well as
place; and I have little doubt that it was not least the *age* of this place that
gave it much of its significance for me. Shakespeare—and his brother,
Edmund, buried there in the chancel—Chaucer, Lancelot Andrewes,
John Harvard—peopled this place for me. So it was a world of *people*
too—and living people as well as dead. I would not be here this evening if
it were not for the ministry of people like Cuthbert Bardsley, the then

Provost who most influenced me. He heard my confession often in the Harvard Chapel, and helped me towards ordination.

Place—people—and time—are all inextricably interwoven in my memory of and my gratitude for this place.

That God uses buildings, like this Cathedral I have no doubt. Neither have I any doubt that God uses particular places. It was G. K. Chesterton who said: 'For anything to be real it must be local.' The Church has to take *place* seriously if it is to take God seriously. It has to take locality seriously. Indeed, I should like to say that the Church must take 'the local' seriously. My predecessor as Vicar of St George's, Camberwell, Fr Geoffrey Beaumont, was renowned for his ministry to the *locality* literally through 'the local'—through the pubs of the parish. I first met him in The Waterman's Arms, in Waterloo, in the 1940s. It was at that time a pub on what was later to be the site of the Festival Hall. I remember Geoffrey Beaumont, on that particular occasion, seated at a piano, with a pint pot on top of it, surrounded by twenty or thirty Southern Railway porters, male and female. Geoffrey, of blessed memory, had a wonderful way of getting in touch with the people of the locality through 'the local'.

The whole parochial system is, of course, intended—in theory—to take locality seriously. It was meant to secure a significant *building* for every locality, and not only a building but a trained ministry, a priest, for every locality.

But in these last thirty-four years the parochial system has suffered great strain. That strain had begun long before thirty-four years ago when, in the early Victorian era, village communities, like Camberwell, suddenly became hugely populous areas. But then there were large numbers of ordained priests. Even when I was ordained, in 1951, I was part of a large staff of six clergy in Westminster. Priests—male priests—served and penetrated the place, the parish, the locality, to some extent. But now, of course, curates are a rarity, and the ordained ministry has been halved since I was ordained.

Place, people and time.

So far, I have seemed to suggest that locality is confined to where people *live*. But in these last years an important phrase has become current. People often talk now of 'the *plural* society'; by which they mean that locality at one time—at one *time*—was simple. It was simply where people lived. But now there is also the locality where people *work*— maybe miles away. And somehow the Church has to relate to *that* world.

When I was fourteen, as I have said, I first came to Southwark, and came here, to this Cathedral, to this place. But then I was out at work on Bankside, at Emerson Wharf, near to what is now the Provost's Lodgings, between Southwark Bridge and Blackfriars Bridge. From eight till five each day that was my locality. And that world of the wharf, though only 300 yards away, was a world away from this Cathedral. It was the world of dockers, Trades Unions, bosses: of people who had little or no touch with the Church. Many of them at first lived in Bermondsey, Southwark and Camberwell—the bosses, of course, lived in Richmond!—but the ravages of the war forced many to move out to places like Thornton Heath and Lewisham. The world of work was almost as important to them as the world where they lived.

And there were other worlds which were and are important parts of this 'plural' society. The highly influential world of radio soon became the world of television; and there was the world of the *Mirror* and the *Sun*—and *The Times* and *The Telegraph*—which also shaped the thoughts of people.

Place, the place where people lived, was only one world which the Church had to serve and penetrate: the world of work, the world of other institutions—like the Press—and Parliament—the world of leisure, the world of education: all these, somehow, the Church, which at one time only had to relate to the one world of the local village, now had to try to serve and penetrate. It had long been accepted that hospitals and universities were separate worlds and needed priests of their own—chaplains. But it has taken much longer for people to accept that each world of our *plural* society has now to be served and penetrated by the gospel and the Church.

If the *building* which had once upon a time seemed appropriate—like St George's, Camberwell, built in 1824 to seat 1,750—was now in trouble, so too was the shape of the ministry often inappropriate to *plural* locality as we now know it.

But there were *people*—we sometimes call them 'prophets'—like Bishop John Robinson, Bishop of Woolwich 1959 to 1969—to name but one—who would speak powerfully to the Church to suggest ways and means of relating the Church of our time to the world of our time: to the worlds—plural—of our time.

Place—people—and time.

You might have thought from what I have said so far that the only people on my heart and mind are *clergy*! I can assure you that is far from the case.

Twenty-five years ago, in 1968, I was the lowest form of life at that year's Lambeth Conference. I was what's called a Consultant to the Conference, and had to write one of the preparatory essays for the bishops to read. In that essay I made a suggestion which the bishops discussed in their groups during the Conference. My suggestion was treated seriously by most of the overseas bishops. It was not treated seriously by most of the English bishops, for whom at that time there were few problems of finance or indeed of *man*power—and I use that word advisedly. What was the suggestion? Well, I'll repeat it tonight because I believe it still has great relevance to Southwark and to people in the Church in Southwark, and the passing of *time* may have made the suggestion more obviously relevant to people in this place, and this country.

I suggested that each year, at a special meeting of each congregation at, for example, Whitsuntide, the whole congregation should be called together to consider who—if any—should be nominated from that parish as candidates for further training for ministry of one sort and another.

I believed then, and still believe, that if the congregation each year were to ask for one or more of their number, men or women, to receive further training, the persons nominated would be likely to treat the suggestion seriously. And it would be for the Diocesan Committee for Training for Ministry to take such nominations seriously. Such requests for further training would shape a good deal of diocesan training. It would also mean that the further training of *every* member of *every* congregation would have to be *considered*, and considered seriously.

Place—people—and time.

In these last thirty-four years, the world has become a place of much greater mobility. Whole populations have moved, for one reason or another—not least economic. When I went to St George's, Camberwell, in 1959, we were seeing the beginning of the racial transformation of South London. The first baby I baptized in St George's I shall never forget. It was Olayemi Olushala Odanye, from Nigeria. I had to learn the name in order to pronounce it!—and it has got stuck in my memory. Soon the members of our congregation from overseas became very important to us. It was of huge importance at that time to help those who had just arrived from another country to feel at home in the Church of England.

Place—people—and *time*. Perhaps it's just worth saying that it is exactly twenty-five years this month since Enoch Powell made his sad speech forecasting 'rivers of blood'.

The training of people from different racial backgrounds has become of course a very important part of Southwark's training—not least through the Simon of Cyrene Institute. Southwark has pioneered much training since John Robinson did so much to initiate the Southwark Ordination Course and Wychcroft.

I do not intend this evening to engage in great controversy concerning the ordination of women; but if we take the subject of 'place—people—and time' seriously we are bound to take women's ministry as seriously as men's.

St George's, Camberwell—the building I knew—has been closed for many years and a new, more appropriate building has replaced it, and there have, of course, been several vicars since I was there.

> Change and decay in all around I see:
> O thou who changest not, abide with me.

'Abide with me' is a good hymn, and says some important things but I'm not certain it gets the gospel and 'place, people and time' quite right. 'Change and *decay*': yes; that's *part* of the truth. But change in the gospel has also to be related to healing, to redemption, to transfiguration, to resurrection.

St Paul says: 'And having done all to stand. Stand therefore . . .' It is within the unchangeable love of God that Christians find their security. It is in that love that, having done all, we can stand. That *unchangeable* love of God has new forms of His love in store for us. We may meet that unchangeable love in new places, new buildings, new people, renewed understandings of ourselves, the Church, the world—and in new worlds—and in new times.

When I first came to work in Southwark I was, as I said, fourteen; when I came back to Southwark, to Camberwell, I was thirty-four. For fifteen years now I have been doing a bit of moonlighting as what's called 'Preacher' to the members of Gray's Inn, where lawyers are trained—men and women. Let me simply read to you the brief letter I had published recently in *The Times*. I wrote:

> As Preacher to Gray's Inn I have needed to study the recent report on sex equality at the Bar and in the judiciary. The Report reveals that: '60 per cent of women barristers surveyed said they had faced discrimination during their career on grounds of sex.' One is bound to wonder how much that is *said* to be *theological* objection to women priests is in fact comparable with the prejudice experienced by women barristers. But how does one get the Church to ask the penetrating questions the Bar has been asking itself?

Place—people—and time.

There is one subject which I think is inescapable once you take these three subjects seriously: the subject of *change*. I reflect, for instance, that Bishop Mervyn Stockwood will be eighty in three weeks' time, and Bishop John Robinson has, alas, been dead for nearly ten years.

When I came to be a Canon of this Cathedral I was forty-one. When I came back to Southwark again, to work alongside the Archbishop's Commission on Urban Priority Areas on *Faith in the City*, I was fifty-eight.

But so many of the problems of our inner cities are even worse now than they were ten years ago when *Faith in the City* was launched. 'Having done all' we must *go on standing* for justice as the primary form of Love. *Now* I am sixty-eight, and it won't be all that long before I meet the unchangeable love of God in *another* world and in other forms of Life, of resurrection life. But in the unchangeable love of God we can all stand—where else can we stand? Having done all, in that love we can and must stand. Stand therefore!

38

THE THOMAS MERTON STORY

Gray's Inn Chapel; 9 May 1993

It should never greatly surprise us that Christian biography plays such an important part in Christian education, in the education of every Christian—through, for instance, the lives of the saints. After all, the life of Jesus Himself is of supreme significance, and spells out to us the meaning of our humanity: of true humanity; and the lives of the followers of Jesus should be, at the least, instructive. So I need not apologize for wanting to set before you another Christian biography.

Today, I want to give you the Thomas Merton Story.

Merton hit the headlines in 1949, with the publication of his best-seller *Elected Silence*. That was the title in this country; it was called *Seven Storey Mountain* in the United States.

It first appeared when I was a theological student; and, I have to say, I did not like Merton's theology. He was writing then as a very Puritanical Cistercian monk. In fact, he spent twenty-seven years as a monk; but what is fascinating and instructive is how Merton changed in those twenty-seven years.

You need to know something about Merton's beginning, however, if you're to understand his middle years—that's to say, the time of his conversion to Catholicism and his entry, in 1941, into the Abbey of Gethsemani in rural Kentucky—and, indeed, if you're to understand his end.

So let's begin at the beginning; at Merton's beginning.

His latest biographer, William Shannon, who is also editing four thousand of Merton's letters, divides his earliest years into what he calls:

> The French years
> The Oakham School years
> The Clare College, Cambridge, year
> and
> The Columbia University
> and
> The St Bonaventure University years.

Each of those years is given a chapter. They cover the years 1915 to 1941; and his biographer makes it clear that for almost half his life Merton lived without any clearly definable religious faith.

The epigraph with which Shannon begins his first chapter is not unimportant. He writes: 'The person we are able to become is hidden in our gifts'; and we are told that Merton said there were three gifts important to him: first, his Catholic faith; second, his monastic vocation; third, his calling to be a writer and to share his beliefs with the world at large. In time, Merton realized his gifts were both blessing and burden.

Merton's father was an artist, born in New Zealand; but he was something of a wanderer. Not long after arriving in London, he moved to Paris, to study art, where he met an American art student, Ruth Jenkins, whom he soon married, at St Anne's, Soho. *Thomas* Merton was born on 31 January 1915 at Prades, in the south of France, where they had settled, temporarily. In the later years of the First World War, the young family went to America, to Ruth Merton's family; but when Tom Merton was six his mother died of cancer. Tom went with his father to Bermuda, Europe and Algeria; for a time there was a possible stepmother but his father did not in the end marry her. Merton's father was a gifted artist: his exhibition here in London at the Leicester Galleries in 1925 was a considerable success.

When his father took the 14-year-old Thomas to Oakham School he was clearly an exceptional young lad, interested chiefly in modern languages and literature, and desperately in need of the home even a small public school like Oakham could provide. Thomas never really had a home. His father died in 1931, but his grandfather—his mother's father—came over from the States and secured Tom's future financially. His school holidays, in Strasbourg, Rome and the States, were important to Tom; and he worked hard enough to secure a scholarship to Clare College, Cambridge.

But the least said about Tom's year at Clare and Cambridge, the better. Shannon calls it 'the nadir of his life'. Drinking, drifting, and generally living it up, led to an unmarried woman bearing their child, and nothing is now known of either the woman or the child.

It is in the fifth chapter of the biography that Shannon describes Merton's 'blossoming' at Columbia University, in New York City, from 1936 to 1940. Aldous Huxley's *Ends and Means* and Etienne Gilson's *The Spirit of Medieval Philosophy*, and the guidance of the Hindu monk, Bramachari, all played their part in Merton's conversion to Catholicism and his reception into the Catholic Church in 1938, as did a Catholic friend, Dan Walsh, who taught part-time at Columbia. From 1940 to 1941, the 26-year-old Merton taught English at St Bonaventure University and began to wrestle with the call to the priesthood. It was in Holy Week 1941 that he first visited the Cistercian Abbey at Gethsemani, Kentucky, and within months he was living within its walls.

As I've said, Merton spent twenty-seven years as a monk. William

Shannon underlines Merton's contradictions: Merton, the Trappist, with a vocation to silence but with the gift of writing; fifty books came from his pen over the years, and as many major articles. But there was also the contrast between the pre-Vatican II Merton who wrote *Elected Silence*—whose theology I didn't like!—and post-Vatican II Merton— whose theology I did like! There was the Merton who travelled in two directions: out of the world, for good, as a Trappist and, indeed, becom- ing a hermit within Gethsemani Abbey, but also returning to the world via (not least) the voluminous fan mail of a world-famous author. He was able to set up ecumenical dialogue at Gethsemani; he developed strong connections with Latin America, particularly with its intellectuals; he entered into profound correspondence with people like Boris Pasternak and D. T. Suzuki, the 94-year-old Zen scholar—whom Merton was allowed by his abbot to visit in New York. He became deeply involved in Gandhian non-violence, and in the Peace Movement.

He writes, for instance:

> It is my belief that all those in the world who have kept some vestige of sanity and spirituality should unite in firm resistance to the movements of power politicians and the monster nations, resist the whole movement of war and aggression, resist the diplomatic overtures of power and develop a strong and coherent 'third world' that can stand on its own feet and affirm the spiritual and human values which are cynically denied by the great powers . . . Natur- ally in the monastery I am not very well versed in politics, but I feel that a certain spiritual outlook does have some value after all. It gives a perspective which is not available to those who think only in terms of weapons and money and the manipulation of political groups.

Merton played a significant part, from Gethsemani Abbey, in the struggle for racial equality in the States, and in the movement for monastic renewal.

He wrote in his introduction to the Japanese edition of one of his books:

> The monastery is not an 'escape' from the world. On the contrary, by being in the monastery, I take my true part in all the struggles and sufferings of the world . . . It is my intention to make my entire life a rejection of, a protest against, the crimes and injustices of war and political tyranny which threaten to destroy the whole race of human beings and the world with them. By the monastic life and vows I am saying NO to all the concentration camps, the aerial bombardments, the staged political trials, the judicial murders, the racial injustices, the economic tyrannies, and the whole socioeconomic appar- atus which seems geared for nothing but global destruction in spite of all its fair words in favor of peace. I make monastic silence a protest against the lies of politicians, propagandists, and agitators, and when I speak it is to deny that my faith and my Church can ever be seriously aligned with these forces of injustice and destruction.

Gradually Merton became involved in the increasing dialogue concerning world religions. His journey to Asia in the last year of his life brought him into contact with leading figures in the world of Buddhism, not least, the Dalai Lama.

William Shannon calls his biography of Merton *Silent Lamp*, which is the name given to Merton by the Chinese philosopher John Wu in the course of their collaboration on the teaching of the early Taoist sage Chuang Tzu. 'You are so deeply Christian that you cannot help touching the vital springs of other religions' wrote John Wu to Merton. Out of the heart of his silent vocation as a Christian monk, all the rich activity of Merton as a writer and teacher overflowed.

In an essay of Merton's that he particularly liked there occurs a profound paragraph which I shall quote as near to the very heart of Thomas Merton:

> This inner 'I', which is always alone, is always universal: for in this inmost 'I' my own solitude meets the solitude of every other man and the solitude of God. . . . It is only this inmost and solitary 'I' that truly loves with the love and the spirit of Christ. This 'I' is Christ Himself, living in us; and we, in Him, living in the Father.

It was on 10 December 1968—twenty-five years ago—that Merton's tragic death occurred. He was in a bungalow owned by the Red Cross in Thailand. He had just delivered a lecture on 'Marxism and Monastic Perspectives'. A nun, who was also a doctor, wrote this report of his death:

> December 10, 1968, just after 4.00 p.m., I suddenly heard someone saying: 'Father Thomas Merton is lying dead in his room.' Hoping that there was still something to be done, I hurried immediately to his room.
>
> Father Merton was lying on the terrazzo floor, his eyes half-open, no breathing, no pulse, no heart sounds, no light reaction of the pupils. The face was deep bluish-red and the lower arms and legs showed spots of the same colour. The arms were lying stretched beside the body. The feet were turned inside like in convulsion. Fr Merton was only in shorts. An electric fan of about 150 cm. [about 5 ft] high was lying across the body. The electric cord was pulled out of the plug lying on the floor. A smell of burnt flesh was in the air.
>
> As I turned the fan somewhat aside, I realized that there was a third degree burn, just in the right upper abdominal region, the place where the middle part of the fan with the switchboard had touched the skin. . . . The cloth of the shorts showed no sign of burning itself. The fan had lain direct on the skin, above the upper part of the shorts. On the lower region of the right upper arm (or on the upper part of the lower arm) were signs of strip-like burns.

Merton was a man full of surprises—to the very last.

He must have been a very difficult monk to handle, and one can only admire the way the subject of authority and freedom was handled by his immediate Cistercian superiors. It is nevertheless important to say that in April 1962 Merton was informed by his abbot that the abbot general of his Order in France had told him he must desist from any further writing on the subject of war and peace.

His biographer tells us that in 1960 Merton had received permission to make regular visits to Dr James Wygal, a psychologist, in Louisville. We are told nothing more, not even why he went. In March, 1966, Merton received serious back surgery in hospital, in Louisville, and fell in love with a young student nurse. Shannon tells us some have blown the story out of all proportion; others have minimized it; but we are not told enough to know how *not* to blow it up *or* to minimize it. It was clearly a significant incident for Merton—and, of course, for the nurse. Whether Merton talked to Dr James Wygal about it we do not know. Merton, in his prolific writings, is strangely silent on the significant subject of sexuality and sanctity: certainly on *his* sexuality and sanctity; and Shannon fails to enlighten us. Yet it is surely an important part of 'The Thomas Merton Story'.

I have preached to you about Thomas Merton today for several reasons.

First: because in our busy world, in which we sometimes divide people into the significant and the insignificant, the way of life of a Trappist monk is often regarded as irrelevant. But Merton's life was clearly one of the most fruitful of all twentieth-century lives.

Second: Merton's life reminds us of the need for each one of us to take care of the silent centre of our own existence.

Third: Merton had many and varied gifts as writer, poet, scholar. His vocation as priest and monk pulled them all together; integrated them.

To my mind, Thomas Merton is another example of the way Christ can and does gather up the fragments of our divided selves, so that nothing is lost of what we were intended to be when we were a twinkle in God's eye.

❦ 39

DOROTHY L. SAYERS

St Paul's Knightsbridge; 23 May 1993

My good friend, your vicar, has encouraged me to think you may be pleased if I share in the celebrations of your 150th anniversary by celebrating in my sermon someone the centenary of whose birth occurs this year, and who played a major part in the life of St Anne's, Soho, in this Deanery, which has just celebrated half a century since it was rebuilt and rededicated.

The person I have in mind is best known now as a writer of detective stories; and even if you haven't read them, you have probably seen some of them, adapted for television. It's the creator of Lord Peter Wimsey I have in mind, Dorothy L. Sayers. (If I'm not mistaken, Lord Peter came here regularly to weddings and memorial services.) But it's not in fact the detective writer but the scholar and theologian who will be the subject of my sermon—though I hasten to say that when Archbishop Temple offered Dorothy L. Sayers the degree of Doctor of Divinity in 1943, she refused it, saying she had 'only served Divinity as it were accidentally, coming to it as a writer'.

Four biographies have now been written of Dorothy L. Sayers: by Ralph Hone, David Brabazon, David Coomes and, most recently, Barbara Reynolds.

As a 'Brief Life' let me simply read you what appears on the dust jacket of Barbara Reynolds' biography:*

Born in 1893 in Oxford, Dorothy Leigh Sayers had a happy childhood in her father's East Anglian parish, then went to Oxford University, where she was one of the first women to be awarded a degree. Unable to make a living by either her poetry or her mediaeval French scholarship, she became one of the few women to be employed writing advertising copy, working on the legendary campaigns for Guinness stout and Colman's mustard. By then she had written her first Lord Peter Wimsey book, *Whose Body?*, and embarked on one of the most enduringly successful writing careers of this century.

In the late 1930s she wrote *Busman's Honeymoon*, her first play and her last full-length detective novel. There were further plays, both secular and religious, particularly *The Man Born To Be King*, which revolutionised the way that religious material was broadcast in Britain. It aroused considerable

---

Dorothy L. Sayers: Her Life and Soul (London: Hodder & Stoughton, 1993).

controversy at the time. She then returned to the scholarly work she had set aside in the 1920s, embarking on a new translation of Dante's *Divine Comedy*.

By the end of her life, Dorothy L. Sayers was fixed in the public imagination as a woman of both great talent and almost terrifying respectability. Only her closest friends knew the woman behind the image: warm, friendly and immensely kind. And it is only since her death that the rest of her story has emerged. It is now well known that she had a child out of wedlock before her marriage, and until now this has been interpreted as a tragedy from which she never quite recovered. Now, after studying her private letters, Barbara Reynolds is able to reveal much more: Sayers' exuberant joy in good times, her indomitable cheerfulness even when things seemed bleakest; the attractive yet flawed men she loved; how she incorporated and transformed her experiences, both happy and unhappy, in her novels and religious writings.

Her biographer, Barbara Reynolds, sums up a great deal of Dorothy Sayers' life when she simply says, in a single sentence: 'Dorothy Sayers became a skilled practitioner of the art of appealing to the imagination as well as to the intellect.'

In one of her books, *Gaudy Night*, there is a fascinating discussion between Harriet Vane and Miss de Vine of the relation of the mind to the emotions. Miss de Vine asks, 'Isn't the writing of good prose an emotional experience?' Harriet replies: 'Yes, of course it is. At least, when you get the thing dead right and know it's dead right, there's no excitement like it. It's marvellous. It makes you feel like God on the Seventh Day—for a bit, anyhow.'

That is almost a throw-away conversation; but I think myself it goes to the heart of Dorothy L. Sayers. She saw her creativity as reflecting, however faintly, the very being of God the Creator.

That is illustrated in a very down to earth way by an article she wrote, entitled: 'How I came to invent the character of Lord Peter Wimsey'.

Lord Peter's large income (the source of which by the way I have never investigated) . . . I deliberately gave him . . . After all it cost me nothing and at that time I was particularly hard up and it gave me pleasure to spend his fortune for him. When I was dissatisfied with my single unfurnished room I took a luxurious flat for him in Piccadilly. When my cheap rug got a hole in it, I ordered him an Aubusson carpet. When I had no money to pay my bus fare I presented him with a Daimler double-six, upholstered in a style of sober magnificence, and when I felt dull I let him drive it. I can heartily recommend this inexpensive way of furnishing to all who are discontented with their incomes. It relieves the mind and does no harm to anybody.

It wasn't only her writing that Dorothy Sayers saw as reflecting the work of the Creator. The work of any maker—architect, craftsman, poet—was for Dorothy a sacramental act. Thus, in her play for the 1937 Canterbury Cathedral Festival, *The Zeal of Thine House*, the Archangel Raphael accepts the work of the architect, William of Sens, in lieu of neglected prayer:

> True as a mason's rule
> And line can make them, the shafted columns rise
> Singing like music; and by day and night
> The unsleeping arches with perpetual voice
> Proclaim in Heaven, to labour is to pray.

Barbara Reynolds writes:

Dorothy was vividly and creatively aware that her Canterbury play owed its being to the collaboration of all who had worked with her to honour the cathedral: the actors, the producer, the composer and the choir, the designer of costumes and all who gave life to her words. There was a third element: the audience, who responded. Meditating on this, she was visited by a revelation: not only the building of the cathedral, not merely the production of a play, but every act of creation had a triune structure which mirrored the Trinity. The words she gives to the Archangel are the expression of her new vision:

Children of men, lift up your hearts. Laud and magnify God, the everlasting Wisdom, the holy undivided and adorable Trinity.

Praise Him that He hath made man in His own image, a maker and craftsman like Himself, a little mirror of His triune majesty.

For every work of creation is threefold, an earthly trinity to match the heavenly.

First: there is the Creative Idea; passionless, timeless, beholding the whole work complete at once, the end in the beginning: and this is the image of the Father.

Second: there is the Creative Energy, begotten of that Idea, working in time from the beginning to the end, with sweat and passion, being incarnate in the bonds of matter; and this is the image of the Word.

Third: there is the Creative Power, the meaning of the work and its response in the lively soul; and this is the image of the indwelling Spirit.

And these three are one, each equally in itself the whole work, whereof none can exist without other; and this is the image of the Trinity.

It was in 1938 that the BBC invited Dorothy Sayers to write a Nativity Play—for the Children's Hour. This gave her the opportunity to try out another conviction which had become uppermost in her mind. The way to bring home the incarnation to people was to use the language of every day: to show that 'His Manhood was a real manhood, subject to the common realities of daily life; that the men and women surrounding Him were living human beings, not just characters in a story; that, in short, He was born, not into "The Bible", but into the world.' *He That Should Come* is set in a crowded inn, with bustling, quarrelling travellers, talking like ordinary people of the present day.

Listeners to radio had never heard anything like it. The story came to life for them as never before.

The Zeal of Thine House as a play had been followed in 1940 by one of Dorothy's greatest works which spelt out her theology of creation, and, indeed, of creativeness: *The Mind of the Maker*. And the nativity play for broadcasting, *He That Should Come,* was followed, also in 1940, by her second great work *The Man Born To Be King*: twelve plays on the life of our Lord.

The time would fail me to tell in any detail the controversy the play caused; but tribute ought to be paid to Dr James Welch, the Director of Religious Broadcasting, who had the courage to invite Dorothy to write *The Man Born To Be King* and no less the courage to stand by her when she was under attack. While that attack was still raging, Dr Welch wrote to her:

> What [it] has revealed to me quite clearly is that at heart most of us are Arians; we are prepared for Our Lord to be born into the language of the A. V., or into stained glass or into paint; what we are not prepared to accept is that He was incarnate. *Incarnatus est* is a phrase; we bow when we say it; but how many of us are prepared really to believe it?

It is not surprising that as the dark clouds of war lowered in the late thirties, it was the problem of good and evil which came to occupy the mind of Dorothy L. Sayers. Her drama *The Devil To Pay* concerns the same story as Marlowe and Goethe had taken as they wrestled with that subject: the legend of Faust. She wrote *The Devil To Pay* for another Canterbury Festival and it was transferred to His Majesty's Theatre Haymarket the month before war broke out. How relevant her work was to what was happening in the world around is made blazingly clear by the Judge at the end of the play:

> All things God can do, but this thing He will not;
> Unbind the chain of cause and consequence . . .

It was not the last time Dorothy would concern herself with Death, Judgement, Heaven and Hell: in the last fourteen years of her life her creative imagination was caught up with *The Divine Comedy* of Dante. Her intellect came to grips with the theology and moral grandeur of Dante's poem, and she accepted the invitation to translate and expound it for Penguin Classics. But behind the intellect was Dorothy Sayers' own experience. In 1948 she delivered a lecture on 'The Meaning of Purgatory'. Just listen to how human that lecture was:

> We will suppose that in a fit of anger or resentment or merely sheer wicked carelessness you damage something belonging to your friend—we will call it a valuable china teapot . . . We shall take it that, seeing the fragments of the teapot at your feet, you are overcome with shame and horror at what you have done and want to put matters right so far as possible. Obviously, there are two things to be done: the first is to restore the right relationship with your friend which has been broken up by your anger or negligence or whatever the sin was. You go to her at once and confess your sinful feeling and the guilty act to which it led; you say how dreadfully sorry you are, and you beg her to forgive you, and promise that you will try to make it up to her in future. That is, you

make an act of penitence, confession, contrition and atonement. She forgives you at once, you kiss and make friends; and that restores the relationship. You are now released at once from the *guilt* of what you did: in technical terms, you have purged the *culpa*.

But, Dorothy goes on to say, something remains to be done, without which the atonement will not be complete:

> You will want, that is, to make an act of compensation, and the technical term for that is purging the *reatus* . . . and if the sinner is truly penitent, he will be eager to purge it in any way God may appoint . . . if we are ever to be happy in His presence again, it is something in us that has to be altered.

To end my tribute to Dorothy L. Sayers, I want to return, as her latest biographer does, to Dorothy as a young woman, still at Oxford. She wrote a poem which bears the marks of her youth yet somehow comprehends her whole life. It may have something to say, I suspect, about your life and mine:

> Lord, if this night my journey end,
> I thank Thee first for many a friend,
> The sturdy and unquestioned piers
> That run beneath my bridge of years.
>
> And next, for all the love I gave
> To things and men this side the grave,
> Wisely or not, since I can prove
> There always is much good in love.
>
> Next, for the power thou gavest me
> To view the whole world mirthfully,
> For laughter, paraclete of pain,
> Like April suns across the rain.
>
> Also that, being not too wise
> To do things foolish in men's eyes,
> I gained experience by this,
> And saw life somewhat as it is.
>
> Next, for the joy of labour done
> And burdens shouldered in the sun;
> Nor less, for shame of labour lost,
> And meekness born of a barren boast.
>
> For every fair and useless thing
> That bids men pause from labouring
> To look and find the larkspur blue
> And marigolds of a different hue;
>
> For eyes to see and ears to hear,
> For tongue to speak and thews to bear,
> For hands to handle, feet to go,
> For life, I give Thee thanks also.

For all things merry, quaint and strange,
For sound and silence, strength and change,
And last, for death, which only gives
Value to every thing that lives;

For these, good Lord that madest me,
I praise Thy name; since verily,
I of my joy have had no dearth
Though this night were my last on earth.

40

MINISTRY AND MYSTERY

*To celebrate the Twenty-Fifth
Anniversary of the Ordination of
the Revd Evan Jones, Vicar of
St James with St Peter,
Islington; 9 June 1993*

Evan: it's a special joy for me to preach at the jubilee of your ordination.

I should like to begin what I have to say by recounting what may seem at first an oddly irrelevant anecdote.

My phone rang a few days ago, and a kindly, rather diffident, voice said: 'Is that Canon James?' I said it was, and he said, even more uncertainly: 'You *are* the author of a book of sermons called *Word Over All*?' 'Yes' I said, 'Well,' he went on, 'on page 74, paragraph 7, line 2, do you mean what you say? Or is it perhaps a misprint?' And then he added: 'I feel awful asking you this; but it *could* be a misprint.' I went and looked up page 74, paragraph 7, line 2; and, alas, it *was* a misprint—and it was my fault. It said, 'After forty years of ordained *mystery* . . .' I was talking about my own *ministry*.

I imagine, Evan, you will agree, that these last twenty-five years have been for you years of mystery as well as of ministry. But I've no doubt you will be thankful to have been—to use St Paul's phrase—a 'steward of the mysteries of God' for a quarter of a century.

I would quite like to have made this a dialogue sermon this evening with you, Evan, and to have asked you to tell us what have been above all the mysteries of God for you in these last twenty-five years of ministry—in Exeter Diocese as well as in London.

I suspect you might say: 'Well, there's the mystery of the jolly old Church of England for a start! What a mystery that is!'

Yes. But after we'd got past that, I wonder how you would go on?

You will, of course, be looking back today with particular thanksgiving to your ordination. But I wonder how your understanding of the mystery of ordination has changed and grown over the years? I suspect you are as glad as I am that you were ordained. Neither you nor I would want to be anything else. But I would be surprised if in earlier years you did not make a much greater distinction between those who are ordained and those who are not ordained; whereas now, if I'm not mistaken, you see it as one of the main tasks of those who are ordained, to help those who are not ordained to realize and discover the mystery of Christ's priesthood which lies at the very heart of their humanity, of all humanity, and which enables all of us, whether ordained or not, to be 'ministers of Christ and stewards of the mysteries of God'.

But I would want to press that question, 'What are the mysteries of God, Evan, which you have found above all to lie at the heart of your ministry?'

I don't doubt, for instance, that today you are devoutly thankful when you remember your first Mass, and not only your first Mass, but all who have been with you at the altar over the years, and who have sustained you in your ministry. But the Mass now takes you—I suspect—right out of the Church into the whole wide world.

It was just two years after you had been ordained, Evan, that Professor John Macquarrie—then, I think, Lady Margaret Professor of Divinity and Canon of Christ Church, Oxford—delivered a lecture which said a great deal to me about mystery and ministry and humanity as a whole.

> There is today [he said] a revival of interest in mystery and of the sense of wonder in our secular society, especially among young people. This may mark the beginning of a revulsion against the long established hostility to mystery in Western philosophy. Now if it is true that the most natural (though not the only) way into mystery is through the exploration of man himself, then the Christian faith is singularly well situated to give a lead in the quest for mystery. By its doctrine of the incarnation, Christianity holds that it is precisely in a human person, Jesus Christ, that the final mystery of being has been opened up. According to Paul, Christ is 'the revelation of the mystery which was kept secret for long ages' (Rom. 16. 25–6). This is commonly taken to mean that Christ has revealed or opened up the mystery of God. But would it not be correct to say that he has done this by opening up the mystery of man? Is there not a deep affinity between the mystery of God and the mystery of humanity? By becoming man in the fullest sense, that is to say, in a measure of fullness that transcends all our ordinary levels of manhood, Christ manifests God in the flesh. He pushes back the horizons of the human mystery so that they open on to the divine mystery, but he does this without ceasing to be man.

'He pushes back the horizons of the human mystery so that they open on to the divine mystery . . .'

I suspect that is just what has been most important for you in the last quarter of a century—in manifold ways.

I imagine, Evan, that like me, from time to time in your ministry, as, for instance, you have held a baby's head in the cup of your hand, as you have baptized it, you have sometimes been overcome with a sense of the incredible miracle of existence; and the human mystery has opened on to the divine.

Or, sometimes, as a young man and young woman have stood side by side before you and taken the marriage vows with utter sincerity, to God Himself, the human mystery has opened on to the divine.

Or when you have stood in a hospital ward or some other room of death at the bedside of someone leaving this world and all they love and you have stood with them and those they love, it has been the human mystery opening on to the divine mystery of which you have been conscious, indeed have been overwhelmed by, and you have experienced the enormous privilege of ministry.

To be a steward of such mysteries is undoubtedly a huge privilege, but we are not stewards like the race-course stewards at Epsom. We are not in charge of something which is handleable and manageable like a possession. And you know well, Evan, how important it is from time to time just to be silent before the mystery; to bow before it—wherever it confronts you; to allow yourself to be bowled over by the mystery, like those disciples on the Mount of Transfiguration. No matter how often you have had to try and put the mystery into words, you are, I know, well aware it just cannot be done. In the end we are all reduced to silence. Words fail.

But to go back to my question: 'What have been above all the mysteries of God for you in these last twenty-five years?' that have 'pushed back the horizons of the human mystery and have opened on to the divine mystery?'

I have little doubt music will often have pushed back those horizons—and, certainly, friendship—and many many human relationships.

I wonder how far in these years the mystery of sexuality has become clearer to you . . . and the mystery of gender and identity, not least your own identity.

I sometimes think myself that why I was ordained is because few other vocations, if any, could enable me as a male to express my femininity, indeed, my identity, so profoundly, so satisfyingly.

And I think that behind all the controversy over the ordination of women is not least the failure of the Church and the failure of people within it, lay and ordained, to be willing to plumb the depths of their own gender and sexuality and identity.

*   *   *

So far, Evan, I've only talked of mysteries as gifts to us, but, you will have learnt as I have learnt, that almost everything in this world is curse as well as blessing, blessing as well as curse and, surely, one of the most baffling mysteries of all is simply the mystery of iniquity, of evil—in each of us as individuals—in Islington—in England—in Europe—in the wide world.

Yet alongside the baffling mystery of iniquity is the mystery of its healing and redemption, and the mystery of that triumphant suffering which Christ Himself exemplified.

You have now spent twenty-five years, Evan, as a steward of the mysteries of God—not just of the joyful mysteries but of the sorrowful mysteries. You will no doubt have had your own experience of the mystery of iniquity and of its redemption.

And now you have gathered us here to give thanks with you for these past years and you have invited us to commit ourselves with you to all that lies ahead—in mystery as well as ministry. And we are grateful. ''Tis good, Lord, to be here.' 'Tis good, Evan, to be here!

Last Monday evening two good friends of mine took me to Stratford-on-Avon to see what I have always believed to be Shakespeare's most profound play, *King Lear*. It was, in fact, the best performance I have ever seen, with Robert Stephens as Lear.

At one point in *King Lear*, one of the characters simply says: 'Thy life's a miracle.' Only Shakespeare can be as profound and as simple as that.

Evan, you would agree with those words of Shakespeare. And so say most of us.

Then, in the last act, Lear invites all those who are with him to

> take upon's the mystery of things
> as if we were God's spies.

I think Evan, that is the heart of what you have invited us all to join with you in doing this evening, as we gather with you, thankfully, at the altar.

That way the horizons of the human mystery will go on for all of us opening on to the divine, be the years ahead of us few or many, come joy, come pain, come death itself:

> to take upon's the mystery of things
> as if we were God's spies.